MS American History Before 1865
Student Guide

Second Edition

Illustrations Credits
All illustrations © K12 Inc. unless otherwise noted

About K12 Inc.
K12 Inc. (NYSE: LRN) drives innovation and advances the quality of education by delivering state-of-the-art digital learning platforms and technology to students and school districts around the world. K12 is a company of educators offering its online and blended curriculum to charter schools, public school districts, private schools, and directly to families. More information can be found at K12.com.

978-1-60153-522-1

Printed by LSC Communications, Harrisonburg, VA, USA, May 2020.

Table of Contents

Unit 4: Thirteen Colonies, Part 2

Unit 5: Road to Revolution

Unit 6: The American Revolution

Unit 7: The Constitution

Unit 8: A New Nation

Unit 9: A New Age and New Industries

Unit 10: Americans Take New Land

Unit 11: Reform and Reflection

Student Guides and Worksheets

Student Guide
Lesson 1: History and *A History of US*

Early Native Americans were as different from one another as any of us are today, but they shared a common respect for nature and the land. Study the physical geography of North America and how it affected their lives. Learn how the first Americans reached this continent, and explore the rich diversity of Native American cultures before European contact.

The history of the United States is the history of every American. It's your history, your story. It's a story people all over the world want to study. It's not like the history of any other place. Americans don't share the same race or religion. We don't all speak the same language. Some American families have been Americans for centuries. Others became Americans last week. Americans are very different from one another. But we all share a belief in democracy. And that makes us one.

Lesson Objectives
- Describe the format and features of the text, including its theme, structure, use of primary sources, and additional information in the margins.
- Identify at least two reasons Joy Hakim gives for studying American history.

PREPARE

Approximate lesson time is 60 minutes.

Advance Preparation
- View the Introduction to MS American History Before 1865, located in the first lesson.

Materials
For the Student

A History Of Us

Getting Started

A History of US (Concise Edition), Volume A (Prehistory to 1800) by Joy Hakim

History Journal

LEARN
Activity 1: Introducing American History A *(Offline)*

Instructions
Getting Started

The book you are about to begin is full of stories. It has pictures and drawings and even some cartoons. But it is different from many storybooks because its stories are all true. The author, Joy Hakim, is a wonderful storyteller. Every one of her stories has something to do with you. How can that be? Chapter 1 will explain.

- First, look at the cover of *A History of US (Concise Edition),* Volume A (Prehistory to 1800). It is the first book in a series called *A History of US.* There are four books in all, but you'll use only two this year.
- The first volume covers prehistory to 1800. Prehistory is all the things that happened before people could write. And who were the first Americans? This first volume will tell you that story.
- Answer the first eight questions on the Getting Started sheet.

You did some detective work to answer those questions. Historians do a lot of detective work to find facts and think about what they find. The thinking you just did about the picture is called *document analysis.* You'll do more of that, but for now, let's get back to detective work.

- Answer the rest of the questions on the Getting Started sheet.
- Check your answers with an adult.
- Put the activity sheet in your History Journal.

Do you know what a *primary source document* is? *Primary* means that it is original, actually from the time and place where something happened. A *document* is anything that is on paper (or something like paper). It could be a deed, a will, a letter, a painting, or a photograph. Even a film taken while something happened is a primary source. So are other things, but they are always from the time and place of the event.

You will see many primary sources in *A History of US.* You'll find definitions, explanations, and extra information, too. Look at those before or after you read the text, or you'll miss things you'll want to know. Now, it's time to get started. Do you know why people study history? There are many reasons. The author, Joy Hakim, will tell you why she thinks history is important. See if you agree.

Read

Stories of the first Americans, of those who came from Europe, Africa, and Asia centuries ago, and of some who came last week are all part of your story. America's story is fascinating—with no end yet. But that's not the only reason to learn it. Chapter 1, "History? Why?" explains.

Read Chapter 1, pages 2–6, and do the following:

- Make a list of reasons for studying American history in your History Journal.
- Complete the History of US sheet.

Vocabulary

Look for the following terms as your read and write a definition for each term in your History Journal.

- democracy
- liberty
- justice

About Your History Journal

The History Journal is a three-ring binder with loose-leaf paper. You will do a lot of writing in your journal this year. You'll also use it to keep the pages that you print from the History lessons. Punch holes in these pages and insert them in order in the History Journal. Set aside a section of the journal for vocabulary. When you are asked to define terms as you read, you will put them in that special section. The journal will be a valuable study guide for you.

Name _____   Date _____

Getting Started

You'll need to become a detective to find the right answers for all the questions below. Get ready to search for the answers. They are all in *A History of US* (Concise Edition), Volume A (Prehistory to 1800).

1. Look at the front cover of the book. Who is the author of *A History of US*?

   _____

2. Who do you think the person shown on the front cover is? _____

   _____ What things in the picture helped you decide?

   _____

3. What time period does this volume of *A History of US* cover? _____

4. Look at the table of contents. Into how many parts is this book divided? _____

5. What is the title of Chapter 26, and on what page does it begin? _____

6. Look at pages 434 and 435. What is a collection of maps called? _____ Name

   a mountain range located in North America. _____

7. On what page does the glossary begin? _____ What is the definition of *democracy*?

   _____

8. Which primary source begins on page 401 of the appendix of primary sources?

   _____

Turn to Chapter 59, which begins on page 276.

9. What is the title of this Chapter? _____

When you read a chapter, make sure you take a look at all of the images. You may see images of paintings, drawings, prints, illustrations, photographs, documents, and other primary or secondary sources. Take a moment to study each image and read its caption.

10. Who is shown in the painting on page 276? _____

    How did this man earn a living? _____

Sidebars are a common element of the chapters in this book. They are located in the margins and are set off from the rest of the text with red lines. Sidebars provide additional information related to the main text.

11. What is the connection between the sidebar on page 277 and the main text? _____

_____

_____

Some chapters include a map. Make sure you read the caption and study the map.

12. In which two towns were battles fought? _____

Sometimes words from the text will be defined in the margns. These keywords are set off from the rest of the text with yellow lines.

13. Look at the keyword on page 281. What are *regulars*? _____

Some chapters have a special feature. Look at page 282 to see what a feature looks like.

14. What is this feature about? _____

Name _____   Date _____

A History of US

Can you remember the theme of *A History of US*? Rewrite it by piecing together the following phrases:

No other nation in	so much freedom, so
that has ever existed.	America is
the most remarkable nation	and so much opportunity
has ever provided	United States of
much justice,	the history of the world,

We believe that the _____

_____

_____

_____

_____ to so many people.

Thinking Cap Question! When Marcus Garvey said, "A man without history is like a tree without roots," he was making an analogy. An analogy is a comparison based on the resemblance between two things. How do you feel about history? Do you think that history is important? Write an analogy that describes what history means to you.

Adapted from *A History of US*

Student Guide
Lesson 2: Maps and Directions

Do you want to know more about the world? Maps and globes are packed with information. Maps are much easier to store and carry around than globes. But it's really tough to show a round earth on flat paper, so all maps are slightly distorted.

Lesson Objectives
- Identify characteristics and uses of maps and globes.
- Explain the reason for distortion on maps and the purpose of projections.
- Identify cardinal and intermediate directions.

PREPARE

Approximate lesson time is 60 minutes.

Materials
> For the Student
>> Understanding Geography: Map Skills and Our World (Level 5)
>> History Journal

LEARN
Activity 1: The Earth on Maps and Globes *(Online)*
Instructions
- Read Activity 1, "The Earth on Maps and Globes" (pages 4–7), in *Understanding Geography*.
- Answer Questions 1–14 in your History Journal.
- If you have time, you may want to answer the Skill Builder Questions on page 7.
- After you have finished, compare your answers with the ones in the Learning Coach Guide.

ASSESS
Lesson Assessment: Maps and Directions (*Online*)
You will complete an online assessment covering the main goals of this lesson. Your assessment will be scored by the computer.

Student Guide
Lesson 3: (Optional) Grids

Imaginary lines of latitude and longitude can help you find any place on earth. Weather forecasters use them to track storms. Rescuers use them to find ships in trouble at sea. They function like a global address. Even though you may skip this lesson, you must complete the **Read On** section before moving on to the next lesson.

Lesson Objectives

- Identify *latitude, longitude, absolute location,* and *hemisphere.*
- Use longitude and latitude to determine absolute location.
- Use maps and globes to locate places.

PREPARE

Approximate lesson time is 60 minutes.

Materials

For the Student

Understanding Geography: Map Skills and Our World (Level 5)

History Journal

A History of US (Concise Edition), Volume A (Prehistory to 1800) by Joy Hakim

LEARN
Activity 1. Optional: Latitude and Longitude *(Online)*
Instructions

- Read Activity 2, "The Coordinate System: Latitude and Longitude" (pages 8–11), in *Understanding Geography*.
- Answer Questions 1–15 in your History Journal.
- If you have time, you may want to answer the Skill Builder Questions on page 11.
- After you have finished, compare your answers with the ones in the Learning Coach Guide.

Activity 2. Optional: Chapters 2 and 3 *(Online)*
Instructions

During the Ice Age, land bridges promoted the movement of people and animals into new regions.
We think the Eskimos are the descendants of the last ancient Asians to reach North America. These people actually call themselves by a different name: the Inuit. They live in Alaska, Greenland, Siberia, and northern Canada. These areas are all part of the icy far North.

Read On

Read Chapter 2, pages 7–11, and Chapter 3, pages 12–16, in *A History of US (Concise Edition),* Volume A (Prehistory to 1800). As you read, think about what geographic features and conditions helped cause the movement of people into North and South America. Also think about how the Inuit adapted to the harsh environments found there.

Vocabulary

You'll see these terms as you read. Write a brief definition in your History Journal for each term as you come to it.

- Eskimo
- igloo
- Inuit

Beyond the Lesson

How do forecasters follow hurricanes? Visit the National Hurricane Center to find out. Learn about history's deadliest hurricanes. Print your own tracking charts and follow the path of a hurricane.

Activity 3. Optional: Hurricanes *(Online)*

Student Guide
Lesson 4: North American Beginnings

The first Americans probably came from Asia. They followed their prey, large mammals, across a land bridge from Asia to North America. That land bridge no longer exists, but their trek thousands of years ago led to the settlement of North and South America.

Lesson Objectives
- Recognize the role of an archaeologist.
- Locate the Bering Sea and land bridge on a map or globe.
- Trace the migration route of the earliest Americans.
- Describe the reason for migration to the Americas as the need to follow herds for food during the Ice Age.
- Describe and categorize Inuit lands, shelter, food, customs, and beliefs.
- Describe the reasons for migration to the Americas as the need to follow herds for food during the Ice Age.

PREPARE

Approximate lesson time is 60 minutes.

Materials
> For the Student
>> Discussion Questions
>> Native American Groups
> A History of US (Concise Edition), Volume A (Prehistory to 1800) by Joy Hakim
> History Journal

Keywords and Pronunciation
taiga (TIY-guh)

LEARN
Activity 1: The First Americans *(Offline)*
Instructions
Check Your Reading (Chapter 2, pages 7–11, and Chapter 3, pages 12–16)

- Try to answer all the questions on the Discussion Questions sheet.
- If you have trouble, read that part of Chapter 2 or 3 again.
- Discuss your answers with an adult.

Native American Groups

In this lesson, you will begin adding information to a table to compare Native American groups. Use the table in the Native American Groups sheet to help you organize what you read about the Inuit in Chapter 3. Fill in the row on the Inuit. If you aren't sure how to fill in a section, review the chapter. Ask an adult to check your work. **Keep the Native American Groups sheet in your History Journal so you can add information to it in later lessons.**

Migration

Do you understand the meaning of the word *migration*? Migration is movement from one area to another. The word has a verb form: *to migrate*.

Here are two definitions of to *migrate*. Both usually apply to large groups of animals or people.

1. To move from one country or place to another
2. To go back and forth from one region or climate to another for feeding or breeding

Why is migration important? Because the "history of us" begins with the migration of human beings from Asia to the Americas. Later, there will be other important migrations as well.

Go back online and click "From Asia to the Americas." Trace the migration route of the earliest Americans.

Assessment

Stay online to complete your assessment.

ASSESS
Lesson Assessment: North American Beginnings (*Online*)

You will complete an online assessment covering the main goals of this lesson. Your assessment will be scored by the computer.

Name _____   Date _____

Discussion Questions

Trace the migration route of the earliest Americans on a globe. To see if you traced the correct route, look at the map in Chapter 2.

Now answer the following questions. Make sure you've read Chapters 2 and 3.

1. Why did people leave Asia and migrate to the Americas?

   _____

   _____

2. What is an archaeologist?

   _____

   _____

3. Why was America a "hunter's heaven"?

   _____

   _____

   _____

   _____

4. At the end of the Ice Age, what happened to North America's glaciers and seas?

   _____

   _____

   _____

5. What happened to the land bridge connecting Asia and North America?

   _____

   _____

6. Where did the name *Indians* come from?

_____

_____

_____

7. What things did the first Americans do well? What did they invent? What did they make?

_____

_____

_____

_____

_____

_____

8. How did the horse affect Indian hunting?

_____

_____

9. Where do Eskimos (the Inuit) live today?

_____

_____

Name _____ Date _____

Native American Groups

Use this graphic organizer to help you gather, organize, and display facts and concepts from Unit 1.

	Economic Activities	Location	Customs/ Beliefs	Food	Shelter
Inuit					
Anasazi					
Indians of the Northwest					
Plains Indians					
Mound Builders					
Eastern Woodland Indians					

Student Guide
Lesson 5: Cliff Dwellers

In Europe, people were building castles and going on crusades. At about the same time, the Anasazi were living in the southwestern United States. The Anasazi were farmers in a desert area. They are gone now, but they left stone ruins that give us clues about their lives.

Lesson Objectives
- Describe the Anasazi as cliff dwellers.
- Locate on a map the area where the cliff dwellers lived.
- Describe Anasazi shelter, food, customs, and beliefs.
- Describe the hardships of farming in a desert region.
- Identify Pueblo peoples as the Anasazi's modern descendants.

PREPARE

Approximate lesson time is 60 minutes.

Materials
For the Student
A History of US (Concise Edition), Volume A (Prehistory to 1800) by Joy Hakim
History Journal

Keywords and Pronunciation
prestige (preh-STEEZH)

LEARN
Activity 1: Remember the Cliff Dwellers *(Offline)*
Instructions
Read

- Read Chapter 4, pages, 17–22. As you read, fill in the row on the Anasazi in your Native American Groups table.
- On a map of the United States, locate the area where the cliff dwellers lived.
- Ask an adult to check your work, and then save the table in your History Journal.

Vocabulary

You'll see these terms as you read. Write a brief definition for each term as you come to it.

- adobe (uh-DOH-bee)
- Anasazi (ah-nuh-SAH-zee)
- drought (drowt)
- mesa (MAY-suh)
- pueblo (PWEH-bloh)

Review

Review what you have learned about the Anasazi using the flash cards online.

Read On

Has learning about the Anasazi made you hot and dry? Let's go somewhere cooler—the American Northwest, where Washington and Oregon meet the Pacific Ocean. This is where the Indians of the Northwest lived, and still do.

- Read Chapter 5, pages 23–26.
- As you read, look for the information for the North American Groups table.
- Be prepared to say if you'd accept an invitation to a potlatch, and why.

Vocabulary

You'll see these words as you read. Write a brief definition for each as you come to it.

- prestige
- potlatch
- totem pole

ASSESS

Lesson Assessment: Cliff Dwellers *(Online)*
You will complete an online assessment covering the main points of this lesson. Your assessment will be scored by the computer.

Student Guide
Lesson 6: Indians of the Northwest

The people of the Pacific Northwest used the ocean, rain, and forest to live well. They formed societies with classes based on wealth and prestige.

Lesson Objectives

- Locate the area where the Northwest Indians lived on a map.
- Describe Northwest Indian shelter, food, beliefs, and customs, including totem poles.
- Use maps and graphs to locate and describe major climate regions of the United States.
- Analyze photographs to gather information on Indian life in the Pacific Northwest.

PREPARE

Approximate lesson time is 60 minutes.

Materials

For the Student

Document Analysis: Life on the Northwest Coast

A History of US (Concise Edition), Volume A (Prehistory to 1800) by Joy Hakim

Understanding Geography: Map Skills and Our World (Level 5)

History Journal

LEARN
Activity 1: Northwest Indians Show Off *(Offline)*
Instructions
Check Your Reading (Chapter 5, pages 23–26)

- Pretend you received an invitation to a potlatch. Tell an adult why you would or would not like to go.
- Complete the row for the Northwest tribes on your Native American Groups table. If you don't know what to write, look for the information in the chapter.
- Keep your table in your History Journal.
- Click Flash Cards to review Chapter 5.

Use What You Know

What can you learn from photographs? Probably more than you think. Study some photographs that show life on the Northwest coast.

- Complete the Document Analysis: Life on the Northwest Coast sheet.
- Discuss your work with an adult.

Climate

Think about the Indians of the American Northwest. The climate there is different from the climates where the Inuit and the Anasazi lived. You can use a climate map to tell what kind of climate different regions of a country or continent have.

- Read Activity 3, "Climate" (pages 12–15), in *Understanding Geography*.
- Answer Questions 1–10 in your History Journal.
- If you have time, you may want to answer the Skill Builder Questions on page 15.
- After you have finished, compare your answers with the ones in the Learning Coach Guide.

Assessment

Complete the assessment online.

ASSESS
Lesson Assessment: Indians of the Northwest (*Online*)

You will complete an online assessment covering the main goals of this lesson. Your assessment will be scored by the computer.

Name _____   Date _____

Document Analysis: Life on the Northwest Coast

You can learn a lot by studying, or analyzing, documents such as photographs. Document analysis is a skill that historians use to learn about the past.

Step 1: Observation

You will analyze four photographs on page 26 of Chapter 5. For each, follow these steps:

1. Study the photograph. Don't just glance at it—really look at it. Form an impression of the whole picture in your mind.
2. Now examine individual objects in the photograph.
3. Divide the photograph into four equal sections, or quadrants. Study each section. Look for details.
4. Complete this chart. List people, objects, and activities you notice in the photograph. You may find there is no information for one or two of the categories.

Photograph	People	Objects	Activities
1. mask			
2. Haida village			
3. Nootka smoking fish			
4. Tlingit salmon rattle			

Step 2: Inference

Based on your observations, list at least two things you might infer from each photograph. To infer is to draw a conclusion based on facts. For example, if you see smoke from a distance, you could infer that there is a fire.

Photograph 1: mask

1. _____

2. _____

Photograph 2: Haida village

1. _____

2. _____

Photograph 3: Nootka smoking fish

1. _____

2. _____

Photograph 4: carved object

1. _____

2. _____

Step 3: Questions

What questions come to mind when you study this photograph? Where could you find the answers to those questions? Select one photograph to ask these questions about.

Photograph: _____

1. What questions come to mind when you study this photograph? _____

_____

_____

2. Where could you find the answers to those questions? _____

_____

_____

Student Guide
Lesson 7: Touring the Continent

Take a trip across North America. See the different kinds of land. The Native Americans who live in various states across the country are different, too. In fact, there is no such thing as a "typical" Native American.

Lesson Objectives

- Demonstrate mastery of important knowledge and skills in this unit.
- Transfer written information on the geography of North America to a map.
- Identify geographic reasons for diversity among Native American groups.
- Recognize that there were hundreds of different Indian peoples, tribes, and languages.
- Locate the Bering Sea and land bridge on a map or globe.
- Describe the reasons for migration to the Americas as the need to follow herds for food during the Ice Age.
- Trace the migration route of the earliest Americans.
- Define the following words: *Eskimo, Inuit, kayak,* and *igloo.*
- Locate the regions where Inuit live on a map.
- Describe and categorize Inuit shelter, food, customs, and beliefs.
- Describe the Anasazi as cliff dwellers.
- Locate on a map the area where the cliff dwellers lived.
- Describe Anasazi shelter, food, customs, and beliefs.
- Locate the area where the Northwest Indians lived on a map.
- Describe Northwest Indian shelter, food, beliefs, and customs, including totem poles.
- Identify Pueblo peoples as the Anasazi's modern descendants.

PREPARE

Approximate lesson time is 60 minutes.

Materials

For the Student

Taking a Tour

A History of US (Concise Edition), Volume A (Prehistory to 1800) by Joy Hakim

Understanding Geography: Map Skills and Our World (Level 5)

LEARN
Activity 1: Take a Tour of North America *(Offline)*

Instructions
Read

Try to imagine an Inuit visiting the Anasazi. These two groups lived in very different places with different climates. The Inuit lived—and still live—in the icy far north of North America. The Anasazi lived in the Southwest. Each had different shelters, food, customs, and beliefs.

There are big differences in the land and climate going south to north between the Southwest and the Arctic. There are also big differences going west to east across North America. For centuries, these differences have affected how people live on different parts of the continent.

- Print the Taking a Tour sheet. Notice what it asks you to look for.
- Read Chapter 6, pages 27–33.
- As you read, look at the map on pages 68 and 69 in *Understanding Geography* and follow the journey.
- Follow the instructions on the Taking a Tour sheet. Look at the Thinking Cap Question. What else can you add to your map?

Read On

When people first migrated to North America, the region called the Great Plains was a hunter's paradise. But the climate changed, and life on the plains became difficult.

- Read Chapter 7, pages 34–37.
- As you read, think about how the land and climate affected the lives of the Plains Indians.
- Figure out how horses changed everything.

Vocabulary

You'll see these terms as you read. Write a brief definition for each term as you come to it.

- plains
- tepee
- nomad

ASSESS

Mid-Unit Assessment: The Earliest Americans, Part 1 *(Online)*
Complete the computer-scored portion of the Mid-Unit Assessment. When you have finished, complete the teacher-scored portion of the assessment and submit it to your teacher.

Mid-Unit Assessment: The Earliest Americans, Part 2 *(Offline)*
Complete the teacher-scored portion of the Mid-Unit Assessment and submit it to your teacher.

Name _____   Date _____

Taking A Tour

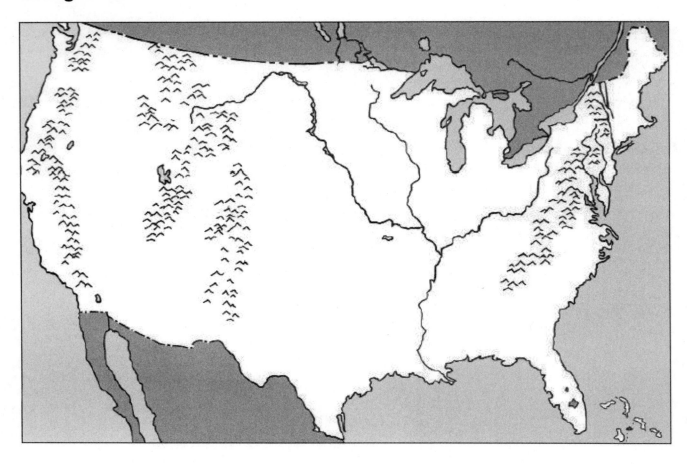

Are you ready for a trip across the United States? As you travel, trace your route and label your stops on the map above. Bon voyage!

1. You start your journey on the West Coast where the giant redwood trees grow. Label the West Coast on the map.

2. Travel east over the rugged mountains of California, and over the desert to the Rocky Mountains. Draw and label both mountain chains on the map.

3. Continue east over grasslands covered with buffalo and prairie dogs to the great river called the Mississippi. Label the river and its two branches, the Missouri River which flows from the west, and the Ohio River from the east.

4. Still traveling east over thick forests, find the ancient Appalachian Mountains. Label this mountain chain on the map.

5. Go east and you should be on the Atlantic Coast. Label it.

Adapted from *A History of US*

Thinking Cap Question! Turn your map into a picture map of the nation. Add redwoods, cactus, grasslands, and forests where they grow. You can also add animals, such as buffalo, grizzly bears, prairie dogs, and whales. Where does each type of animal live?

Student Guide
Lesson 8: The Plains Indians

In the center of the continent, big game animals began to disappear. This changed the lives of the Native Americans who lived there. They had to adapt to the harsh environment of the prairie. Another big change came into their lives much later. The Spanish brought horses to North America.

Lesson Objectives

- Identify and describe Plains Indians shelter, food, customs, beliefs, and nomadic way of life.
- Identify different kinds of regions.
- Analyze maps to gain information about regions.
- Describe three changes that occurred as a result of the Spanish introduction of the horse to North America.
- Explain that the Plains Indians depended on the buffalo for food, clothing, shelter, and tools.

PREPARE

Approximate lesson time is 60 minutes.

Materials

For the Student

A History of US (Concise Edition), Volume A (Prehistory to 1800) by Joy Hakim

Understanding Geography: Map Skills and Our World (Level 5)

History Journal

LEARN
Activity 1: Plains Indians Are Not Plain at All (Offline)
Instructions
Check Your Reading (Chapter 7, pages 34–37)

- Explain to an adult what happened when the Spanish introduced the horse to North America.
- Complete the row for the Plains Indians on your Native American Groups table. If you have trouble, look over Chapter 7 again.
- Go back online and use the Flash Cards to review Chapter 7.
- Stay online and click "On the Plains" to play a game.

Native American Cultural Regions

Historians organize tribes of early Native Americans into different cultural regions. Groups of people in each region had similar ways of life. For example, both the Chinook and Yakima tribes lived in the region called the Northwest Coast. These two groups had many things in common. You can use a cultural region map and a vegetation map to find out why.

- Read Activity 14, "Regions" (pages 56–59), in *Understanding Geography*.
- Answer Questions 1–12 in your History Journal.
- If you have time, you may want to answer the Skill Builder Questions on page 59
- After you have finished, compare your answers with the ones in the Learning Coach Guide.

Read On

You probably know that the ancient Egyptians built large structures thousands of years ago. They weren't the only people to do that. Did you know that east of the Great Plains, a group of Native Americans were great builders too? They had big cities, well-organized governments, and beautiful art, and they built mounds.

Read Chapter 8, pages 38–41. As you read, figure out:

- Why did the "Mound Builders" make mounds?
- Do any remain?
- What happened to the Mound Builders?

ASSESS

Lesson Assessment: The Plains Indians (*Online*)

You will complete an online assessment based on the North American Cultural Regions activity from the lesson. Your assessment will be scored by the computer.

Student Guide
Lesson 9: The Mound Builders

The Mound Builders flourished for more than 2,000 years. They built great structures of earth that rivaled the pyramids. Then, like the Anasazi, they faded from history. They left behind unsolved mysteries.

Lesson Objectives

- Locate the area where the Mound Builders live on a map.
- Describe the findings of archaeologists and historians studying the Mound Builders, including evidence of trade, cities, and slavery.
- Explain that mounds were built as burial sites, temple platforms, and religious symbols.
- Summarize key theories on the disappearance of the Mound Builders, including disease and outside attack.

PREPARE

Approximate lesson time is 60 minutes.

Materials

For the Student

A History of US (Concise Edition), Volume A (Prehistory to 1800) by Joy Hakim

History Journal

Keywords and Pronunciation

Algonquian (al-GAHN-kwee-uhn)

LEARN
Activity 1: Dig Those Mound Builders *(Offline)*
Instructions
Check Your Reading (Chapter 8, pages 38–41)

- Go online and click Flash Cards to review Chapter 8.
- Complete the row for the Mound Builders on your Native American Groups sheet.

Use What You Know

There are several theories that try to explain the disappearance of the Mound Builders. You can read about them in Chapter 8. In your History Journal, write a short newspaper article with the headline: "Mound Builders Disappear!"

The first paragraph should be the *lead*. The lead is a short paragraph that answers most or all of the "five W's and how." The five W's are *who, what, where, when,* and *why*. The lead should also explain *how* things happened. Most newspaper articles begin with a lead.

There are two reasons to write a lead. One is to get the reader's attention. The other is to help readers learn the most important facts quickly. There are several ways to write a lead. Here are some of them:

- Write a sentence or two summing up the whole event.
- Start with a quotation from someone involved in the event.
- Describe the scene where the event took place.
- Ask an interesting question to catch the reader's attention.

The second paragraph should give more details about the topic. Include general information about the Mound Builders in this paragraph. Compare your paragraph with the sample in the Learning Coach Guide.

Read On

Between the Atlantic coast and the Mississippi River was a land carpeted with trees. The forests there teemed with life. Beaver, deer, raccoon, opossum, and bear made easy targets for the hunters who shared the woods. This is where the peoples of the eastern forests lived—the Algonquian tribes. We call them Woodland Indians. To the north of the Algonquians was a confederation of Indian nations, known as the Iroquois. Although they were enemies of the Algonquians, they believed in peace and brotherhood.

Read Chapter 9, pages 42–46. As you read, see if you can find the answers to these questions:

1. How were the Woodland Indians grouped?
2. Did the different groups get along?
3. What was the purpose of the Iroquois League?

Vocabulary

You'll see these words as you read. Write a brief definition for each as you come to it.

- Algonquian (al-GAHN-kwee-uhn)
- wigwam
- wampum
- confederacy

ASSESS

Lesson Assessment: The Mound Builders (Online)

You will complete an online assessment covering the main points of this lesson. Your assessment will be scored by the computer.

Student Guide
Lesson 10: The Eastern Woodland Indians

The Algonquian peoples lived in the Eastern Woodlands. They lived in groups who spoke similar languages. They traded with one another. They hunted and gathered. They also practiced slash-and-burn farming. They had few enemies except for the Iroquois, whom they called the "terrible people."

Lesson Objectives
- Locate the area where the Eastern Woodland Indians lived on a map.
- Identify and describe the shelter, food, customs, and beliefs of the Eastern Woodland Indians.
- Analyze drawings to gather information about some Eastern Woodland Indians.
- Explain that the purpose of the Iroquois League was to bring independent nations together for mutual defense and common concerns.
- Describe the role of women among the Iroquois as tribal leaders.

PREPARE

Approximate lesson time is 60 minutes.

Materials
For the Student
Document Analysis: Eastern Woodland Indians
A History of US (Concise Edition), Volume A (Prehistory to 1800) by Joy Hakim
History Journal

LEARN
Activity 1: Indians of the Eastern Forests (Offline)
Instructions
Check Your Reading (Chapter 9, pages 42–46)
The Eastern Woodland Indians spoke an Algonquian language. They had a good life, but they had enemies to the north. Do you know who these enemies were?

- Go online and review Chapter 9 with the Flash Cards.
- Complete the row for the Eastern Woodland Indians in your Native American Groups table. Review Chapter 9 if you have trouble remembering the information you need.
- On a map of the United States, locate the area where the Eastern Woodland Indians lived.

Use What You Know

You analyzed photographs of life on the Northwest coast. Now do the same with drawings of Eastern Woodland Indians. Analyzing drawings is a lot like analyzing photographs. Just follow the directions on the Document Analysis sheet. Discuss your work with an adult.

ASSESS

Lesson Assessment: The Eastern Woodland Indians *(Online)*

You will complete an online assessment covering the main points of this lesson. Your assessment will be scored by the computer.

Name _____   Date _____

Document Analysis: Eastern Woodland Indians

You can learn a lot by studying, or analyzing, historical drawings. Drawing analysis, like photograph analysis, is a skill that historians use to learn about the past.

Step 1: Observation

On page 43 of Chapter 9 there are two pictures that were drawn by sixteenth-century artists who traveled to the New World. The one on the top shows Indians hunting deer. The one on the bottom shows Indians cultivating (farming) their land. We can learn a lot about the lives of the first Americans by studying historical drawings like these.

For each drawing, follow these steps.

1. Study the drawing. Form an impression of the whole drawing in your mind.
2. Now examine individual objects in the drawing.
3. Divide the drawing into four equal sections, or quadrants. Study each section. Look for details.
4. Complete the following chart. List people, objects, and activities you notice in the drawing.

Drawing	People	Objects	Activities
1. farming			
4. hunting			

Step 2: Inference

Based on your observations, list at least two things you might infer from each drawing. To infer is to draw a conclusion based on facts. For example, if you see a drawing of a person wearing lots of jewelry, you could infer that the person likes jewelry.

Drawing 1: farming

   1. _____

   2. _____

Drawing 2: hunting

   1. _____

   2. _____

Step 3: Questions

What questions come to mind when you study these drawings? Where could you find the answers to these questions? Select one drawing to ask these questions about.

Drawing: _____

   1. What questions come to mind when you study this drawing? _____

_____

_____

   2. Where could you find the answers to those questions? _____

_____

_____

Student Guide
Lesson 11: Unit Review

You've completed Unit 1, The Earliest Americans. It's time to review what you've learned. You'll take the Unit Assessment in the next lesson.

Lesson Objectives

- Review major characteristics of Native American groups.
- Compare and contrast Native American groups in terms of location, food, clothing, shelter, economic activity, and government.

PREPARE

Approximate lesson time is 60 minutes.

Materials

For the Student

A History of US (Concise Edition), Volume A (Prehistory to 1800) by Joy Hakim

History Journal

LEARN
Activity 1: A Look Back *(Offline)*
Instructions
Online Review

Review the Big Picture and the Flash Cards to get started.

History Journal Review

Continue reviewing by going through your History Journal.

- Look at the sheets you completed for this unit.
- Review your vocabulary words.
- Read over the writing assignments you completed.

Take your time. Your History Journal is a great resource for a unit review!

Student Guide
Lesson 12: Unit Assessment

You've finished this unit! Now take the Unit Assessment.

Lesson Objectives

- Recognize the role of an archaeologist.
- Locate the Bering Sea and land bridge on a map or globe.
- Trace the migration route of the earliest Americans.
- Locate the regions where Inuit live on a map.
- Describe and categorize Inuit shelter, food, customs, and beliefs.
- Locate on a map the area where the cliff dwellers lived.
- Describe Anasazi shelter, food, customs, and beliefs.
- Locate the area where the Northwest Indians lived on a map.
- Describe Northwest Indian shelter, food, beliefs, and customs, including totem poles.
- Identify and describe Plains Indians shelter, food, customs, beliefs, and nomadic way of life.
- Describe the findings of archaeologists and historians studying the Mound Builders, including evidence of trade, cities, and slavery.
- Locate the area where the Eastern Woodland Indians lived on a map.
- Identify and describe the shelter, food, customs, and beliefs of the Eastern Woodland Indians.
- Define *sachem* and *wampum*.
- Explain that the purpose of the Iroquois League was to bring independent nations together for mutual defense and common concerns.
- Use maps and globes to locate places.
- Identify Pueblo peoples as the Anasazi's modern descendants.
- Describe three changes that occurred as a result of the Spanish introduction of the horse to North America.
- Explain that the Plains Indians depended on the buffalo for food, clothing, shelter, and tools.

PREPARE

Approximate lesson time is 60 minutes.

Materials

 For the Student

  place mat map

ASSESS

Unit Assessment: The Earliest Americans, Part 1 *(Online)*

Complete the computer-scored portion of the Unit Assessment. When you have finished, complete the teacher-scored portion of the assessment and submit it to your teacher.

Unit Assessment: The Earliest Americans, Part 2 *(Offline)*

Complete the teacher-scored portion of the Unit Assessment and submit it to your teacher.

Student Guide
Lesson 1: Navigating Uncharted Waters

The 16th century was a time of tremendous change and excitement in much of Europe. A growing thirst for knowledge, power, and wealth led to remarkable voyages of exploration. Those voyages, in turn, led to unimaginable discoveries for Europeans and the greatest exchange of plant and animal life in history. The period begins before the tomato in Italy, the potato in Ireland, or the horse on the Great Plains. It ends with huge population growth in Europe, decimation of populations in the Americas, and the eventual forced migration of 12 million Africans.

Most historians believe the Vikings were the first Europeans to sail to North America. How far they explored is still a mystery. Four centuries later, other Europeans set sail across oceans. New learning and technology had opened the world to Europeans. The printing press made books and maps affordable, so ideas spread. An improved compass helped ships sail farther from home. Many Europeans wanted to trade with the rich lands of Asia. They wanted to find a route that would let them sail there.

Lesson Objectives
- Identify the Vikings as the first Europeans to make settlements in North America.
- Use maps to plot longitude, latitude, and direction.

PREPARE

Approximate lesson time is 60 minutes.

Materials
For the Student

A History of US (Concise Edition), Volume A (Prehistory to 1800) by Joy Hakim

map, world

LEARN
Activity 1: The Vikings (Offline)
Instructions
Read

Read Chapter 10, pages 47–49.

Vocabulary

You'll see these terms as you read. Write a brief definition for each term as you come to it:

- Scandinavia
- anthropology

Use What You Know

Use the place mat map of the world to trace routes and write navigation log entries in your History Journal.

Both Viking, and later European, explorers could tell how far north or south they had traveled by sighting known stars to identify their position. They had to guess how far they had traveled east or west, however. A compass would tell them which direction they were traveling, but it wouldn't tell them how far they had gone.

Pretend that you're a Viking on a journey from Norway to North America. Write at least four navigation log entries in your History Journal. Include the following:

1. The day (guess how long it would take to get to each point)
2. The land you sighted (as it is labeled on the world map)
3. The direction you traveled
4. Your approximate position in degrees of latitude.

Here is your first entry as an example. (You've reached the United Kingdom.)

Day 2
First land sighted since we left home. It is the United Kingdom.
Traveled southwest.
Position is 59° N.

Read On

On the place mat map of the world, point to Spain, Cuba, and China. Columbus wanted to sail west from Spain to China. You see what got in his way.

Read about Christopher Columbus and how he believed that the world was round. You will learn about his search for support for his plans, his first voyage, and what he discovered.

- Read Chapter 11, pages 50–55, and Chapter 12, pages 56–59.
- Be prepared to evaluate Columbus on the success of his efforts.

Vocabulary

You'll see these words as you read. Write a brief definition for each in your History Journal as you come to it.

- hemisphere
- parallel
- meridian
- astrolabe (AS-truh-layb)
- Taino (TIY-noh)

Student Guide
Lesson 2: Discovering New Lands

As a child, Christopher Columbus dreamed of sailing to China. As an old man, he died thinking he had done just that. He knew a lot about geography, but missed some clues that would have prevented a big mistake. He believed the world was round, but he misjudged how big it was. He set sail on an exciting and frightening journey across the Atlantic Ocean to find China. Instead, on October 12, 1492, Columbus landed in America and met the native peoples who lived there.

Lesson Objectives

- Identify Columbus as the first explorer to attempt to reach East Asia by sailing west from Europe.
- Recognize Columbus's errors in understanding the distance around the Earth and in thinking he had reached Asia.
- Define primary source and analyze a primary source to gain information.
- Explain the significance of new knowledge and inventions in fifteenth-century Europe, including Gutenberg's press and the compass.
- Explain the reasons for European desire to go to Asia, including an interest in learning and the desire for power, wealth, and goods.
- Identify the Vikings as the first Europeans to make settlements in North America.

PREPARE

Approximate lesson time is 60 minutes.

Materials

For the Student

Document Analysis: Columbus's Letter

A History of US (Concise Edition), Volume A (Prehistory to 1800) by Joy Hakim

Understanding Geography: Map Skills and Our World (Level 5)

map, world

LEARN
Activity 1: Columbus "Discovers" America—By Mistake *(Offline)*
Instructions
Check Your Reading (Chapter 11, pages 50–55, and Chapter 12, pages 56–59)

Answer the following questions in your History Journal. Use a world map to help you answer questions 1 and 2.

1. Find the Tropic of Cancer on your globe. This line of latitude is at 23½° N. What is another name for lines of latitude?
2. Columbus's plan was to follow the parallel of the Tropic of Cancer to China. Why would he choose to navigate that route? How did the navigational instruments he had influence that decision?
3. Why did Columbus believe he had reached Asia when he had actually sailed less than halfway there?
4. How did the improved compass help Europeans explore farther from their home ports?
5. Columbus and other European explorers read about Marco Polo's adventures in China. They studied maps and read about new scientific discoveries. That new knowledge helped promote European exploration. What invention, made in 1456, allowed that knowledge and information to spread quickly?

Document Analysis

Primary sources are one of the things historians use to learn about the past. Primary sources are documents made by people who actually saw or participated in an event and recorded that event soon afterward. They can be drawings, paintings, photographs, or written documents such as letters, reports, diaries, or newspaper articles.

Complete the Document Analysis: Columbus's Letter sheet.

Map Scales

Learn how to calculate distances on maps.

- Read Activity 4, "Map Scales" (pages 16–19), in *Understanding Geography*.
- Answer questions 1–11 in your History Journal.
- If you have time, you may want to answer the Skill Builder Questions on page 19.
- After you have finished you should compare your answers with the ones in the Learning Coach Guide.

Read On

Columbus made several more journeys to the Americas. In doing so, he brought many things with him from Europe and took many things back to Europe from the Americas. The world has never been the same since.

- Read Chapter 13, pages 60–65.
- Prepare to discuss what happened as a result of the Columbian Exchange.

Beyond the Lesson

Go online to learn more about Christopher Columbus.

ASSESS

Lesson Assessment: Discovering New Lands *(Online)*

You will complete an online assessment covering the main points of this lesson. Your assessment will be scored by the computer.

LEARN

Activity 2. Optional: More on Columbus *(Online)*

Name _____   Date _____

Document Analysis: Columbus's Letter

You can learn a lot by studying, or analyzing, documents such as letters. Document analysis is a skill that historians use to learn about the past. Primary source documents are created by people who actually saw or participated in an event and recorded that event soon afterward. When considering the value of a primary source document, these are some of the things it is important to know:

- What type of document it is
- The name and position (title) of the person who wrote it
- When it was written
- Whom it was written for

Answer the following questions based on the primary source "From Columbus's Pen" in Chapter 12.

1. What type of document is this? _____

2. Is this a primary source document? _____

3. When was it written? _____

4. Who was the author? _____

5. What was the author's position or title? _____

6. For whom was the document written? _____

7. List three things the author said that you think are important.

   _____

   _____

   _____

8. Why do you think this document was written? _____

   _____

   _____

9. What evidence in the document helps you know why it was written? Quote from the document. _____

_____

_____

_____

10. List two things the document tells you about life in the Americas at the time that it was written. _____

_____

_____

_____

11. Write a question to the author that the document leaves unanswered.

_____

_____

_____

Student Guide
Lesson 3: Columbus Journeys On

Columbus didn't find gold or a route to China on his second voyage. And he still didn't realize he was not in Asia. Instead he brought the first of a flood of Europeans and Africans to the Americas. These people brought plants, animals, and diseases that were new to the Western Hemisphere. Then they introduced plants, animals, and diseases of the Americas to Europe and Africa. The world was changed forever.

Lesson Objectives

- Use maps to gain information on the Columbian Exchange.
- Recognize that plants, animals and diseases were exchanged among continents as a result of European exploration.
- Explain the reason for the introduction of African slavery into the Americas as a way to fill the need for field workers.
- List at least four plants, three animals, and one disease that were part of the Columbian Exchange.
- Demonstrate knowledge gained in previous lessons.
- Define *hemisphere, parallel*, and *meridian*.
- Identify Columbus as the first explorer to attempt to reach East Asia by sailing west from Europe.
- Recognize Columbus's errors in understanding the distance around the Earth and in thinking he had reached Asia.
- Define primary source and analyze a primary source to gain information.

PREPARE

Approximate lesson time is 60 minutes.

Materials

For the Student

A History of US (Concise Edition), Volume A (Prehistory to 1800) by Joy Hakim

History Journal

LEARN
Activity 1: When Two Worlds Collide *(Online)*
Instructions
Check Your Reading (Chapter 13, pages 60–65)

Review Chapter 13 by answering the following questions in your History Journal:

1. What was exchanged among continents as a result of European exploration of North and South America?
2. Why were black people from Africa brought to the Caribbean Islands as slaves?

Ask an adult to check your answers.

Use What You Know

Life existed for thousands of years with little contact between the Eastern Hemisphere and the Western Hemisphere. When Columbus bridged those two worlds, the exchange between the Old World and the New World began. Some parts of that exchange happened right away, while others are still going on.

Go back online to read Worlds of Change—The Columbian Exchange to learn more about this exchange. Be prepared to identify at least four plants, three animals, and one disease that were part of the Columbian Exchange.

When you've finished, write the answers to the following questions in complete sentences in your History Journal. Check your answers with an adult.

1. Identify four plants, three animals, and one disease that were a part of the Columbian Exchange.
2. In North and South America, most people are of European or African descent. Can you explain why so few Native Americans exist in their own land?
3. Explain how and why millions of African slaves were brought to the New World.
4. In the sixteenth and seventeenth centuries, huge population shifts occurred in the Americas that related to four continents—two in the Eastern Hemisphere and two in the Western Hemisphere. Identify the continents and describe the population shifts.
5. One Native American group in North America was particularly changed by the introduction of an animal to the New World. Which Indian group was changed by what animal? How was it changed?
6. Two large animals that were introduced to the New World changed whole societies and helped create cultures and industries in both North and South America. What were these animals? What culture did they help create? What two industries did one of those animals help create?

Look Back

Advances in technology, a European desire to sail to Asia, and a visionary named Columbus came together to start a whole new chapter in the history of the world.

Review the following to prepare for an assessment:

- Chapters 10–13 in *A History of US (Concise Edition),* Volume A (Prehistory to 1800)
- History Journal

Online, review:

- Worlds of Change—The Columbian Exchange
- Columbus Flash Cards

If you have difficulty with any part of the material, review it with an adult.

Read On

Aztec civilization was sophisticated, with a magnificent capital city and the largest army in the world. What happened when the Aztecs met the Spaniards? Where did all that magnificence and power go?

- Read Chapter 15, pages 71–75.
- Prepare to discuss what happened to the Aztecs after they met the Spaniards.

Vocabulary

You'll see these terms as you read. Write a brief definition for each term in your History Journal.

- artisans
- Mesoamerica

Optional: Beyond the Lesson

Read Chapter 14, pages 66–70, to learn about some of the explorers that sailed into uncharted waters in the early sixteenth century.

ASSESS
Mid-Unit Assessment: Columbus Journeys On, Part 1 *(Online)*
Complete the computer-scored portion of the Mid-Unit Assessment. When you have finished, complete the teacher-scored portion of the assessment and submit it to your teacher.

Mid-Unit Assessment: Columbus Journeys On, Part 2 *(Offline)*
Complete the teacher-scored portion of the Mid-Unit Assessment and submit it to your teacher.

LEARN
Activity 2. Optional: Finding the Pacific and Sailing Around the World *(Online)*

Student Guide
Lesson 4: The Spanish Conquest

Two worlds came together when the Spaniard Hernando Cortés met the Aztec ruler Moctezuma. The battle fought in Tenochtitlán, the Aztec capital, decided the fate of this mighty Mesoamerican civilization.

Lesson Objectives
- Locate the Aztec Empire on a map.
- Identify Moctezuma as the leader of the Aztecs and Cortés as their Spanish conqueror.
- Describe the Aztec Empire as a complex civilization.
- Identify Mesoamerica and three Mesoamerican civilizations before the Spanish conquest.

PREPARE

Approximate lesson time is 60 minutes.

Materials
> For the Student
>> European Explorers
>>
>> Map of European Exploration
>>
>> Senor Hernando Cortes
>
> A History of US (Concise Edition), Volume A (Prehistory to 1800) by Joy Hakim
>
> History Journal

LEARN
Activity 1: New Spain *(Offline)*
Instructions
Check Your Reading (Chapter 15, pages 71–75)

Review Chapter 15 by looking at a map and completing an activity sheet.

- On the map of European Exploration, find the route Cortés took from Cuba to Tenochtitlán. Add his route to the European Explorers sheet using a colored pencil or marker. Then add that color to the legend. Keep the sheet in your History Journal. You will need it for later lessons.
- Complete the Señor Hernando Cortés sheet. Have an adult check your answers.

A Very Short History of Mesoamerica

Answer the following questions in your History Journal. Have an adult check your work.

1. What does *Mesoamerica* mean?
2. Which was the first Mesoamerican civilization to develop? What agricultural contribution did that group make to Mesoamerican civilization?
3. What kind of system of writing did the Maya develop?
4. What were some of the accomplishments of the Mayan civilization?
5. Which Mesoamericans were warriors who built monumental pyramids?

Read On

Ponce de León, the "brave lion," discovered Florida while searching for the Fountain of Youth. Francisco Pizarro defeated the large and powerful Inca Empire with just 180 men. Francisco Vasquez de Coronado searched for cities of gold. Read about these explorers and learn why the Spanish were so eager to explore the New World.

- Read Chapter 16, pages 76–80, and Chapter 17, pages 81–84.
- Be prepared to explain why people in Europe accepted the brutal destruction of Native American civilizations.

Optional: Beyond the Lesson

Visit a website to read an article about the discovery of an ancient Mesoamerican ball court.

Activity 2. Optional: The Spanish Conquest *(Online)*

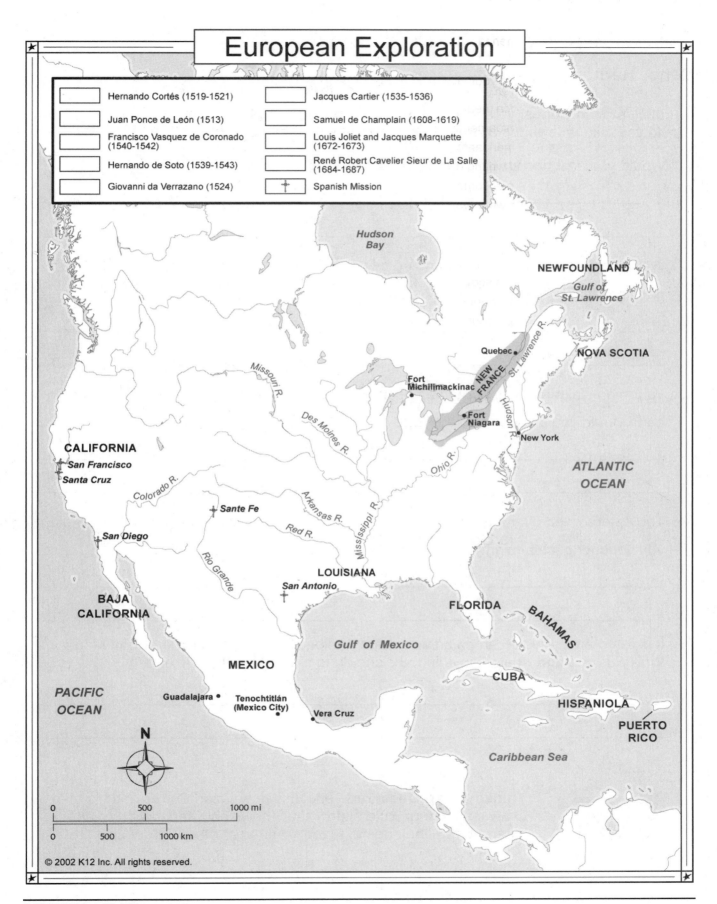

European Exploration

Hernando Cortés (1519-1521)	Jacques Cartier (1535-1536)
Juan Ponce de León (1513)	Samuel de Champlain (1608-1619)
Francisco Vasquez de Coronado (1540-1542)	Louis Joliet and Jacques Marquette (1672-1673)
Hernando de Soto (1539-1543)	René Robert Cavelier Sieur de La Salle (1684-1687)
Giovanni da Verrazano (1524)	✝ Spanish Mission

© 2002 K12 Inc. All rights reserved.

Name _____   Date _____

Señor Hernando Cortés

Señor Hernando Cortés, you have just returned from your trip to the lands in the West. Would you mind answering a few questions about your experiences?

1. Would you describe for us what impressed you most about Tenochtitlán?

   _____

   _____

2. We understand that you were horrified by some Aztec customs. Would you describe the practices that bothered you most? _____

   _____

   _____

3. Your men claim that you burned and sank your own ships! Is this true, and if so, why on earth would you do such a thing? _____

   _____

   _____

4. The Aztecs ruled over a great empire and were much feared by their enemies. How did you conquer such a mighty enemy with only 400 men? _____

   _____

   _____

5. It is rumored that your campaign was greatly helped by a woman named Doña Marina. Who was she and what, if anything, did she do to aid you against the enemy?

   _____

   _____

Thinking Cap Question! Tenochtitlán amazed Cortés and his men. Draw a picture or write a story that shows how Tenochtitlán was different from their home, Madrid, and from other European cities.

Adapted from *A History of US*

Student Guide
Lesson 5: Ponce de León and Coronado

Spanish conquistadors dreamed of finding another rich empire to conquer. They drove deeper into the Americas. Spain's thirst for gold did not end with the brutal conquest of the Incas. It was the reason for Coronado's 7,000-mile journey in search of the fabled city of Cíbola.

Lesson Objectives
- Identify Ponce de León as a Spanish explorer of Florida.
- Locate Puerto Rico, Florida, and Cuba on a map.
- Identify Francisco Vasquez de Coronado as a Spanish explorer of the southwestern United States and trace his route on a map.

PREPARE

Approximate lesson time is 60 minutes.

Materials
For the Student

Picture Puzzles

A History of US (Concise Edition), Volume A (Prehistory to 1800) by Joy Hakim

History Journal

LEARN
Activity 1: Spain Seeks Riches in the New World *(Offline)*
Instructions
Check Your Reading (Chapter 16, pages 76–80, and Chapter 17, pages 81–84)

- Add the routes of Ponce de León and Francisco Vasquez de Coronado to the European Explorers sheet from the Spanish Conquest lesson. (Refer to the map of European Exploration from the same lesson.) Also label Florida, Cuba, and Puerto Rico. Keep these sheets in your History Journal.
- Complete the Picture Puzzles sheet. Discuss your answers with an adult.

Use What You Know

During their journeys, many explorers kept diaries or journals in which they recorded their observations, thoughts, and feelings. Some explorers also drew maps showing where they went.

Imagine you are traveling with Coronado as he leads his expedition to find Cíbola. In your History Journal, write a journal entry about your adventure.

The journal entry should:

- Describe the makeup of the expedition (who went, how they traveled, what they ate, what they brought, etc.).
- Describe at least one encounter with Indians.
- Describe the findings of one exploring party that Coronado sent out.
- Express your opinion as to whether the expedition was a success or not and why.
- Include a map showing the expedition's route.

Read On

Ponce de León and Coronado weren't the last conquistadors to come to America. Hernando de Soto came to explore Florida and ended up discovering the Mississippi River. The dream of finding Cíbola hadn't died, either. Juan de Oñate would set out to find the golden city. Of course we know he didn't find it. But he would start a Spanish colony in New Mexico—Santa Fe.

- Read Chapter 18, pages 85–88, and Chapter 19, pages 89–92.
- Prepare to trace Hernando de Soto's route of exploration across the southeastern United States.

Name _____   Date _____

Picture Puzzles

Study the pictures and review Chapters 16 and 17 to answer these questions.

1. The place is Peru. Who is fighting? Who won? What conquistador was in charge?

_____

_____

_____

_____

_____

2. The place is Cuzco. Why are the people gathering all of their gold?

_____

_____

_____

_____

3. Who made this silver alpaca? What happened to most of their

artwork? _____

_____

4. What happened to about three-quarters of all Native Americans after Europeans arrived in the Americas?

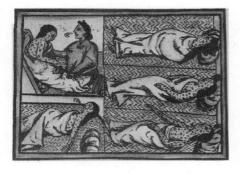

_____

_____

Thinking Cap Question! In the sixteenth century, Europeans were looking for gold and not much else. What if they had valued the arts and culture of the people they met? Explain how you think history might have been different.

Adapted from *A History of US*

Student Guide
Lesson 6: More Conquistadors

Conquistadors continued to explore North America. Cabrillo and de Soto explored California and the southeastern United States. They failed to find gold. Finally, one Spaniard did what no other had done. Juan de Oñate established a Spanish colony north of New Spain—Santa Fe.

Lesson Objectives

- Identify Hernando de Soto as a Spanish explorer of the southeastern United States and trace on a map his route of exploration.
- Describe the behavior of the conquistadors toward the Native Americans.
- Identify one city in the United States that started as a Spanish mission.
- Locate the Aztec Empire on a map.
- Identify Moctezuma as the leader of the Aztecs and Cortés as their Spanish conqueror.
- Describe the Aztec Empire as a complex civilization.
- Identify Mesoamerica and three Mesoamerican civilizations before the Spanish conquest.
- Identify Ponce de León as a Spanish explorer of Florida.
- Locate Puerto Rico, Florida, and Cuba on a map.
- Identify Francisco Vasquez de Coronado as a Spanish explorer of the southwestern United States and trace his route on a map.

PREPARE

Approximate lesson time is 60 minutes.

Materials

For the Student

A History of US (Concise Edition), Volume A (Prehistory to 1800) by Joy Hakim

map, U.S.

History Journal

LEARN
Activity 1: Giving Way to Priests and Settlers *(Offline)*
Instructions
Check Your Reading (Chapter 18, pages 85–88, and Chapter 19, pages 89–92)

Add Hernando de Soto's route to the European Explorers sheet in your History Journal. Then update the legend.

Review Chapters 18 and 19 by answering these questions:

1. How did De Soto treat Native Americans he encountered during his westward trek out of Florida?
2. Suppose De Soto and Coronado had met. What would they have learned from each other?
3. What was the significance of the expedition led by Juan de Oñate?
4. How did the Spanish arrival in the American Southwest affect Native Americans living in the area?
5. How would you describe the behavior of the conquistadors toward Native Americans?
6. Name two U.S. cities that started as Spanish missions.

Use What You Know

Questions for Conquistadors

Write one or more questions in your History Journal that you would like to ask the conquistadors about their behavior toward Native Americans. Then decide whether you would have wanted to be a conquistador if you had lived at that time. Explain your decision.

Use the Flash Cards to review for the Mid-Unit Assessment.

Read On

Why were the French interested in a pirate base in Florida? And what were they up to in Canada?
Read Chapter 20, pages 93–98, and Chapter 21, pages 99–105.

Beyond the Lesson

Visit PBS online to further explore the Spanish conquest.

ASSESS
Mid-Unit Assessment: European Exploration *(Online)*
You will complete an online assessment covering the main points of this unit. Your assessment will be scored by the computer.

LEARN
Activity 2. Optional: More Conquistadors *(Online)*

Student Guide
Lesson 7: The French Explore America

The French came to the Americas as explorers and pirates. Some came to build settlements and escape religious persecution. They pushed north into Canada. Finally, their explorations took them down the Mississippi River to the doorstep of New Spain. We can still see their footsteps on maps today.

Lesson Objectives

- Describe the economic and religious motives for French exploration and colonization in North America.
- Identify the area of North America claimed by the French and the routes of major explorers.
- Locate on a map the Mississippi River, Great Lakes, St. Lawrence River, Gulf of Mexico, and the Atlantic and Pacific Oceans.
- Identify major types of bodies of water.

PREPARE

Approximate lesson time is 60 minutes.

Materials

    For the Student

        A History of US (Concise Edition), Volume A (Prehistory to 1800) by Joy Hakim

        Understanding Geography: Map Skills and Our World (Level 5)

        History Journal

LEARN
Activity 1: Pirates, Adventurers, and New France (Offline)
Instructions
Check Your Reading (Chapter 20, pages 93–98, and Chapter 21, pages 99–105)

Add the following explorers to the European Explorers sheet in your History Journal. (Refer to the map of European Exploration.)

- Giovanni da Verrazano
- Samuel de Champlain
- Louis Joliet and Jacques Marquette
- René Robert Cavelier Sieur de La Salle
- Jacques Cartier

Label *New France* and the *Mississippi River*.

Use the following words to describe the location of the Northwest Passage: Cathay, Eastern Ocean, river passage, Europe, North America. Have an adult check your description.

Bodies of Water

In the late 1600s, Europeans crossed the ocean and began exploring the New World and making claims to the lands they "discovered." Maps can help you understand historical events such as these. Maps can also give you clues about the history of a place.

- Read Activity 6, "Bodies of Water," pages 24–27, *Understanding Geography*.
- Answer Questions 1–22 in your History Journal.
- If you have time, you may want to answer the Skill Builder Questions on page 27.
- After you have finished, compare your answers with the ones in the Learning Coach Guide.

ASSESS

Lesson Assessment: The French Explore America (*Online*)

Answer the online geography questions for this assessment. Your assessment will be scored by the computer.

Student Guide
Lesson 8: From England to America

Queen Elizabeth sparked a new spirit of patriotism among the English. They were drawn to North America by dreams of wealth and by religious ideals. Although they soon learned that colonization would not be easy, land-hungry Europeans were ready to write new chapters in the history of the Western Hemisphere.

Lesson Objectives

- Demonstrate mastery of important knowledge and skills taught in previous lessons.
- Identify Elizabeth I as a queen of England who sponsored exploration.
- Summarize the achievements and failures of early English attempts at settlement.
- Identify the area of North America claimed by England.
- Describe England's motives for exploration and colonization as the desire to gain wealth and form model societies.
- Describe the economic and religious motives for French exploration and colonization in North America.
- Identify the area of North America claimed by the French and the routes of major explorers.
- Locate on a map the Mississippi River, Great Lakes, St. Lawrence River, Gulf of Mexico, and the Atlantic and Pacific Oceans.

PREPARE

Approximate lesson time is 60 minutes.

Materials

> For the Student
>> Guided Reading: Chapters 22 and 23
>>
>> A History of US (Concise Edition), Volume A (Prehistory to 1800) by Joy Hakim
>>
>> History Journal

LEARN
Activity 1: England's Attempts in the New World *(Offline)*
Instructions
Read

Read Chapter 22, pages 106–111, and Chapter 23, pages 112–114. Answer the questions on the Guided Reading: Chapters 22 and 23 sheet as you work. When you've finished, discuss your answers with an adult.

Use the Flash Cards to review Lessons 7 and 8 for the online assessment in this lesson.

ASSESS

Lesson Assessment: From England to America (*Online*)

You will complete an online assessment covering the main points for Lessons 7 and 8. Your assessment will be scored by the computer.

Name _____   Date _____

Guided Reading: Chapters 22 and 23

Read Chapters 22 and 23. Use this sheet to guide your reading and to record important facts and information.

1. Who became queen of England in 1558? _____

2. Describe England's new monarch. _____

   _____

   _____

3. What country was England most concerned about in the sixteenth century? _____

4. What were the two dreams that motivated Europeans to explore and colonize North America? _____

   _____

5. Who was the first Englishman to receive a royal charter for land in America?

   _____

6. Who wrote Utopia, and what was it about? _____

   _____

7. What favorite of Queen Elizabeth sent three expeditions to the New World?

   _____

8. What did this man name the land described by the captain of the first expedition?

   _____

9. Was the second expedition a success? Why or why not? _____

   _____

10. Describe the attitude of most Europeans toward the New World and its inhabitants.

    _____

    _____

    _____

11. What happened to the colony that was established on Roanoke Island in 1587?

_____

_____

12. Were England's early attempts at settling North America successful? Why or why not?

_____

_____

_____

Student Guide
Lesson 9: (Optional) Another Look

You have learned about the European exploration of North America. Now review the geography of this continent.

Lesson Objectives
- Idenfity major geographical features and landforms of North America.

PREPARE

Approximate lesson time is 60 minutes.

Materials
For the Student

Map of North America

A History of US (Concise Edition), Volume A (Prehistory to 1800) by Joy Hakim

History Journal

LEARN
Activity 1. Optional: North American Geography *(Offline)*
Instructions
Use What You Know

Locate and label the following on the map of North America. Use a pencil. See what you can do from memory first. Use the atlas in your book as a reference as needed.

Bodies of water:

- Atlantic Ocean and Pacific Ocean
- Hudson Bay
- Great Salt Lake
- The Great Lakes
- Gulf of St. Lawrence
- Gulf of Mexico
- Caribbean Sea

Rivers:

- St. Lawrence
- Hudson
- Mississippi
- Missouri
- Ohio
- Rio Grande
- Colorado

Islands:

- Greenland
- Cuba
- Bahamas
- Hispaniola
- Puerto Rico

Regions/territories/places:

- Newfoundland
- Nova Scotia
- Florida
- Louisiana
- Mexico
- California

Mountain ranges (add mountain symbols):

- Rockies
- Appalachians
- Sierra Madre Occidental
- Sierra Madre Oriental
- Sierra Nevada
- Coast Ranges

North America

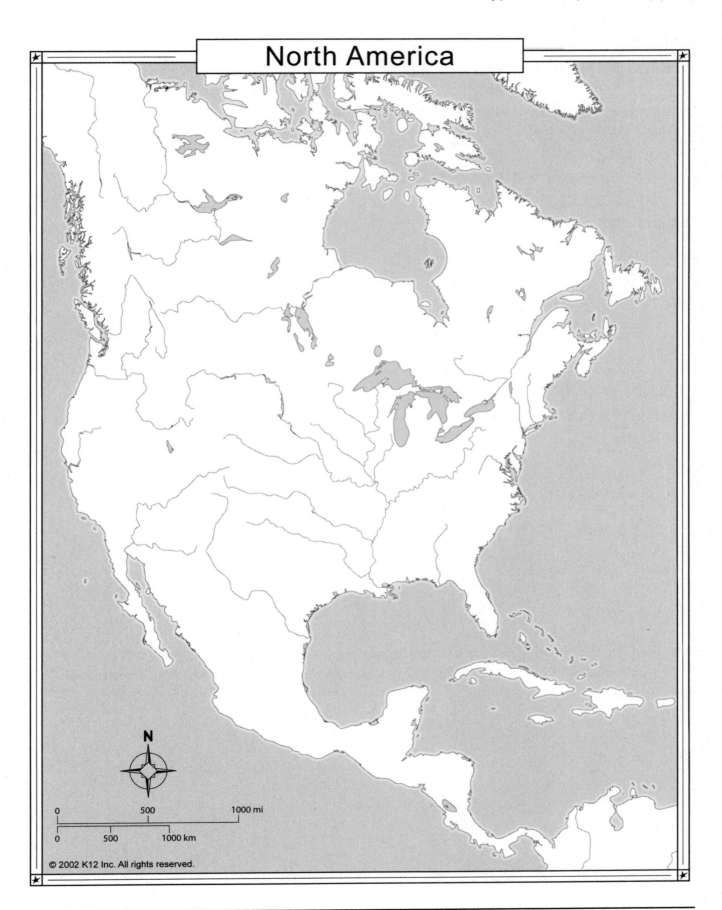

N

0 500 1000 mi

0 500 1000 km

Student Guide
Lesson 10: Unit Review

You've completed Unit 2, European Exploration. It's time to review what you've learned. You'll take the unit assessment in the next lesson.

Lesson Objectives

- Demonstrate mastery of important knowledge and skills taught in previous lessons.

PREPARE

Approximate lesson time is 60 minutes.

Materials

For the Student

A History of US (Concise Edition), Volume A (Prehistory to 1800) by Joy Hakim

History Journal

LEARN
Activity 1: A Look Back *(Offline)*
Instructions
Online Review

Stay online and use the following to review this unit:

- The Big Picture
- Flash Cards
- Time Line

History Journal Review

Now, review more by going through your History Journal. Look at the sheets you completed for this unit. Review your vocabulary words. If you completed writing assignments, read them. Don't rush through. Take your time. Your History Journal is a great resource for a unit review.

Student Guide
Lesson 11: Unit Assessment

You've finished this unit on European exploration! Now take the Unit Assessment, and then read an assignment.

Lesson Objectives

- Demonstrate mastery of important knowledge and skills taught in previous lessons.
- Explain the significance of new knowledge and inventions in fifteenth-century Europe, including Gutenberg's press and the compass.
- Locate the Aztec Empire on a map.
- Describe the Aztec Empire as a complex civilization.
- Identify Mesoamerica and three Mesoamerican civilizations before the Spanish conquest.
- Locate Puerto Rico, Florida, and Cuba on a map.
- Identify Francisco Vasquez de Coronado as a Spanish explorer of the southwestern United States and trace his route on a map.
- Identify Hernando de Soto as a Spanish explorer of the southeastern United States and trace on a map his route of exploration.
- Describe the behavior of the conquistadors toward the Native Americans.
- Identify one city in the United States that started as a Spanish mission.

PREPARE

Approximate lesson time is 60 minutes.

Materials

For the Student

A History of US (Concise Edition), Volume A (Prehistory to 1800) by Joy Hakim

History Journal

ASSESS

Unit Assessment: European Exploration, Part 1 (Online)

Complete the computer-scored portion of the Unit Assessment. When you have finished, complete the teacher-scored portion of the assessment and submit it to your teacher.

Unit Assessment: European Exploration, Part 2 (Offline)

Complete the teacher-scored portion of the Unit Assessment and submit it to your teacher.

LEARN
Activity 1: Chapters 24 and 25 *(Offline)*

Instructions
Read On

Who lived on the land that would one day be called Virginia? And what happened when English settlers arrived? The Woodland Indians lived well in that area. Why, then, did the English suffer from disease and starvation? Learn about both groups and what happened when English settlers arrived in 1607.

- Read Chapter 24, pages 116–120, and Chapter 25, pages 121–125.
- Prepare to compare the Powhatans and the English settlers at Jamestown.

Student Guide
Lesson 1: A Beginning in Virginia

English businessmen wanted to make money by sending settlers to Virginia to find gold. There was no gold, and disease and starvation killed most of the early settlers. But in time they did make money âby raising tobacco. A few years later, Pilgrims arrived on shores to the north, looking for a place to practice their religion. Puritans followed, and New England grew.

A Woodland Indian culture thrived on the land that would be called Virginia. This well-organized Indian culture consisted of hunters and farmers. When English settlers arrived they faced troubles from the start. The Indians attacked them. Their settlement was in a poor location. They faced disease and starvation.

Lesson Objectives
- Locate the Chesapeake Bay, the James River, and Jamestown on a map.
- Assess the needs of a group of settlers in a new place and list the kinds of people and equipment needed for success, including builders, doctors, and farmers.
- Describe the men and boys who sailed for Jamestown as gentlemen unprepared for hard work, their motivation as their desire for gold, and the difficulties they faced such as disease, starvation, and poor location and leadership.
- Explain that the Powhatans were able to live well by hunting, fishing, and farming the great resources of Virginia, while the early English settlers suffered because of poor planning and lack of skills.

PREPARE

Approximate lesson time is 60 minutes.

Materials
For the Student

      Map of Early American Settlements

      A History of US (Concise Edition), Volume A (Prehistory to 1800) by Joy Hakim

      History Journal

LEARN
Activity 1: Virginia Settlements *(Offline)*
Instructions
Check Your Reading (Chapter 24, pages 116-120, and Chapter 25, pages 121-125)

The first Virginians were Woodland Indians who hunted, fished, farmed, and fought in a region of great abundance. But their lives changed dramatically with the arrival of English settlers.

In your History Journal, write "Powhatans" at the top of the page, "English Settlers" one-third of the way down, and "Both" at the two-thirds mark. Then write the following phrases under the name of the group or groups they describe. Check your answers with an adult.

- Arrived by ship
- Searched for gold
- Lived in dozens of villages in eastern Virginia
- Hunted deer and raised vegetables
- Spent too little time planning and planting
- Settled in a swampy area
- Men hunted, fished, and fought; women farmed
- Waged war on enemies
- Used bear grease to ward off mosquitoes
- Ate berries, grapes, and seafood

Discuss

Use the map of Early American Settlements to discuss the following:

- Locate Jamestown on the map. What river is it on? Describe the location of this river.
- What larger body of water brought the settlers to the Chesapeake Bay?

Read On

John Smith was a tough leader. Not everyone liked him, but he led the colonists through their first months in Jamestown.

Read Chapter 26, pages, 126-130, and Chapter 27, pages 131-133. Before you read, think about how you might have handled the lazy, unskilled settlers at Jamestown. What do you think could have happened to cause a "starving time"? Write your thoughts in your History Journal.

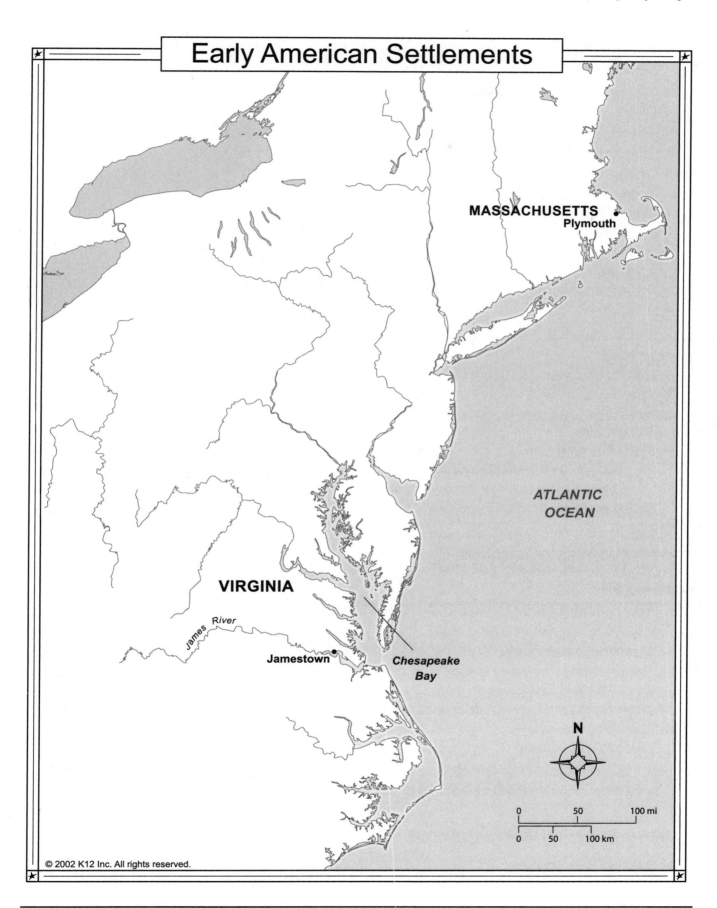

Early American Settlements

MASSACHUSETTS
Plymouth

VIRGINIA

James River

Jamestown

Chesapeake
Bay

ATLANTIC
OCEAN

N

0   50   100 mi

0   50   100 km

69

Student Guide
Lesson 2: John Smith and Jamestown

John Smith was a tough leader. He dealt with the local Indians. He dealt with the settlers, too. He pulled the colony through its first faltering months. But the winter of 1609-1610 almost wiped Jamestown out. The settlers ran out of food. Starvation shrank the settlement from 500 men to just 60.

Lesson Objectives
- Summarize the story of John Smith.
- Identify adjectives to describe John Smith, and explain the reasons he was able to save the colony, including his work policy and relationship with the Indians.
- Identify Pocahontas as the daughter of the chief Powhatan, and compare fictional accounts of her with historical fact.
- Explain how the Jamestown colony was saved from extinction when English ships arrived after a starving time.

PREPARE

Approximate lesson time is 60 minutes.

Materials
For the Student

The Settlers Settle

A History of US (Concise Edition), Volume A (Prehistory to 1800) by Joy Hakim

History Journal

LEARN
Activity 1: Pocahontas Plus *(Offline)*
Instructions
Check Your Reading (Chapter 26, pages 126-130, and Chapter 27, pages, 131-133)

When you read Chapters 26 and 27, you probably noticed a familiar name--Pocahontas. How did what you read compare with what you already knew?

Which of these statements are true and which are false?

1. Pocahontas was an Indian princess.
2. She saved John Smith's life twice.
3. She was about 12 years old when the settlers arrived.
4. Her father wanted her to marry John Smith.
5. Powhatan was Pocahontas's father.

Use What You Know

The Starving Time

In your History Journal, record background information--who, what, when, where, why, and how--that a reporter would need to write an article on the Starving Time. Discuss your answers with an adult.

The Biography of Captain John Smith

Suppose you wanted to write a biography of Captain John Smith. How would you organize your information?

The Settlers Settle page will help you think about and organize the important information you would need. Answer all the questions. Have an adult check your answers.

Read On

What does tobacco have to do with silk? Nothing now, but it did in the early history of Jamestown.

Read Chapter 28, pages 134-136, and Chapter 29, pages 137-141. Think about the things that happened in Virginia that year. List the three things you think are most important.

Vocabulary

You'll see these terms as you read. Write a brief definition for each term as you come to it.

- burgess
- colony
- indentured servant
- slave

Name _____   Date _____

Bio Facts Suppose that you want to write a biography of Captain John Smith. Before you begin writing, you have to organize some of the important information that you need. Fill in what you've learned below.

About Jamestown

1. What business group sent the Englishmen to Virginia in 1607? _____

2. What were the Englishmen looking for? _____
_____

3. Why didn't the settlers want to work? _____
_____

4. What was good and bad about Jamestown's location? _____
_____

About John Smith

5. Why was John Smith in chains when the ships arrived in Virginia? _____
_____

6. How did Smith get the settlers to work? _____
_____

7. What did Smith trade with the Indians? _____

8. Why did the Indians respect John Smith? _____
_____

9. What did John Smith think about America? _____
_____

Adapted from *A History of US*

Writing the Biography

10. You have to give your biography a title. Chose one of the following titles and circle it. Why do you think yours is the better title? Why didn't you choose the other one? You may write your answer on the back of this sheet.

• Captain John Smith, Brave and Smart
• John Smith, the Most Popular Man in Jamestown

Thinking Cap Question! What if Powhatan were writing a biography of John Smith? What would he say? In your History Journal, write a paragraph that Powhatan might have written about the new white leader.

Student Guide
Lesson 3: Tobacco and Turning Points

The Virginia colonists did not find riches in gold. They found them in tobacco! The colony needed workers. Indentured servants, and then slaves, were brought in to fill that need. The year 1619 marked three important events in the course of American life: (1) The first boatload of Englishwomen arrived in Virginia. (2) The English colonies in America became permanent and the people gained important rights. (3) African workers were brought to Virginia. This led to centuries of slavery.

Lesson Objectives
- Identify the role of tobacco in the economic success of Jamestown.
- Explain the beginnings of slavery in Virginia as a way to fill the need for field workers, and the difference between an indentured servant and a slave.
- Describe the significance of the Virginia Charter in guaranteeing the rights of Englishmen to all settlers of the Jamestown colony.
- Identify the House of Burgesses as the first representative assembly in the European colonies.

PREPARE

Approximate lesson time is 60 minutes.

Materials
For the Student

A History of US (Concise Edition), Volume A (Prehistory to 1800) by Joy Hakim

History Journal

paper, construction, 9" x 12"

pencils, colored, 16 colors or more

Keywords and Pronunciation
stygian (STIH-jee-uhn)

LEARN
Activity 1: What Doesn't Belong? (Offline)
Instructions
Check Your Reading (Chapter 28, pages 134–136, and Chapter 29, pages 137–141)

What doesn't belong? Read each numbered word or phrase. Then read the phrases underneath. Figure out which phrase does not belong in each group. Check your answers with an adult.

1. tobacco

- hated by King James
- not very profitable
- required a lot of workers to grow
- new variety developed by John Rolfe

2. indentured servants

- worked from four to seven years for freedom
- some were criminals
- some were treated like slaves
- called that because of bad teeth

3. boatload of Africans

- first came to Virginia on a Dutch ship
- immediately became slaves forever
- some owned their own land
- originally treated like indentured servants

4. House of Burgesses

- a group of lawmakers first elected in 1619
- an assembly in Virginia like Parliament in England
- a huge plantation home belonging originally to the Burgesses
- America's first representative government

Use What You Know

King James used some strong words to describe how he felt about tobacco. Read the quotation in the sidebar on page 135 aloud. Ask for help with any words you don't understand. Or listen to someone else reading it aloud. Can you almost hear King James talking?

Now create an anti-tobacco advertisement for the king. Reread what he had to say about tobacco before you begin.

Read On

The colonists and the Indians went from good intentions to violent conflict. Why do you think this happened?

Read Chapter 30, pages 142–145. Before you begin reading, predict the answer to the first of these questions. Then read to see if you were right. Answer the second question in your History Journal.

1. What was the major reason that the Europeans and Indians had no hope of living in peace with each other?
2. What factors in England helped Jamestown succeed?

Student Guide
Lesson 4: Conflict

Conflict was brewing between the Europeans and the Indians. The Europeans wanted to control more land. The Indians knew that losing land would destroy their way of life. The conflict soon became violent. Still, more people arrived from England. Slavery increased as well.

Lesson Objectives
- Identify James I as the king of England at the time Virginia was settled.
- Describe the factors in England that pushed people to come to America, including poverty and a growing population.
- Explain the reasons for conflict between English settlers and Native Americans as racism and the disagreement over land use and ownership.
- Explain that slavery had existed in Africa long before slavery came to America but that there were major differences.

PREPARE

Approximate lesson time is 60 minutes.

Materials
For the Student

Act 1: Jamestown

A History of US (Concise Edition), Volume A (Prehistory to 1800) by Joy Hakim

History Journal

LEARN
Activity 1: Indians vs. English (Offline)
Instructions
Check Your Reading (Chapter 30, pages 142–145)

Talk over the following with an adult:

1. Did you predict what happened in Chapter 30? Don't worry if you didn't—predictions can't always be right.
2. What was the main reason for conflict between English settlers and Native Americans?
3. How did the Great Massacre of 1622 lead to more violence?
4. Why were people leaving England to settle in Virginia?
5. King James thought he was absolutely divine and always right. King James also thought he ruled by "divine right," which is different. What is divine right?
6. Before the first African slaves were brought to America, slavery had existed for a long time. Where? When? How? What happened in America to make slavery develop into "a terrible and degrading system"?

Use What You Know

Complete the Act I: Jamestown sheet and see if you think history is like a play. Check your answers with an adult.

Read On

Read Chapter 31, pages 146–150, and Chapter 32, pages 151–155. Look for the answers to these questions as you read.

1. Who were the Saints?
2. Who were the Strangers?
3. What was a Puritan?
4. Who was Squanto?

Look for these things and people, too. Write something about each of them in your History Journal.

- Pilgrim
- Mayflower
- William Bradford
- Constitution
- Mayflower Compact

ASSESS

Lesson Assessment: Conflict *(Online)*

You will complete an online assessment covering the main points of this lesson. Your assessment will be scored by the computer.

Name _____   Date _____

Act 1: Jamestown

Some people say that history is like a play. There is a setting—a place such as Jamestown. There is a time—such as the early 1600s. And there is a cast of characters—the people who take part in the events, whose lives are the real story of history. Answer these questions as if you were a member in the cast of characters at Jamestown. Use the back of this sheet if necessary.

You are a woman from England. It is 1619:

1. Why did you come to Jamestown? _____

_____

2. What are some of the ways you would like to change Jamestown? _____

_____

_____

You are a burgess. It is 1619:

3. What is your job? _____

4. In what way is the House of Burgesses a "first"? _____

_____

You are an African. It is 1619:

5. How and why were you taken from your home? _____

_____

6. How did the African slave trade start? _____

_____

You are a Powhatan Indian. It is 1622:

7. Do you and the Europeans disagree about land? Why? _____

_____

Adapted from *A History of US*

8. The Europeans are Christian. How do they view your people and your beliefs?

_____

_____

9. What did some of your people do in March 1622? _____

_____

Thinking Cap Question! The play is entitled "Jamestown Days." Of the above characters, which one would you most like to be? In your History Journal, either write one scene that involves your character or draw a picture of your character. If you need help, refer to your book. It contains many details about the everyday life of various Jamestown dwellers.

Student Guide
Lesson 5: Pilgrims and Promises

A group of people in England was unhappy with the established church. They no longer wanted to be part of it. First they fled to Holland. Then, in 1620, the Pilgrims settled in America. They struggled through their first year because they arrived after the planting season was over. The Indians helped them. Meanwhile, times grew harder for another religious group in England—the Puritans.

Lesson Objectives
- Describe the goals of the Separatists, or Pilgrims, including religious freedom.
- Describe the Mayflower Compact as an early form of self-government in Plymouth and William Bradford as the governor.
- Identify Squanto as an Indian who taught the Pilgrims how to survive in their new home.
- Describe the hardships faced by the Pilgrims, including starvation and cold.

PREPARE

Approximate lesson time is 60 minutes.

Materials
For the Student

A Land of Differences Activity Sheet

A History of US (Concise Edition), Volume A (Prehistory to 1800) by Joy Hakim

History Journal

LEARN
Activity 1: Strangers, Saints, and Pilgrims (Offline)
Instructions
Check Your Reading (Chapter 31, pages 146–150, and Chapter 32, pages 151–155)

You read about many people, ideas, and adventures in Chapters 31 and 32. The Land of Differences sheet will help you sort them out. After you answer each question, turn the paper over and write down the reason behind your choice.

For the Thinking Cap Question, write a caption for the picture. Be sure to look carefully at the picture and think about what it means.

Use What You Know

Imagine that you were a Pilgrim—one who kept a diary. Write three short diary entries in your History Journal. Each entry should describe one of the following:

- problems in the trip, or life in the new colony
- the way the settlement was governed
- the help the Indians gave, especially Squanto

Read On

In 1630 the first Puritans arrived in the New World. What do you remember about the Puritans and what they wanted to do?

Read Chapter 33, pages 156–158, and Chapter 34, pages 159–163. Predict the answers to the following questions and write them in your History Journal. Check them and change them as you read.

1. How is a charter like a constitution?
2. What did toleration mean to the Puritans?
3. Why did the Puritans dislike the Quakers?
4. What does *theocracy* mean?
5. What was the *common* in a Puritan village?
6. What did the Puritans think about education?

ASSESS

Lesson Assessment: Pilgrims and Promises (*Online*)

You will complete an online assessment covering the main points of this lesson. Your assessment will be scored by the computer.

Name _____   Date _____

A Land of Differences

Different Ideas, Different Ways When the Pilgrims and Puritans came to America, they brought many different customs and ideas. Read each statement below. Circle the name of the person or group who might have said it.

1. "My church is the established church in England."

   a Roman Catholic   an Anglican

2. "We believe that we can worship God on our own, without priests."

   Catholics   Separatists

3. "I am unhappy in England and hope to find a life of adventure in America."

   a Saint   a Stranger

4. "We want to build a perfect society."

   Pilgrims   indentured servants

5. "I will tell the story of the Pilgrims."

   William Bradford   John Winthrop

6. "My people agree to a peace treaty with the Pilgrims."

   Powhatan   Massasoit

The Pilgrims' ideas about government were different from King James's ideas. Answer the following questions about the Pilgrims' form of government:

7. The Pilgrims agreed to live together under a government of laws. The document they signed is called: _____

8. Why do you think this document is considered one of the great documents of American history?_____

_____

Thinking Cap Question! Write a caption for this picture.

Adapted from *A History of US*

Student Guide
Lesson 6: What's a Puritan?

In 1630, Puritans began the Massachusetts Bay Colony. They set up a new government there. Now they were free to follow their own religious beliefs. But they did not accept other religions. New England villages were well planned. They had places for living, working, and teaching. They had places for worship and for public meetings.

Lesson Objectives
- Define *Puritan* and describe the problems Puritans faced in England, including religious persecution.
- Describe the Puritan settlement of Massachusetts Bay, including the colony's charter, leadership, and religious policy.
- Explain the importance of education to the Puritans as the need to read the Bible, and give examples of the kinds of education established in Massachusetts Bay, including town schools and Harvard College.
- Describe the towns in Massachusetts Bay.

PREPARE

Approximate lesson time is 60 minutes.

Materials
For the Student
> Puritan Life Activity Sheet
> A History of US (Concise Edition), Volume A (Prehistory to 1800) by Joy Hakim
> History Journal

LEARN
Activity 1: Puritans and More Puritans (Offline)
Instructions
Check Your Reading (Chapter 33, pages 156–158, and Chapter 34, pages 159–163)

- Complete the Puritan Life sheet.
- Ask an adult to check your answers.

Use What You Know

Draw a map of your own New England town. Include:

- A New England setting
- At least three of the most important buildings in a New England town
- The commons
- A name for the town

Name _____ Date _____

Puritan Life

By 1640, 20,000 Puritans had come to New England. When they settled, they adopted many new customs and incorporated changes in their daily lives. Write a sentence to explain how each of the following things or places was part of Puritan life in America.

1. the Charter: _____

_____

2. religious freedom: _____

_____

3. ministers: _____

_____

4. stockades: _____

_____

5. the meetinghouse: _____

_____

6. the common: _____

_____

7. Harvard College: _____

_____

8. schoolteachers: _____

_____

9. sermons: _____

_____

Adapted from *A History of US*

Student Guide
Lesson 7: Waterways or Waterwheels

There were big differences between life in Jamestown and life in Massachusetts. One reason for the differences was geography.

Lesson Objectives
- Analyze the geography of the eastern seaboard of the United States.
- Predict economic activity based on the geography of a region.

PREPARE

Approximate lesson time is 60 minutes.

Materials
> For the Student
>> Collecting Evidence
>> Map of U.S. Fall Line
> History Journal

LEARN
Activity 1: Geography Makes a Difference *(Offline)*
Instructions
Waterfalls and Waterways

Imagine traveling in a boat up a river. If you started where the river meets the ocean, or the mouth of the river, what would happen when you got near a waterfall? Could you continue going up the river?
The waterfall is there because there is a steep drop in the elevation of the land. The river falls from the higher elevation to the lower. If you step out of your boat onto the shore and try to walk, you will find yourself climbing from rock to rock—moving into the mountains where the river started.

In colonial times, there were very few roads and no tunnels in North America. Most people stopped going inland when they came to a waterfall. It was just too hard to go any farther. And the rocky, hilly land just beyond the waterfalls was not very good for farming. Usually people stayed between the Atlantic Ocean and the foothills, or beginnings, of the Appalachian Mountains. This area is called a coastal plain. If the mountains are far from the ocean there can be a very wide coastal plain. But if the mountains are close to the ocean there may be no coastal plain at all. The land in the Chesapeake is very different from the land in New England. So is the climate. Geography is one reason life was so different in the two regions.

Use the map of the U.S. Fall Line and answer these questions in your History Journal.

1. How many miles wide is the coastal plain near the Virginia-North Carolina border at the southernmost end of the Chesapeake Bay? Use the scale shown on the map and a ruler to measure the coastal plain, shown in dark gray on the map.

2. How wide is the coastal plain (the dark gray area) on the mainland of Massachusetts?

3. Look at the location of the waterfalls in Massachusetts and Virginia. Find them by matching the symbol in the map key to the map itself. What do you think the land is like in the area between the coastal plain and the mountains? This area is shown in light gray on the onscreen map. Remember what causes a waterfall. Is the land in that area likely to be flat or hilly? Smooth or rocky?

4. Look at the direction in which the rivers flow. Remember, rivers always flow toward a larger body of water such as a bay or an ocean. If you floated on a river in Virginia, in what direction would you go?

5. If you floated on most rivers in New England, in what direction would you go?

6. If you wanted to travel a long way west from the ocean on a river, would you choose to do it in Virginia or Massachusetts? Why?

7. If you wanted to pack your belongings and move far away from your neighbors on the coast, would it be easier in Massachusetts or Virginia?

8. Now think about how people might live in the two regions. If you wanted to have a big farm with thousands of acres and many workers, would you settle in Virginia or Massachusetts? Why?

9. If you wanted to live in a town with close neighbors and other towns nearby, would you settle in Virginia or Massachusetts? Why?

10. Water is powerful. It can turn waterwheels that move other wheels for energy. If you wanted to build a waterwheel that had a lot of waterpower to turn it, would you build it near or far from a waterfall? Why?

Use What You Know

Some early settlers had trouble finding a good way to earn a living. They could have used advice from someone who knew the geography of the region.

The king wants to know how to make the colonies successful. He knows it was a mistake for settlers in Jamestown to spend their time looking for gold.

Here is the scenario for your assignment. Pretend to be an adviser to the king. Write a letter to him suggesting what the colonists in Virginia should do. Then describe what economic activities the settlers in Massachusetts should consider. Use the Collecting Evidence sheet to help you organize your information.

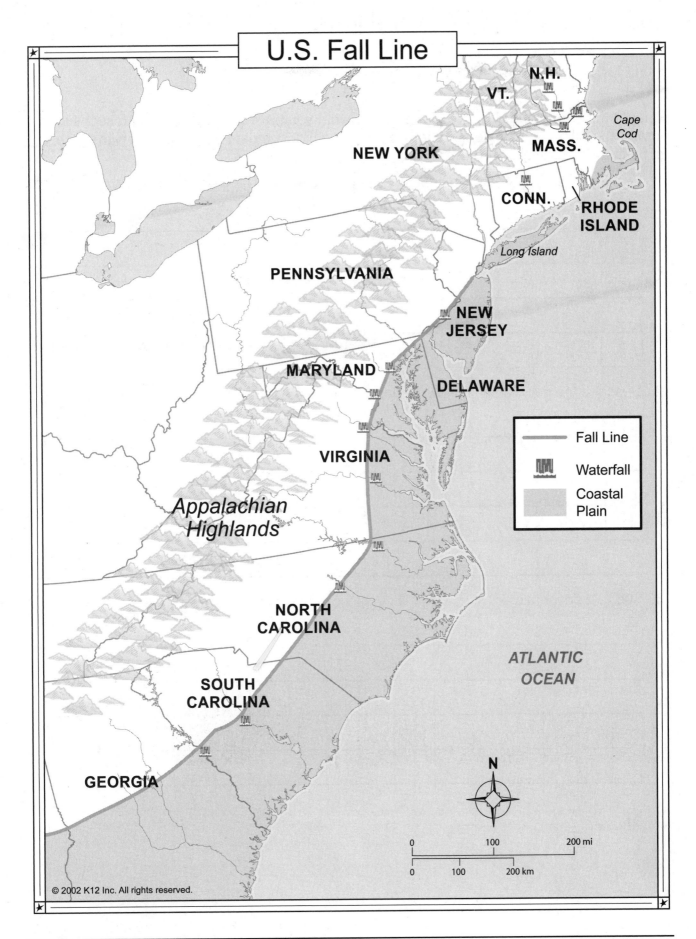

U.S. Fall Line

N.H.
VT.
MASS.
Cape Cod
NEW YORK
CONN.
RHODE ISLAND
Long Island
PENNSYLVANIA
NEW JERSEY
MARYLAND
DELAWARE
VIRGINIA
Appalachian Highlands
ATLANTIC OCEAN
NORTH CAROLINA
SOUTH CAROLINA
GEORGIA

Fall Line
Waterfall
Coastal Plain

N

| 0 | 100 | 200 mi |
| 0 | 100 | 200 km |

Name _____   Date _____

Collecting Evidence

Refer to the map of the U.S. Fall Line and use what you have learned in earlier lessons to answer the following questions. When you are finished, compare your answers with those found in the Learning Coach Guide.

1. List three ways geography influences what kinds of work people do.

_____

_____

_____

_____

2. Describe the geography of New England. Include the land, rivers, and climate.

_____

_____

_____

_____

3. Suggest economic activities that will be successful in New England.

_____

_____

_____

_____

4. Describe the geography of Virginia. Include the land, rivers, and climate.

_____

_____

_____

_____

_____

5. Suggest economic activities that will be successful in Virginia.

_____

_____

_____

_____

_____

Student Guide
Lesson 8: (Optional) Thankful for Feasting

Lesson Objectives
- Explore the history and traditions of Thanksgiving.

PREPARE

Approximate lesson time is 60 minutes.

LEARN
Activity 1. Optional: A Plymouth Celebration *(Online)*

Instructions
Go online to the Plimoth Plantation's "You Are the Historian" activity and learn more about the American Thanksgiving tradition (http://www.plimoth.org/learn/just-kids/thanksgiving-interactive-you-are-historian).

Student Guide
Lesson 9: Unit Review

You have completed Unit 3, Thirteen Colonies, Part 1. It's time to review what you've learned. You'll take the Unit Assessment in the next lesson.

Lesson Objectives
- Review early English settlement in North America.

PREPARE

Approximate lesson time is 60 minutes.

Materials
For the Student

A History of US (Concise Edition), Volume A (Prehistory to 1800) by Joy Hakim

History Journal

LEARN
Activity 1: A Look Back *(Offline)*
Instructions
Online Review

Go online and use the following to review this unit:

- The Big Picture
- Flash Cards
- Time Line

History Journal Review

Review some more by going through your History Journal. Look at the activity sheets you completed for this unit. Review your vocabulary words. If you completed any writing assignments, read them. Don't rush through; take your time. Your History Journal is a great resource for a unit review.

Student Guide
Lesson 10: Unit Assessment

You've finished this unit. Take the unit assessment. Then take a break!

Lesson Objectives

- Demonstrate mastery of important knowledge and skills taught in previous lessons.
- Locate the Chesapeake Bay, the James River, and Jamestown on a map.
- Describe the men and boys who sailed for Jamestown as gentlemen unprepared for hard work, their motivation as their desire for gold, and the difficulties they faced such as disease, starvation, and poor location and leadership.
- Explain how the Jamestown colony was saved from extinction when English ships arrived after a starving time.
- Identify the role of tobacco in the economic success of Jamestown.
- Explain the beginnings of slavery in Virginia as a way to fill the need for field workers, and the difference between an indentured servant and a slave.
- Describe the Mayflower Compact as an early form of self-government in Plymouth and William Bradford as the governor.
- Describe the Puritan settlement of Massachusetts Bay, including the colony's charter, leadership, and religious policy.
- Explain the importance of education to the Puritans as the need to read the Bible, and give examples of the kinds of education established in Massachusetts Bay, including town schools and Harvard College.
- Analyze the geography of the eastern seaboard of the United States.
- Predict economic activity based on the geography of a region.
- Describe the significance of the Virginia Charter in guaranteeing the rights of Englishmen to all settlers of the Jamestown colony.
- Identify the House of Burgesses as the first representative assembly in the European colonies.
- Identify James I as the king of England at the time Virginia was settled.
- Describe the factors in England that pushed people to come to America, including poverty and a growing population.
- Explain the reasons for conflict between English settlers and Native Americans as racism and the disagreement over land use and ownership.
- Describe the hardships faced by the Pilgrims, including starvation and cold.
- Describe the Puritan settlement of Massachusetts Bay, including the colony's charter, leadership, and religious policy.
- Explain the importance of education to the Puritans as the need to read the Bible, and give examples of the kinds of education established in Massachusetts Bay, including town schools and Harvard College.

PREPARE

Approximate lesson time is 60 minutes.

ASSESS

Unit Assessment: Thirteen Colonies, Part 1, Part 1 *(Online)*

Complete the computer-scored portion of the Unit Assessment. When you have finished, complete the teacher-scored portion of the assessment and submit it to your teacher.

Unit Assessment: Thirteen Colonies, Part 1, Part 2 *(Offline)*

Complete the teacher-scored portion of the Unit Assessment and submit it to your teacher.

Student Guide
Lesson 1: Breaks with Tradition: Roger Williams

Geography and values both play a big part in the way people live. In the southern colonies, good soil and warm weather led to the growth of plantations. In New England, towns and industry grew near fast rivers and the coast. The middle colonies had both cities and farms. Different kinds of people lived there, many of them tolerant of other religions.

Roger Williams was a Puritan minister with some non-Puritan ideas and beliefs. Williams's beliefs led to the founding of a new colony. Some of his ideas are central to American life even today.

Lesson Objectives

- Identify Roger Williams as the founder of Rhode Island and a supporter of religious toleration and fair treatment of Native Americans.
- Explain the advantages of relative location to natural harbors in the settlement of Providence.
- Locate the colony of Rhode Island on a map and list its founder, his motives, and his accomplishments.

PREPARE

Approximate lesson time is 60 minutes.

Materials

For the Student

The Thirteen Colonies

A History of US (Concise Edition), Volume A (Prehistory to 1800) by Joy Hakim

History Journal

LEARN
Activity 1: Roger Williams (Offline)
Instructions
Read

You've learned that the Separatists and the Puritans had been involved with religious conflicts in England. The Separatists wanted to separate themselves from the Church of England, and the Puritans wanted to purify the Church of England. As a result of these conflicts new colonies were founded in North America. Now you will meet a man who had religious conflicts with the Puritans from the Massachusetts Bay Colony. These religious conflicts lead to the founding of another new colony. In today's reading you will learn about Roger Williams and how his ideas and beliefs led to the founding of a new colony.

Read Chapter 35, pages 164–167. As you read, prepare to discuss the answers to these questions:

1. Who was Roger Williams?
2. How did his beliefs differ from traditional Puritan beliefs?
3. How did these beliefs lead to the founding of a new colony?

4. What was the new colony called?
5. Was there conflict or cooperation between this new colony and the Native Americans?

Vocabulary

You'll see these terms as you read. Write a brief definition for each term in your History Journal.

- freedom of conscience
- atheist (AY-thee-ist)
- separation of church and state

Check Your Reading (Chapter 35, pages 164–167)

Discuss Chapter 35 with an adult.

Use What You Know

- Locate and label Rhode Island and Providence on the map on the Thirteen Colonies sheet.
- Complete the section in the chart for Rhode Island.
- In your History Journal, explain why Williams might have chosen the geographic location of the new colony. Explain his motive for establishing the new colony, and list the colony's accomplishments.

Read On

You learned how the Puritans banished Roger Williams from the Massachusetts Bay Colony because of religious conflict. Williams founded the Rhode Island colony and allowed others to practice the religion of their choice. But religious conflict in Massachusetts Bay did not stop after Roger Williams was banished. Anne Hutchinson and Mary Dyer were two women who broke with Puritan religious beliefs and practices.

Read Chapter 36, pages 168–171. As you read, think about how the beliefs of Anne Hutchinson and Mary Dyer were different from the beliefs of most Puritans.

Vocabulary

You'll see these terms as you read. Write a brief definition for each as you come to it.

- chattel
- Quaker
- divine right of kings
- martyr

Name _____   Date _____

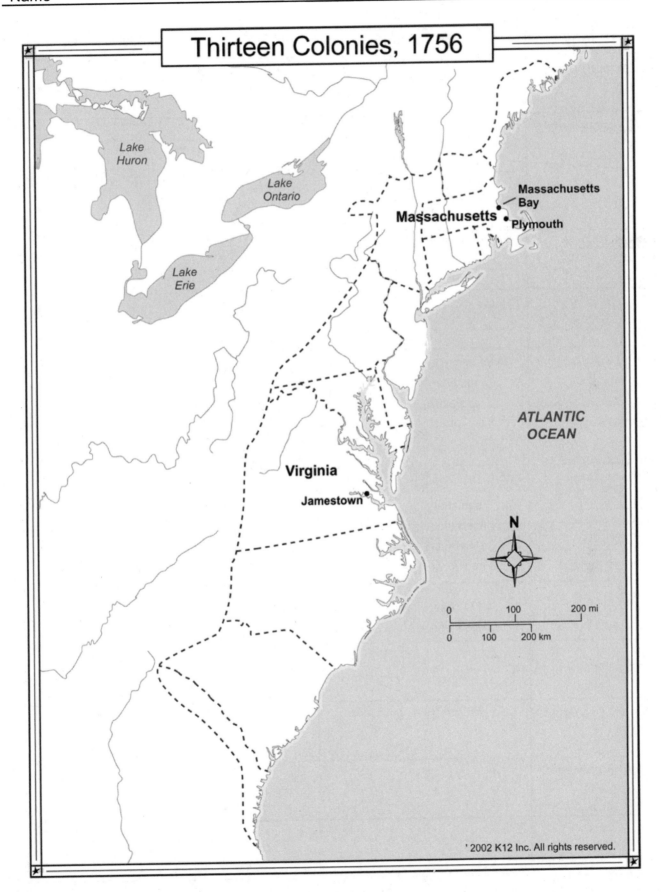

Thirteen Colonies, 1756

Lake Huron

Lake Ontario

Lake Erie

Massachusetts

Massachusetts Bay

Plymouth

Virginia

Jamestown

ATLANTIC OCEAN

N

0		100		200 mi
0	100		200 km	

Colony	Date Founded	Founder(s)
New Hampshire	1680	
Massachusetts	Plymouth: 1620	Pilgrims
	Massachusetts Bay Colony: 1630	Puritans
Connecticut	1636	
Rhode Island	1647	
New York	1664	
New Jersey	1664	
Pennsylvania	1681	
Delaware	1638	
Maryland	1632	
Virginia	1607	
North Carolina	1663	
South Carolina	1712	
Georgia	1733	

Student Guide
Lesson 2: Breaks with Tradition: Anne Hutchinson and Mary Dyer

Anne Hutchinson and Mary Dyer were two women who defied Puritan beliefs and practices. Rebels with a cause, they had the courage to face some terrible consequences for what they believed.

Lesson Objectives

- Describe the status of women in Puritan society.
- Describe the consequences of Anne Hutchinson's break with Puritan tradition.
- Identify Mary Dyer as a Puritan who became a Quaker and was executed for her beliefs.
- Compare and contrast the views of New England dissenters, including Hutchinson and Dyer.

PREPARE

Approximate lesson time is 60 minutes.

Materials

For the Student

Rebels with a Cause

A History of US (Concise Edition), Volume A (Prehistory to 1800) by Joy Hakim

History Journal

LEARN
Activity 1: Anne Hutchinson and Mary Dyer *(Offline)*

Instructions

Check Your Reading (Chapter 36, pages 168–171)

- Complete the Rebels with a Cause sheet.
- Ask an adult to check your answers.

Discuss

Discuss with an adult the ways the Puritan view of women and the Quaker view of women differed from each other.

Read On

Suppose a neighbor for some reason didn't like you and announced to the neighborhood that you were a witch. Would you be thrown in jail or put to death? Probably not, but in 1692 that event did happen in a small village in Massachusetts. In today's reading, you will learn how suspicion and mass hysteria led to the witchcraft trials in Salem.

Read Chapter 37, pages 172–175.

Vocabulary

You'll see the term "city upon a hill" as you read. Write a brief definition in your History Journal when you come to it.

Name _____   Date _____

Rebels with a Cause

Three Rebels Roger Williams, Anne Hutchinson, and Mary Dyer all disagreed with certain Puritan beliefs. But what beliefs did each one hold? What did each one oppose? How did each one stand up for his or her own beliefs? Write the correct name after each of the following descriptions:

1. Believed in freedom of conscience: _____

2. Believed that ordinary people could interpret the Bible: _____

3. Believed in the separation of church and state: _____

4. Refused to swear allegiance to the king: _____

5. Believed that the king had no right to take Indian land: _____

6. Founded the colony that became Rhode Island: _____

7. Was hanged on Boston Common: _____

8. Was killed in New York: _____

9. Wrote a book to teach others the language of the Narraganset Indians: _____

10. Became a Quaker: _____

Thinking Cap Question! Anne Hutchinson and Mary Dyer were friends. Write a conversation that they might have had with one another in your History Journal. Make sure that their conversation reflects how they felt about the Puritans.

Student Guide
Lesson 3: Visiting Salem

In 1692 trouble started brewing in the Salem area. Neighbors became suspicious of one another and began to accuse each other of being witches. Mass hysteria led to witch trials, hangings, and burnings.

Lesson Objectives
- Explain the origins and results of the witchcraft trials in Salem.
- Explain the meaning of the phrase "city upon a hill."

PREPARE

Approximate lesson time is 60 minutes.

Materials
For the Student

A Visit to Salem

A History of US (Concise Edition), Volume A (Prehistory to 1800) by Joy Hakim

History Journal

paper, construction, 9" x 12"

pencils, colored, 16 colors or more

LEARN
Activity 1: Of Witches and Dinosaurs (Offline)
Instructions
Check Your Reading (Chapter 37, pages 172–175)

- Discuss Chapter 37 with an adult.
- Complete the Visit to Salem sheet.
- Ask an adult to check your answers.

Use What You Know

Create a Time Line

- Visit the Salem Witch Trials website:
  http://school.discoveryeducation.com/schooladventures/salemwitchtrials/
- Create a time line of the accusations, examinations, trials, and hangings.
- Print images or illustrate the different events on the time line.
- Put the time line in your History Journal.

Read On

The Puritans were good, strong, intelligent people, even though they made some terrible mistakes. They were independent thinkers, too, and sometimes they disagreed with each other. America was big enough that those who wanted to could move on and start a new settlement. Some people started new settlements for religious reasons. Others did it because they wanted more farmland. Of course, moving to new areas meant pushing into Indian land. Would this cause conflicts between the Indians and the settlers?

Learn how the Connecticut and New Hampshire colonies were founded and how the growth of English settlement led to war.

Read Chapter 38, pages 176–179, and Chapter 39, pages 180–183. As you read the chapters, prepare to discuss the following:

1. How were the people who colonized Maine and New Hampshire different from earlier New England colonists?
2. How did the European idea of land ownership differ from the Indian idea?
3. Why was Connecticut founded?
4. Who were John Mason and Ferdinando Gorges?
5. What caused the Pequot War?
6. What led to King Philip's War, and what was the outcome?

Name _____   Date _____

A Visit to Salem

Pretend that you are a traveler who is visiting the new colonies in the 1690s. You have just arrived in Salem. Fill in the missing words in your diary.

Dear Diary,

Well, here I am in Salem, in the (1) _____ Colony. Most people here belong to one religious group, and call themselves (2) _____ . They can be very judgmental and self-(3) _____ people who are sure that they and only they know the truth! They read the (4) _____ every day and believe that only a few people are saved by God. Those who are saved are members of God's (5) _____ , and must lead very good, religious lives. Those who are not saved will go to a terrible hell filled with fires.

Life was pretty scary here recently. Several young girls were acting very strange. They said that their servant, a poor woman from the West Indies named (6) _____ was a (7) _____ , possessed by evil spirits. Many were accused of being possessed and more than one hundred people were put on (8) _____ . Altogether (9) _____ people were put to death.

Off to Boston tomorrow. I hope things are a little more peaceful there!

Thinking Cap Question! Suppose the traveler were able to interview the judges that presided over the witch trials. Write three interview questions the traveler would ask in your History Journal. Answer them as you think the judges might have answered.

Student Guide
Lesson 4: Elsewhere in New England

A growing number of English settlers spread farther onto Indian land. The Indians believed land was to be shared, not owned, but the settlers thought they had taken control from the Indians. Indian resentment of spreading English settlement soon led to war.

Lesson Objectives

- Demonstrate mastery of important knowledge and skills in previous lessons.
- Chart the founding of Connecticut and New Hampshire.
- Describe the differences in European and Native American attitudes toward land ownership and land use.
- Explain the origins and results of the Pequot War and King Philip's War.
- Explain the reasons for the lack of Indian unity in fighting Europeans.
- Describe the status of women in Puritan society.
- Describe the consequences of Anne Hutchinson's break with Puritan tradition.
- Identify Mary Dyer as a Puritan who became a Quaker and was executed for her beliefs.
- Explain the origins and results of the witchcraft trials in Salem.
- Explain the meaning of the phrase "city upon a hill."
- Identify Roger Williams as the founder of Rhode Island and a supporter of religious toleration and fair treatment of Native Americans.
- Locate the colony of Rhode Island on a map and list its founder, his motives, and his accomplishments.

PREPARE

Approximate lesson time is 60 minutes.

Materials

> For the Student
>> The Pequot War and King Philip's War
>> A History of US (Concise Edition), Volume A (Prehistory to 1800) by Joy Hakim
>> History Journal

LEARN
Activity 1: Connecticut, New Hampshire, and Maine (Offline)

Instructions
Check Your Reading (Chapter 38, pages 176–179, and Chapter 39, pages 180–183)
Discuss Chapters 38 and 39 with an adult.
Use What You Know

- Label New Hampshire and Connecticut on the map on the Thirteen Colonies sheet from the Breaks with Tradition: Roger Williams lesson.
- Complete the sections for New Hampshire and Connecticut on the chart on the same sheet.

- Color the New England colonies green on the map.
- Use the Pequot War and King Philip's War sheet to create a storyboard explaining the causes and results of these two wars. Present the storyboard to an adult. (A storyboard is a tool that filmmakers, multimedia designers, and animators use to visually represent a storyline. A storyboard does not use a lot of detail. Instead, it sketches out the story in a brief, skeleton-like way. One idea is to use a "cartoon" format with characters and speech bubbles.)

Look Back

Use the flash cards to review information on New England before you take the mid-unit assessment.

Read On

The New England colonies were New Hampshire, Massachusetts, Connecticut, and Rhode Island. These colonies were English colonies. But in the 1600s, Holland and Sweden founded colonies in America, too. Men nicknamed Silvernails and Big Tub were the leaders of New Netherland and New Sweden. Do you know where these colonies were and what they are called today? Here's a clue: In 1664 the English took control of them and renamed New Netherland in honor of the Duke of York.

Read Chapter 40, pages 184–187, and Chapter 41, pages 188–190. Find the answers to the following questions.

1. What role did trading play in both New Netherland and New Sweden?
2. What happened to the Dutch and Swedish colonies in America?
3. How did New Netherland become New York and New Jersey?
4. Give some examples of the ways in which the New Jersey colony was more democratic than many colonies.

Vocabulary

You'll see these words as you read. Write a brief definition for each term as you come to it.

- patroon
- proprietor
- quit rent

ASSESS

Mid-Unit Assessment: Thirteen Colonies, Part 1 *(Online)*
Complete the computer-scored portion of the Mid-Unit Assessment. When you have finished, complete the teacher-scored portion of the assessment and submit it to your teacher.

Mid-Unit Assessment: Thirteen Colonies, Part 2 *(Offline)*
Complete the teacher-scored portion of the Mid-Unit Assessment and submit it to your teacher.

Name _____   Date _____

The Pequot War and King Philip's War

Use the boxes to show the causes and results of the wars between settlers and Indians in New England. If you need more boxes, use the back of this sheet.

The Pequot War

1.

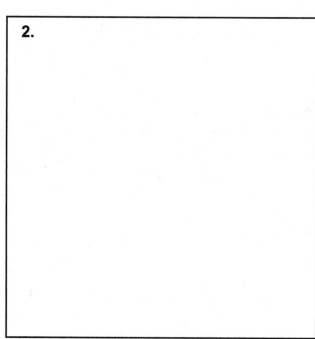

2.

3.

4.

King Philip's War

1.

2.

3.

4.

Student Guide
Lesson 5: The Middle Colonies

In the 1600s, both Holland and Sweden founded colonies in America. Peter Stuyvesant was the leader of New Netherland, and Johan Printz was the leader of New Sweden. The Duke of York sent a fleet of ships to America to take control of these colonies. Once the English had control, the land was divided and renamed New York and New Jersey.

Lesson Objectives
- Locate the middle colonies of New York and New Jersey on a map.
- Summarize the transition from New Amsterdam to New York.
- Give examples of the ways in which the New Jersey colony was more democratic than many colonies.
- Complete the chart for New York and New Jersey.

PREPARE

Approximate lesson time is 60 minutes.

Materials

For the Student

Make the Connection

A History of US (Concise Edition), Volume A (Prehistory to 1800) by Joy Hakim

History Journal

LEARN
Activity 1: Silvernails and Big Tub, Then West to Jersey *(Offline)*
Instructions
Check Your Reading (Chapter 40, pages 184–187, and Chapter 41, pages 188–190)

Discuss Chapters 40 and 41 with an adult.

Use What You Know

- Label New York and New Jersey on the map on the Thirteen Colonies sheet.
- Complete the sections for New York and New Jersey on the chart on the same sheet.
- Complete the Make the Connection sheet.
- Ask an adult to check your answers.

Read On

The English colonies of New York and New Jersey were part of the middle colonies. They had representative government and practiced religious freedom. There were other middle colonies as well. They, too, had some form of representation and religious toleration. Which colonies were they? Who were their founders? How much religious toleration was allowed in these colonies?

Read Chapter 44, pages 201–202, and Chapter 42, pages 191–195. Prepare to answer the following questions for discussion.

1. What was the Calvert family's reason for founding a colony? What was the colony called?
2. What was the Calverts' attitude toward religious freedom?
3. Why was England's class system a reason why many came to the New World?
4. Why did William Penn want a colony?
5. How was Penn's colony different from most of the other colonies?
6. How did Delaware become a colony?

Vocabulary

You'll see the term "Toleration Act" as you read. Write a brief definition for this term in your History Journal.

Name _____ Date _____

Make the Connection

Explain how each pair of names are related to one another. The first pair has been done for you as an example.

1. Henry Hudson/New Netherland

   Henry Hudson was an explorer who claimed land in America for the Netherlands in 1609. The Dutch called the land New Netherland.

2. Dutch West India Company/New Amsterdam

   _____

   _____

   _____

   _____

3. New Netherland/New York

   _____

   _____

   _____

   _____

4. New York/East and West Jersey

   _____

   _____

   _____

   _____

5. East and West Jersey/Jersey

   _____

   _____

   _____

   _____

Student Guide
Lesson 6: Toleration Triumphs

The Calvert family founded the Maryland colony as a safe place for Catholics and Protestants to practice religious freedom. William Penn, a Quaker, founded Pennsylvania as a haven for Quakers and people of all religions.

Lesson Objectives

- Demonstrate mastery of important knowledge and skills in previous lessons.
- Identify Lord Baltimore and the Calverts as the Catholic founders of Maryland as a haven for Catholics.
- Identify William Penn as the Quaker founder of Pennsylvania and the difficulties he and other Quakers faced in England.
- Give examples of toleration and its limits in Pennsylvania and Maryland.
- Chart the founding of Pennsylvania, Delaware, and Maryland.

PREPARE

Approximate lesson time is 60 minutes.

Materials

For the Student

Map of the Thirteen Colonies, 1756

A History of US (Concise Edition), Volume A (Prehistory to 1800) by Joy Hakim

History Journal

LEARN
Activity 1: Toleration in Various Forms (Online)

Instructions

Check Your Reading (Chapter 44, pages 201–202, and Chapter 42, pages 191–195)

- Discuss Chapters 44 and 42 with an adult.
- Label Pennsylvania, Delaware, and Maryland on the map on the Thirteen Colonies sheet.
- Color the middle colonies red.
- Complete the sections for Pennsylvania, Delaware, and Maryland on the chart on the same sheet.

Use What You Know

- Decide whether you would rather live in England, Pennsylvania, or Maryland in the 1600s.
- Write a speech explaining your choice and include why you rejected the other two.
- Practice your speech with an adult.

Look Back

Use the flash cards to review the middle colonies.

Read On

William Penn was a Quaker and the founder of Pennsylvania. Religious freedom, equality for all, and a representative government were just a few of the ideals he used to establish the colony. He also designed the city of Philadelphia. Do you know who Philadelphia's most famous citizen was? He was born in Boston, wrote an almanac, invented many things, signed our Declaration of Independence, and enjoyed flying kites.

Read Chapter 43, pages 196–200. Be prepared to answer the following questions.

1. Name three things Ben Franklin invented.
2. Who was Silence Dogood?
3. Why did Ben Franklin leave Boston and go to Philadelphia?
4. What was *Poor Richard's Almanack?*

ASSESS
Lesson Assessment: Toleration Triumphs *(Online)*

You will complete an online assessment covering the main points of this lesson. Your assessment will be scored by the computer.

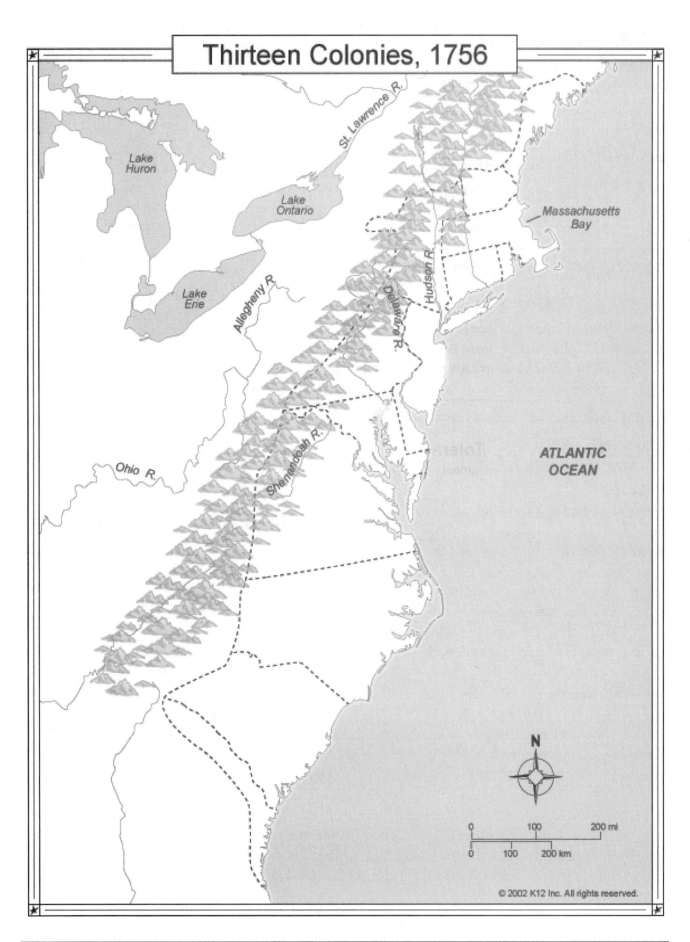

Thirteen Colonies, 1756

Lake Huron

Lake Ontario

Lake Erie

St. Lawrence R.

Massachusetts Bay

Allegheny R.

Delaware R.

Hudson R.

Ohio R.

Shenandoah R.

ATLANTIC OCEAN

N

0   100   200 mi
0   100   200 km

© 2002 K12 Inc. All rights reserved.

Student Guide
Lesson 7: Benjamin Franklin: An American Renaissance Man

Ben Franklin spent most of his life inventing things, including himself. He was a scientist, an inventor, a writer, and a great patriotic American.

Lesson Objectives
- Read and respond to a brief biography of Benjamin Franklin.
- Analyze Franklin's most important accomplishments.
- Analyze the wisdom of Benjamin Franklin and apply it to today.

PREPARE

Approximate lesson time is 60 minutes.

Materials
> For the Student
>> A History of US (Concise Edition), Volume A (Prehistory to 1800) by Joy Hakim
>> History Journal

LEARN
Activity 1: Benjamin Franklin: A Jack-of-All-Trades *(Offline)*
Instructions
Check Your Reading (Chapter 43, pages 196–200)

Review Chapter 43 using the following questions.

1. Name three things Ben Franklin invented.
2. Who was Silence Dogood?
3. Why did Ben Franklin leave Boston and go to Philadelphia?
4. What was *Poor Richard's Almanack*?

Use What You Know

Go online and visit the following website: *Benjamin Franklin: Glimpses of the Man.* Research one of Benjamin Franklin's many accomplishments. Then write one or more paragraphs on the accomplishment and how it has improved the United States. You may use one of the following suggestions or choose your own topic.

- Franklin's success as a printer and author (*Poor Richard's Almanack*)
- His success as a public servant (fire department, public library, hospital)
- His role as an inventor and scientist (electricity, lightning rod, bifocals, Franklin stove)
- His role in politics (coauthor of the Declaration of Independence, diplomat during the American Revolution)

Read On

As the people of the middle colonies took control of more land, they changed it in any way they saw fit. They also changed the cultures they brought with them from Europe by allowing greater religious freedom and more representative government. The southern colonies were quite different from the New England and middle colonies. Find out what English traditions the leaders in the South kept. Explore the different pieces of the southern class system. Why was slavery so much more important in the South than in the other colonies as time went on?

Read Chapter 45, pages 203–207, and Chapter 46, pages 208–212.

Student Guide
Lesson 8: Colonization Heads South

A large plantation was like a small village. The land and workers provided everything, including housing, food, clothing, education, work, and entertainment for the owner and his family. Life for southern tradesmen, small farmers, and slaves was very different from the life of the rich plantation owners. The rich ruling class made strict laws and enjoyed far more privileges than other people in the South.

Lesson Objectives
- Locate on a map the southern colonies of Virginia, North Carolina, South Carolina, and Georgia.
- Describe plantation life for owners, women, slaves, and small farmers.

PREPARE

Approximate lesson time is 60 minutes.

Materials
For the Student
> Living the Good Life
> A History of US (Concise Edition), Volume A (Prehistory to 1800) by Joy Hakim
> History Journal

LEARN
Activity 1: Life in the South (Offline)
Instructions
Check Your Reading (Chapter 45, pages 203–207, and Chapter 46, pages 208–212)

- Complete the Living the Good Life sheet.
- Discuss your answers with an adult.

Read On
This reading prepares you for the next lesson, which is an OPTIONAL lesson.
In the South, the wealthy class made the laws for the small farmers, skilled workers, and slaves. Do you remember the House of Burgesses in Virginia? It met in the state's capital, Williamsburg. Some of these lawmakers would one day be founders of the United States.

Read Chapter 47, pages 213–216.

Name _____   Date _____

Living the Good Life

What If? What if you had lived in Virginia in the early 1700s? What would your life have been like? Pretend that you are each of the people below. Answer the questions about your life.

A Plantation Owner's Daughter

1. What does your plantation look like? List five buildings on your plantation: _____

_____

_____

2. Do you think your father is like a business executive? How? _____

_____

_____

3. There is a party tonight. What are you going to wear? What will your brother wear?

_____

_____

4. Did you go to school today? Where? What did you study? _____

_____

_____

A Young Indentured Servant in Williamsburg

5. You work for a silversmith. List three things you did in the shop today. _____

_____

_____

6. Are you free to change jobs? Why or why not? _____

_____

_____

Adapted from *A History of US*

A Child of a Virginia Farmer

7. Describe the house you live in. _____

_____

_____

8. Are there any laws about religion? What are they? How do your parents feel about these

laws? _____

_____

_____

9. How much schooling do you have? What might you do at the age of 15?

_____

_____

An Eleven-Year-Old Slave Girl

10. You share two houses with other slaves. Describe your living conditions, such as

housing and food. _____

_____

_____

11. What type of schooling do you have? _____

_____

_____

Adapted from *A History of US*

Student Guide
Lesson 9: (Optional) A Visit to Williamsburg

Williamsburg was the capital of Virginia. The members of the House of Burgesses held their meetings in Williamsburg. Several members of the House of Burgesses would one day be the founders of the United States.

Even though you may skip this lesson, you must complete the **Read On** activity before moving on to the next lesson.

Lesson Objectives
- Use the Internet to acquire information on Williamsburg.
- Describe Williamsburg in colonial times.

PREPARE

Approximate lesson time is 60 minutes.

Materials
For the Student

A History of US (Concise Edition), Volume A (Prehistory to 1800) by Joy Hakim

History Journal

LEARN
Activity 1. Optional: A Visit to Williamsburg (Offline)
Instructions
Use What You Know

Take a virtual field trip to Williamsburg using the following website: *Colonial Williamsburg History.* Explore the following sections:

- Meet the People
- See the Places
- Experience the Life
- Clothing

After exploring the website, complete the following sentence in your History Journal: I would / would not (choose one) have enjoyed living in Colonial Williamsburg because _____.

Read On

In Virginia, many of the wealthy colonists kept the customs and traditions of England. The wealthy also made the laws that governed the small farmers, tradesmen, and slaves. Tobacco was the major cash crop. In this activity, you will read about life in the Carolinas.

Read Chapter 48, pages 217–221, and Chapter 49, pages 222–227.

Vocabulary

You'll see these terms as you read. Write a brief definition for each term as you come to it.

- indigo
- Gullah

Student Guide
Lesson 10: Colonial Life in the South

South Carolina was a prosperous colony. Its economy was based on rice and indigo. Slave labor was used to grow these cash crops. The upper class was in control of both the economy and the government. North Carolina was different. The colony consisted of free-spirited farmers, religious rebels, and pirates. The last of the 13 colonies to be formed was Georgia. James Oglethorpe was the founder. He wanted a haven for debtors who were jailed in England because they could not pay their debts.

Lesson Objectives
- Demonstrate mastery of important knowledge and skills taught in previous lessons.
- Identify Charleston on a map and describe the social structure there in colonial times as a mixture of aristocracy, poor whites, and slaves.
- Give examples of democratic practices in North Carolina, including religious toleration.
- Identify James Oglethorpe as the founder of Georgia as a haven for debtors.
- Chart the founding of North Carolina, South Carolina, and Georgia.
- Locate on a map the southern colonies of Virginia, North Carolina, South Carolina, and Georgia.
- Identify Gullah as the language developed by African Americans in South Carolina.

PREPARE

Approximate lesson time is 60 minutes.

Materials
For the Student

The Carolinas

A History of US (Concise Edition), Volume A (Prehistory to 1800) by Joy Hakim

History Journal

LEARN
Activity 1: The Final Three Southern Colonies *(Offline)*
Instructions
Check Your Reading (Chapter 48, pages 217–221, and Chapter 49, pages 222–227)

Complete the Carolinas sheet to check what you learned in Chapter 48. Have an adult check your answers.

Discuss the following questions to review Chapter 49:

1. What was James Oglethorpe's motive for founding Georgia?
2. What did James Oglethorpe want the people to do? What were some of the laws Oglethorpe wanted passed?
3. What were some of the reasons why Oglethorpe's plans didn't work?

Use What You Know

- Label North Carolina, South Carolina, Georgia, and Charleston on the map on the Thirteen Colonies sheet.
- Color the southern colonies blue.
- Complete the sections for North Carolina, South Carolina, and Georgia on the chart on the same sheet.

Look Back

It's time for a review on the southern colonies—use the flash cards. When you've finished, click Student Activity to visit a typical plantation.

ASSESS

Lesson Assessment: Colonial Life in the South (Online)

You will complete an online assessment covering the main points of this lesson. Your assessment will be scored by the computer.

Name _____ Date _____

The Carolinas

North and South Carolina may be neighbors, but they made for very different colonies. Fill in North or South to identify the correct colony. Supply any other missing words to complete each sentence.

1. Named for the English king, _____ Town (Charleston) was the capital

   of _____ Carolina.

2. Many leaders in _____ Carolina came from the Caribbean island

   of _____ .

3. As a place where people left one another alone, _____ Carolina may

   have been the most _____ of all of the colonies.

4. _____ Carolina was a very _____ colony, where a few
   wealthy people held most of the power.

5. The famous pirate _____ operated off the coast of

   _____ Carolina.

6. In 1677, some people in _____ Carolina refused to pay

   _____ to England.

7. Africans probably taught the people in _____ Carolina how to grow

   _____ , the crop that made slavery profitable there.

8. Unlike other Southern colonies, _____ Carolina had a great city,

   _____ .

9. Colonists in _____ Carolina tried to set up their own

   _____ to be free of England.

10. _____ is a language developed by African Americans in

    _____ Carolina.

Thinking Cap Question! Would you rather have lived in North or South Carolina in colonial times? Explain your answer.

Student Guide
Lesson 11: Triangles of Trade

New England shipping developed triangular trade routes. These routes linked New England with England, Africa, the West Indies, and America's Atlantic ports. Some of the trade items included forest products, rice, indigo, furs, and tobacco. Slaves were also traded and transported from Africa to the West Indies and America.

Lesson Objectives

- Analyze a map of colonial trade and trace the major routes and products of the triangular trade.
- Summarize information gained from the diary of Olaudah.
- Categorize resources as fossil fuels or animal, plant, or mineral resources.
- Categorize resources as renewable or nonrenewable.
- Interpret maps for information about natural resources.

PREPARE

Approximate lesson time is 60 minutes.

Materials

For the Student

Map of Triangle Trade

Triangular Journeys

A History of US (Concise Edition), Volume A (Prehistory to 1800) by Joy Hakim

Understanding Geography: Map Skills and Our World (Level 5)

History Journal

LEARN
Activity 1: Triangular Journeys (Offline)
Instructions
Read

Read Chapter 50, pages 228–234.

Check Your Reading (Chapter 50, pages 228–234)

Complete the Triangular Journeys sheet. You may use the map of Triangle Trade as a reference. Have an adult check your answers.

Use What You Know

- In your History Journal, list some things you learned about Olaudah by reading the excerpts from Olaudah's diary.
- Read your list to an adult. Point out information from the excerpts that support your list.

Resources and Trade

In colonial times, colonists got many things they needed from their own community. Most people grew their own food, made their own clothes, and even built their own furniture. They also brought in some manufactured products from Great Britain. Maps can help you learn more about an area's economy.

- Read Activity 7, "Resources and Trade" (pages 28–31), in *Understanding Geography*.
- Answer Questions 1–13 in your History Journal.
- If you have time, you may want to answer the Skill Builder Questions on page 31.
- After you have finished you should compare your answers with the ones in the Teacher Guide.

ASSESS

Lesson Assessment: Triangles of Trade (*Online*)

Answer the online geography questions for this assessment. Your assessment will be scored by the computer.

Name _____ Date _____

Triangular Journeys

Suppose that you are traveling by ship in the year 1700. Answer these questions about the stops on your journey from Massachusetts to the West Indies:

New England

1. You left your family's farm in Massachusetts because you couldn't make a living. Why was it so hard to farm in New England? _____

_____

2. Was it hard to find a job in industry? Why? _____

_____

_____

3. How did codfish influence Yankee trade? _____

_____

_____

England

4. Your ship is part of the Triangular Trade. Why has it come to England? _____

_____

5. Name two products your ship has brought to England. _____

_____

Africa

6. What cargo does your ship carry from England to Africa? Why? _____

_____

_____

7. What cargo does your ship carry from Africa to the West Indies? Why? _____

_____

_____

West Indies

8. What is the African cargo traded for in the West Indies? _____

_____

9. What is the West Indian cargo used for in New England? _____

_____

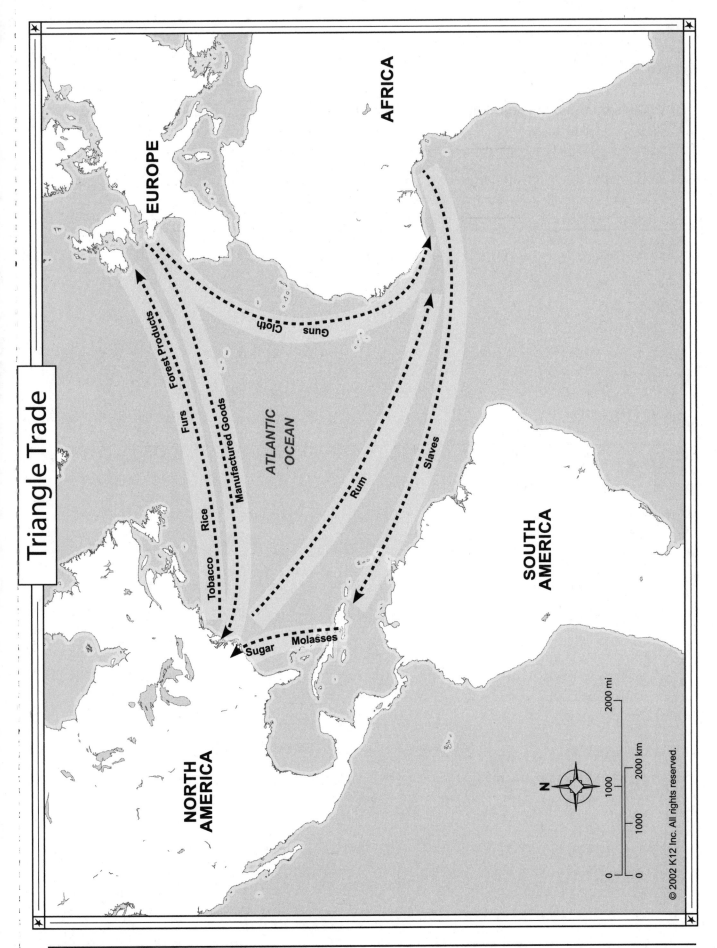

Triangle Trade

EUROPE

AFRICA

ATLANTIC OCEAN

Forest Products

Furs

Manufactured Goods

Rice

Tobacco

Sugar

Molasses

Rum

Slaves

Cloth

Guns

NORTH AMERICA

SOUTH AMERICA

N

2000 mi

2000 km

1000

1000

0

0

© 2002 K12 Inc. All rights reserved.

Student Guide
Lesson 12: Unit Review

You've completed Unit 4, Thirteen Colonies, Part 2. It's time to review what you've learned. You'll take the Unit Assessment in the next lesson.

(This review might refer to topics presented in optional lessons in this unit.)

Lesson Objectives
- Demonstrate mastery of important knowledge and skills taught in previous lessons.

PREPARE

Approximate lesson time is 60 minutes.

Materials
For the Student
- Thirteen Colonies, 1756
- Triangles of Trade

A History of US (Concise Edition), Volume A (Prehistory to 1800) by Joy Hakim

History Journal

LEARN
Activity 1: A Look Back *(Offline)*
Instructions
Online Review

Use the following to review this unit:

- The Big Picture
- Flash Cards
- Time Line
- Thirteen Colonies, 1756 map
- Triangle Trade map

History Journal Review

Now go offline and review more by going through your History Journal. Look at the sheets you completed for this unit. Review your vocabulary words. If you completed any writing assignments, read them. Take your time. Your History Journal is a great resource for a unit review.

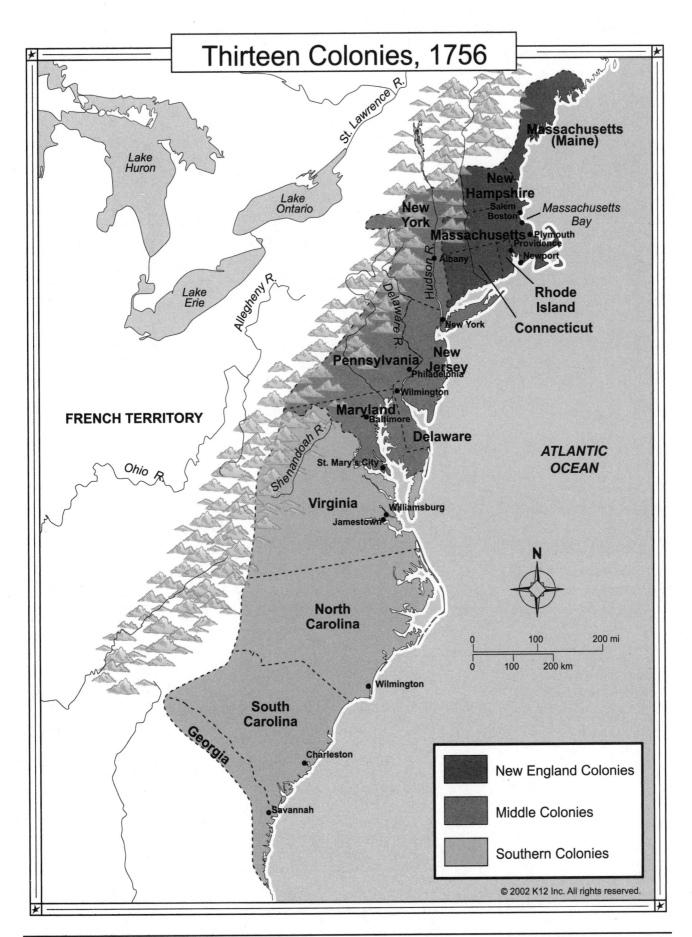

Thirteen Colonies, 1756

Lake Huron

Lake Ontario

Lake Erie

St. Lawrence R.

Allegheny R.

Ohio R.

Shenandoah R.

Delaware R.

Hudson R.

FRENCH TERRITORY

Massachusetts (Maine)

New Hampshire

New York
• Albany

Salem
Boston

Massachusetts Bay

Massachusetts

Plymouth
Providence
Newport

Rhode Island

Connecticut

• New York

Pennsylvania
• Philadelphia

New Jersey

• Wilmington

Maryland
• Baltimore

Delaware

• St. Mary's City

ATLANTIC OCEAN

Virginia
• Williamsburg
Jamestown

N

0   100   200 mi
0   100   200 km

North Carolina

• Wilmington

South Carolina

Georgia

• Charleston

• Savannah

New England Colonies

Middle Colonies

Southern Colonies

© 2002 K12 Inc. All rights reserved.

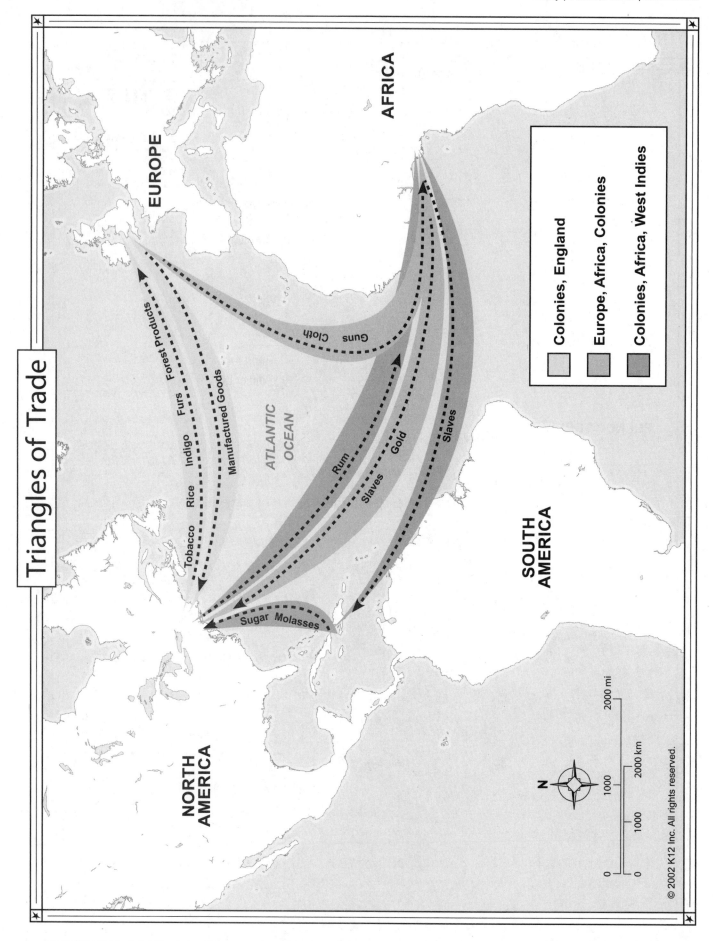

Triangles of Trade

ATLANTIC OCEAN

EUROPE

AFRICA

NORTH AMERICA

SOUTH AMERICA

Forest Products
Furs
Indigo
Rice
Tobacco
Manufactured Goods

Cloth
Guns

Rum
Slaves
Gold
Slaves

Sugar Molasses

Legend:
- Colonies, England
- Europe, Africa, Colonies
- Colonies, Africa, West Indies

N

2000 mi
1000
0

2000 km
1000
0

© 2002 K12 Inc. All rights reserved.

Student Guide
Lesson 13: Unit Assessment

You've finished this unit on the 13 colonies. Now take the Unit Assessment, and then read today's assignment.

Lesson Objectives
- Analyze the geography of the eastern seaboard of the United States.
- Describe the status of women in Puritan society.
- Describe the consequences of Anne Hutchinson's break with Puritan tradition.
- Explain the origins and results of the witchcraft trials in Salem.
- Chart the founding of Connecticut and New Hampshire.
- Explain the origins and results of the Pequot War and King Philip's War.
- Locate the middle colonies of New York and New Jersey on a map.
- Complete the chart for New York and New Jersey.
- Identify Lord Baltimore and the Calverts as the Catholic founders of Maryland as a haven for Catholics.
- Identify William Penn as the Quaker founder of Pennsylvania and the difficulties he and other Quakers faced in England.
- Chart the founding of Pennsylvania, Delaware, and Maryland.
- Analyze Franklin's most important accomplishments.
- Locate on a map the southern colonies of Virginia, North Carolina, South Carolina, and Georgia.
- Identify James Oglethorpe as the founder of Georgia as a haven for debtors.
- Identify Roger Williams as the founder of Rhode Island and a supporter of religious toleration and fair treatment of Native Americans.
- Locate the colony of Rhode Island on a map and list its founder, his motives, and his accomplishments.

PREPARE

Approximate lesson time is 60 minutes.

Materials
> For the Student
>> A History of US (Concise Edition), Volume A (Prehistory to 1800) by Joy Hakim
>>
>> History Journal

ASSESS

Unit Assessment: Thirteen Colonies, Part 2, Part 1 *(Online)*
Complete the computer-scored portion of the Unit Assessment. When you have finished, complete the teacher-scored portion of the assessment and submit it to your teacher.

Unit Assessment: Thirteen Colonies, Part 2, Part 2 *(Offline)*
Complete the teacher-scored portion of the Unit Assessment and submit it to your teacher.

LEARN
Activity 1: Chapter 51 *(Offline)*
Instructions
Read On

The assigned reading prepares you for the next lesson, which is an OPTIONAL lesson.

Peter Zenger founded a newspaper called the *New York Weekly Journal.* He used the newspaper to criticize the New York governor and his politics. The governor had Zenger arrested and tried. Who was Zenger's attorney? What was the outcome of the trial? How does the Zenger trial affect life in the United States today?

Read Chapter 51, pages 236–239.

Student Guide
Lesson 1: (Optional) Peter's Press

John Adams said that the real American Revolution took place in the "minds and hearts of the people." Those people began as loyal and proud citizens of the most powerful and democratic nation in the world—"Great Britain. They ended by taking up arms against the king. Their journey toward independence started years before any shots were fired.

The trial of John Peter Zenger may seem unimportant today. But Zenger, his lawyer, and the people of New York did something very good for all of us. They defended their rights to freedom of the press and trial by jury. Those are rights we have today. And the trial helped bring the colonies together.

Even though you may skip this lesson, you must complete the **Read On** activity before moving on to the next lesson.

Lesson Objectives
- Identify Peter Zenger.
- Define *libel*.
- Summarize the importance of the Peter Zenger Trial

PREPARE

Approximate lesson time is 60 minutes.

Materials
For the Student

Hamilton Said It First!

A History of US (Concise Edition), Volume A (Prehistory to 1800) by Joy Hakim

History Journal

LEARN
Activity 1. Optional: Freedom of the Press *(Offline)*
Instructions
Check Your Reading (Chapter 51, pages 236–239)

Go over what you learned in Chapter 51 using the Hamilton Said It First! sheet.

Read On

The French and Indian War changed the future of the North American continent. Do you know who were allies and who were enemies in that war? Did you know that George Washington was a soldier in the British army during that war? He and others learned valuable lessons that helped them shake off British rule over 20 years later. How did that happen? And why?

Read Chapter 52, pages 240–245, and Chapter 53, pages 246–251.

Vocabulary

You'll see these terms as you read. Write a brief definition for each term in your History Journal.

- frontier
- Huguenot
- surveyor
- lay siege

Name _____   Date _____

Hamilton Said It First!

At Peter Zenger's trial, Andrew Hamilton said:

> *"Free men have the right to oppose arbitrary power by speaking and writing truths… to assert with courage the sense they have of the blessings of liberty, the value they put upon it, and their resolution… to prove it one of the greatest blessings heaven can bestow… There is no libel if the truth is told."*

In questions 1–4, your mission is to locate the word or words from Hamilton's quote that best fit in the blanks.

1. In his newspaper, Peter Zenger published articles criticizing the Governor's use of

   _____ _____."

2. Because it was against the law to criticize the king or his appointees, the Attorney

   General accused Peter Zenger of committing "_____."

3. Hamilton believed Zenger was not guilty of this charge because in Zenger's newspaper

   articles the "_____ _____ _____."

4. Hamilton felt that more than just Peter Zenger was on trial. He felt that the larger concept

   of American "_____" was at stake.

5. Gouverneur Morris, one of the writers of the Constitution, said: "The trial of Zenger in 1735 was the germ of American freedom, the morning star of that liberty which subsequently revolutionized America." What did Hamilton and Morris agree about?

   _____

   _____

   _____

Thinking Cap Question! Do you think that television and newspaper reporters should be free to criticize the president as much as they like? Why or why not? Write your answer in your History Journal.

Adapted from *A History of US*

Student Guide
Lesson 2: The French and Indian War

The French and Indian War changed the future of the North American continent. It also taught colonial leaders, such as George Washington, valuable lessons that would later help them against the British. With help from their colonial and Native American allies, the British won the war. But another conflict soon began—this time over who would pay for the war.

Lesson Objectives

- Analyze Franklin's "Join or Die" to gain understanding of political cartoons.
- Explain the causes of the French and Indian War as competition between France and England for land and power.
- Identify George Washington as a soldier in the British Army during the French and Indian War.

PREPARE

Approximate lesson time is 60 minutes.

Materials

For the Student

Understanding Political Cartoons

A History of US (Concise Edition), Volume A (Prehistory to 1800) by Joy Hakim

History Journal

LEARN
Activity 1: British Victory (Offline)

Instructions

Check Your Reading (Chapter 52, pages 240–245, and Chapter 53, pages 246–251)

Review Chapters 52 and 53 by discussing the following questions with an adult:

1. What was the major cause of the French and Indian War?
2. What lessons did George Washington learn from the French and Indian War?
3. How did the British expect to pay for the high cost of the war?
4. Look at the map on page 249. What do the locations of the forts have in common? Why do you think that is?

Use What You Know

Diary Entry

It's time for battle! You're part of the Virginia militia that served with George Washington in the Ohio River Valley. In your History Journal, write a diary entry that describes how you planned to drive the French out of Fort Duquesne. Describe what happened during your campaign to rid the frontier and Fort Duquesne of the French. Did it all go as planned?

Document Analysis

Discuss Franklin's "Join or Die" political cartoon with an adult. Then complete the Understanding Political Cartoons sheet.

Read On

Learn what Great Britain got as a result of winning the war. What do you think Britain's Indian allies, the Iroquois, got for helping the British? And who do you think wanted to move into all that land west of the Appalachians?

Read Chapter 54, pages 252–257. As you read, keep these questions in mind:

- Did the British encourage the colonists to take land west of the Appalachians?
- What did the colonists think of the British proclamation?

Vocabulary

You'll see these terms as you read. Write a brief definition for each in your History Journal.

- mission
- speculator
- pioneer

Name _____   Date _____

Understanding Political Cartoons

Benjamin Franklin, 1754

Answer the following questions after studying Benjamin Franklin's cartoon.

1. What is the title of the cartoon? _____

2. What does each segment of the serpent represent? _____

   _____

3. The section of the snake nearest the head is labeled "N.E." for New England (New Hampshire, Massachusetts, Rhode Island, and Connecticut). Travel south from there to the snake's tail and list the colonies represented in the cartoon.

   _____

   _____

   _____

4. Which of the 13 colonies are not represented? _____

5. Explain the message of Benjamin Franklin's cartoon. _____

   _____

6. How many years passed between the time Franklin drew this cartoon and the start of the Revolutionary War? _____

Student Guide
Lesson 3: Looking West

After the French and Indian War, British colonists expected to settle west of the Appalachians. Native Americans knew this would mean the end of their lands. The British tried to stop the migration of colonists with the Proclamation of 1763, which said that no colonists could settle west of the Appalachian Mountains. But the pioneer spirit was too strong.

Lesson Objectives

- Summarize the outcome of the French and Indian War as the end of the French presence in most of North America.
- Describe the problems faced by Native Americans in the Ohio River Valley after 1763, including encroachment by white settlers.
- Describe the problems the British government faced after 1763 in trying to limit westward migration and why many Americans wanted to go west.
- Locate the Appalachian Mountains on a map and explain that the British did not want migration across them for reasons of economics and security.

PREPARE

Approximate lesson time is 60 minutes.

Materials

For the Student

Map of Land Claims in the New World, 1750

Map of Land Claims in the New World, 1763

Talking Heads: Proclamation of 1763

The French and Indian War: Before and After

A History of US (Concise Edition), Volume A (Prehistory to 1800) by Joy Hakim

History Journal

LEARN
Activity 1: Heading West? *(Offline)*
Instructions
Check Your Reading (Chapter 54, pages 252–257)

Go over Chapter 54 by discuss the following questions with an adult.

1. Did Native Americans benefit from the French and Indian war?
2. Why did England forbid settlement west of the Appalachian Mountains?
3. How did colonists respond to the Proclamation of 1763? Why?
4. How do you think Native Americans might have viewed the Proclamation of 1763? Why?
5. What routes did pioneers travel to reach the West?
6. Who was Daniel Boone?

Use What You Know

French and Indian War: Before and After

Use the maps provided to complete the French and Indian War: Before and After sheet. Check your work with an adult.

Talking Heads: Proclamation of 1763

Review the Proclamation of 1763 by completing the Talking Heads: Proclamation of 1763 sheet. Check your answers with an adult.

Name _____   Date _____

The French and Indian War: Before and After

Color the land the British controlled before the French and Indian War in red. Color the land the French controlled in yellow. Label the English colonies, Mexico, Florida, Newfoundland, Boston, Montreal, Great Lakes, Mississippi River, Ohio River, and Fort Duquesne.

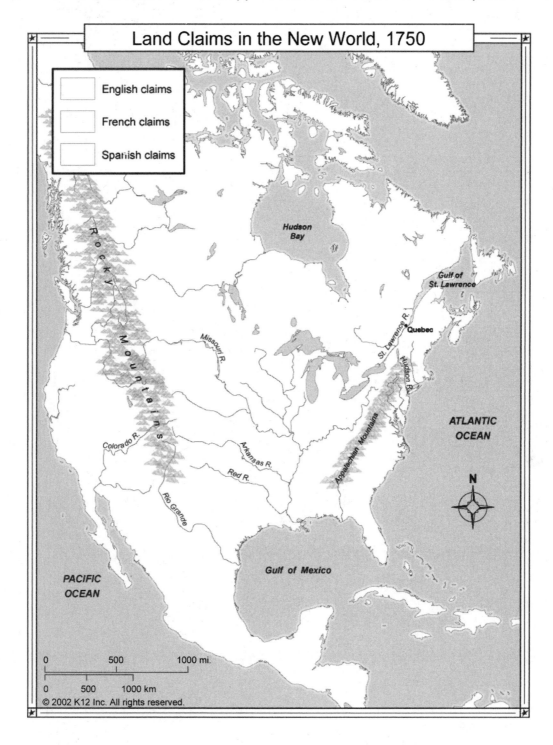

Color the land the British controlled after the French and Indian War in red. Color the land the French controlled in yellow. Label the English colonies, Mexico, Florida, Newfoundland, Boston, Montreal, Great Lakes, Mississippi River, Ohio River, and Fort Duquesne.

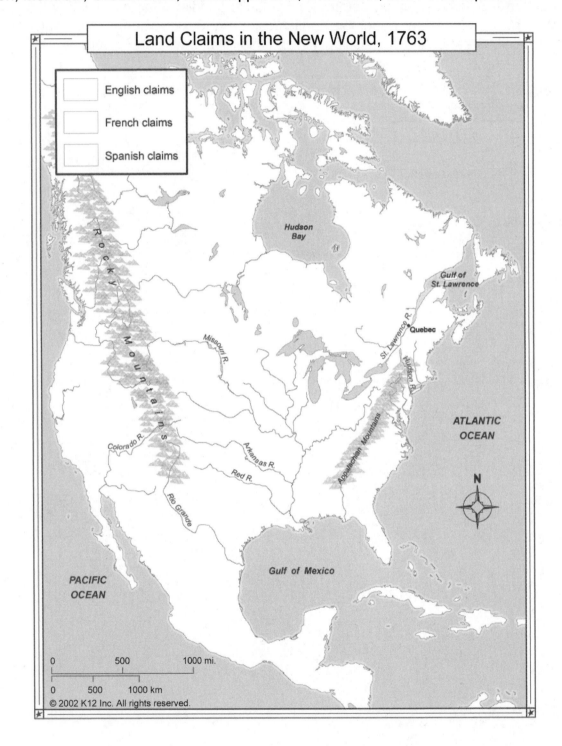

Land Claims in the New World, 1763

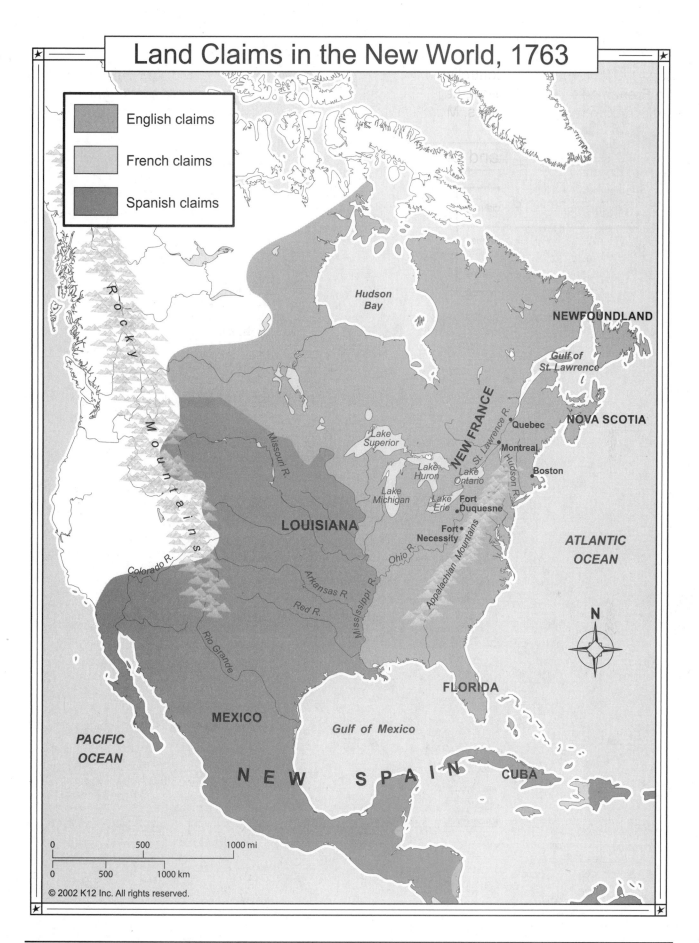

Land Claims in the New World, 1763

English claims

French claims

Spanish claims

Rocky Mountains

Hudson Bay

NEWFOUNDLAND

Gulf of St. Lawrence

NOVA SCOTIA

NEW FRANCE

Quebec

Montreal

St. Lawrence R.

Hudson R.

Boston

Lake Superior

Lake Huron

Lake Michigan

Lake Ontario

Lake Erie

Fort Duquesne

Fort Necessity

Missouri R.

LOUISIANA

Ohio R.

Appalachian Mountains

ATLANTIC OCEAN

Arkansas R.

Red R.

Mississippi R.

Colorado R.

Rio Grande

MEXICO

FLORIDA

PACIFIC OCEAN

Gulf of Mexico

N E W   S P A I N

CUBA

N

0   500   1000 mi

0   500   1000 km

© 2002 K12 Inc. All rights reserved.

145

Land Claims in the New World, 1750

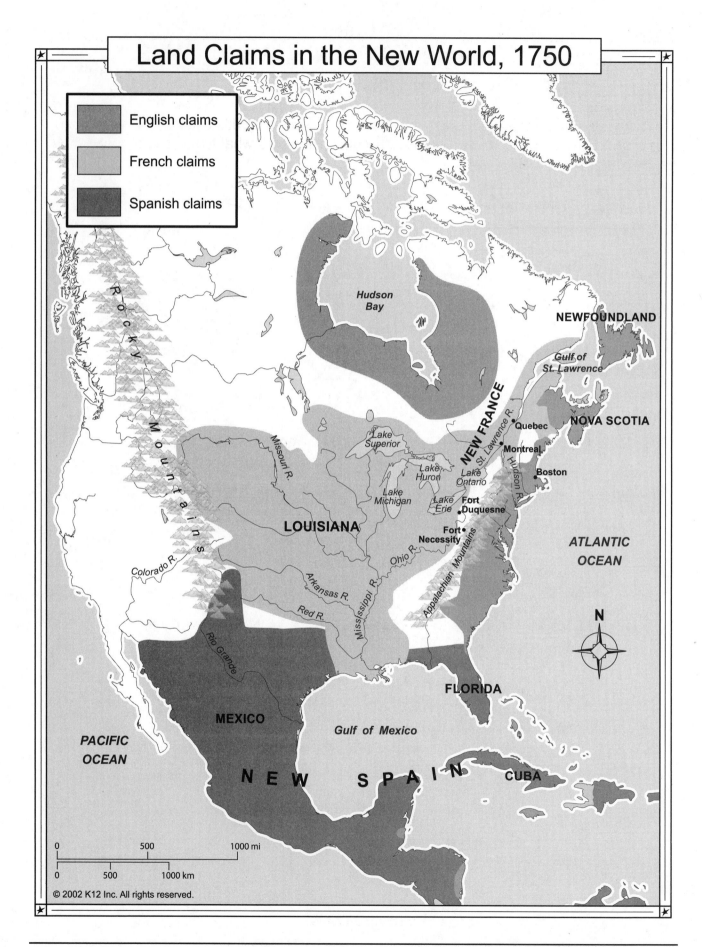

146

Name _____   Date _____

Talking Heads: Proclamation of 1763

These three heads represent Native Americans, colonists, and British officials. In each head, write a sentence, draw a picture, or make a symbol that states what that group thought about the Proclamation of 1763.

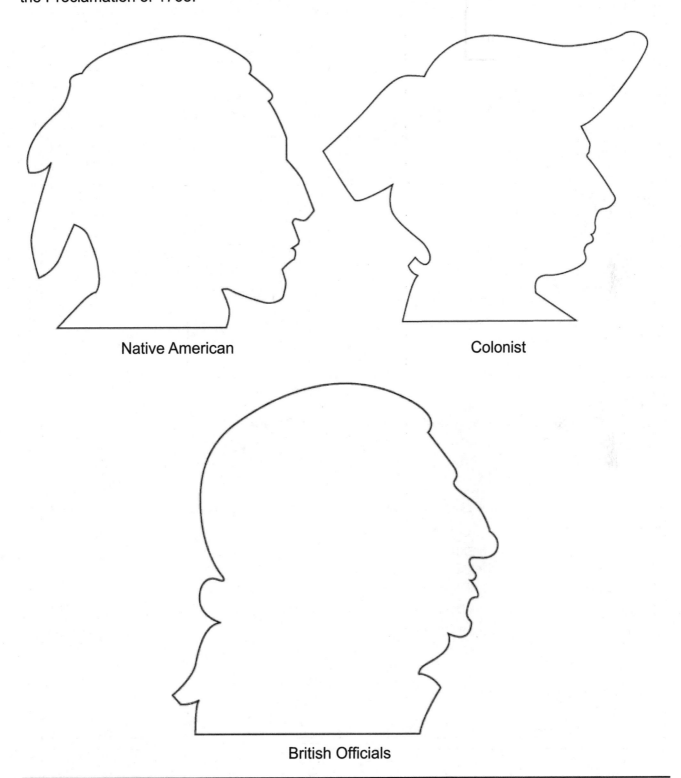

Native American

Colonist

British Officials

Student Guide
Lesson 4: (Optional) Boone Went Over the Mountain

Imagine heading into the wilderness on your own. You are going through native hunting grounds, so there is a threat of Indian attack. There is danger from wild animals as well. Would you keep pushing forward? Daniel Boone, one of the most famous pioneers in American history, dealt with these and many other hazards as he went deep into the American frontier.

Even though you may skip this lesson, you must complete the **Read On** section before moving on to the next lesson.

Lesson Objectives
- Demonstrate mastery of important knowledge and skills taught in previous lessons.
- Analyze primary sources to gain information.
- Identify Daniel Boone as an early American pioneer.

PREPARE

Approximate lesson time is 60 minutes.

Materials
> For the Student
>> Document Analysis: Daniel Boone
>> A History of US (Concise Edition), Volume A (Prehistory to 1800) by Joy Hakim
>> History Journal

LEARN
Activity 1. Optional: Adventures of Daniel Boone *(Offline)*
Instructions
Use What You Know

Use your document analysis skills as you read Daniel Boone's own story. Do you remember what someone's journal or diary about an event is called? It's a *primary source*.

- Go online and visit Archiving Early America (http://www.earlyamerica.com/lives/boone/).
- Read Parts 1 and 2 of "The Adventures of Colonel Daniel Boone."
- Answer the questions on the Document Analysis: Daniel Boone sheet.
- Have an adult check your work.

Read On

Americans believed English rights were their rights, rights the Magna Carta had given them in 1215. The English disagreed. This set the stage for a step-by-step progression of events that led to the American Revolution. Read Chapter 55, pages 258–260, and Chapter 56, pages 261–264. Meet King George III and begin the journey to revolution.

Vocabulary

You'll see these terms as you read. Write a brief definition for each term in your History Journal.

- Magna Carta
- habeas corpus
- repealed
- minister

Name _____   Date _____

Document Analysis: Daniel Boone

After reviewing "The Adventures of Colonel Daniel Boon," answer the following questions.

1. Type of document (check one):

   _____ Newspaper   _____ Report

   _____ Letter   _____ Map

   _____ Telegram   _____ Journal/Diary

2. Date of document: _____

3. Author of document: _____

4. For what audience was the document written? _____

5. Why do you think Daniel Boone wrote this document? _____

   _____

6. List two things the document tells you about life on the Appalachian frontier at that time.

   _____

   _____

   _____

   _____

7. Do you think Daniel Boone gave a fair account of his run-ins with the Native Americans?
   Why or why not? _____

   _____

   _____

   _____

Student Guide
Lesson 5: The Stamp of English Rights

The English were used to conflict with their rulers. It helped build their government. But they weren't prepared for conflict with the colonists. After the British government tried to raise money by taxing stamps and tea, the colonists sent the British a message: "No taxation without representation."

Lesson Objectives

- Explain the significance of Magna Carta and the "rights of Englishmen."
- Identify George III as the king of England in the mid-eighteenth century.
- Identify and describe the Stamp Act.
- Describe the reasons for and results of the Boston Tea Party.

PREPARE

Approximate lesson time is 60 minutes.

Materials

For the Student

Revolutionary Action and Reaction

A History of US (Concise Edition), Volume A (Prehistory to 1800) by Joy Hakim

History Journal

LEARN
Activity 1: Stamp It Out (Offline)
Instructions
Check Your Reading (Chapter 55, pages 258–260, and Chapter 56, pages 261–264)

Check what you learned in Chapters 55 and 56 using the following questions.

1. Why is the Magna Carta so important in the history of democracy?
2. Why did George III and Parliament tax the colonies?
3. Why did taxes imposed by Britain anger the colonists?
4. How did the conflict over British taxes bring the colonies together?

Use What You Know

Complete the Revolutionary Action and Reaction sheet.

Read On

A *firebrand* is someone who stirs things up and gets people excited or angry. Three firebrands helped spark the war with their actions and words. From north to south, people soon knew the names of Samuel Adams, Thomas Paine, and Patrick Henry.

Draw a chart with three columns in your History Journal. At the top of each column, write the name of one of these leaders: Samuel Adams, Thomas Paine, and Patrick Henry.

Read Chapter 57, pages 265–270. As you read, look for ways in which these leaders were firebrands. On the chart, list the ways in which each leader was revolutionary.

Beyond the Lesson

Go back online to visit the Boston Tea Party website (http://www.pbs.org/ktca/liberty/chronicle_boston1774.html).

Activity 2: The Stamp of English Rights *(Online)*

Name _____ Date _____

Revolutionary Action and Reaction

Complete the action and reaction chart. You may need to fill in the action, date, or reaction for an event. You may use your book. The first two have been done for you.

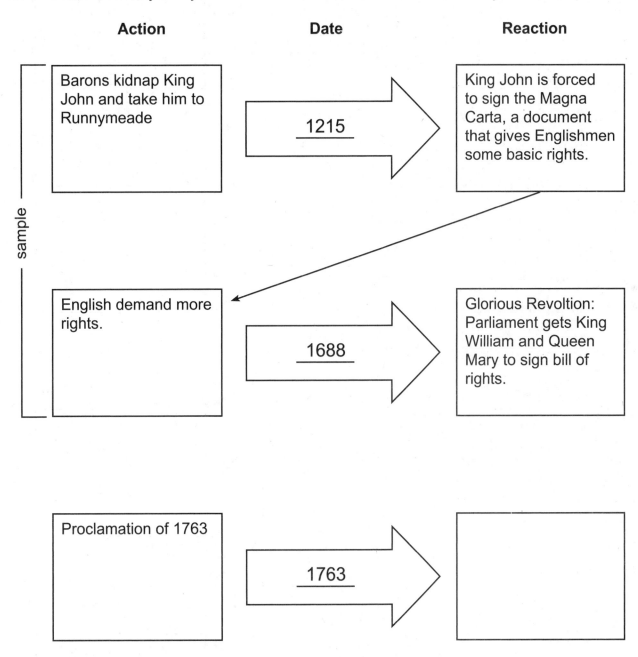

Action	Date	Reaction
sample Barons kidnap King John and take him to Runnymeade	1215	King John is forced to sign the Magna Carta, a document that gives Englishmen some basic rights.
English demand more rights.	1688	Glorious Revoltion: Parliament gets King William and Queen Mary to sign bill of rights.
Proclamation of 1763	1763	

Action	Date	Reaction

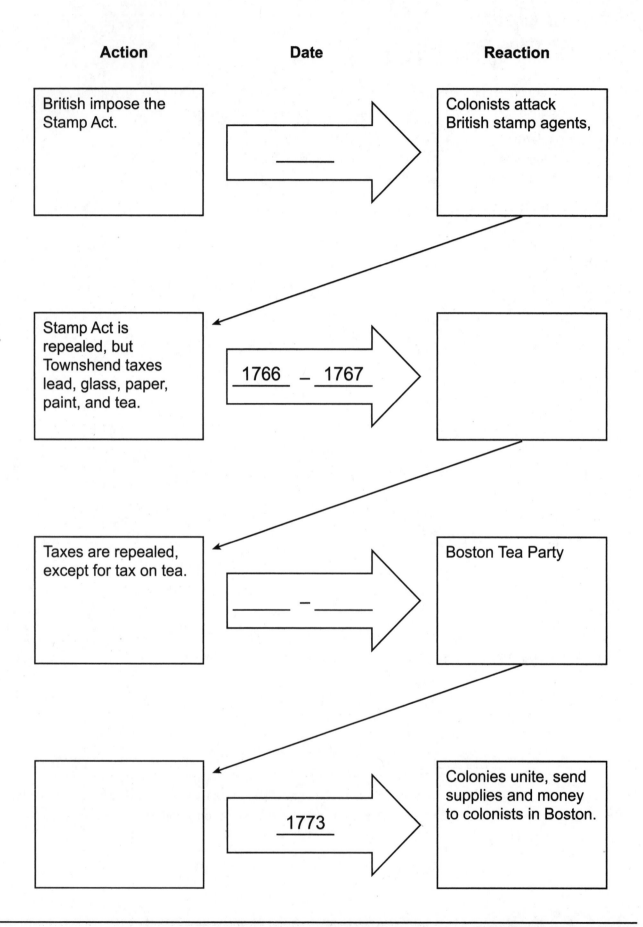

British impose the Stamp Act.

_____

Colonists attack British stamp agents,

Stamp Act is repealed, but Townshend taxes lead, glass, paper, paint, and tea.

1766 – 1767

Taxes are repealed, except for tax on tea.

_____ – _____

Boston Tea Party

1773

Colonies unite, send supplies and money to colonists in Boston.

Student Guide
Lesson 6: Give Us Liberty!

Words can be very powerful. Three fiery men used words and actions to help spark the Revolutionary War. People from north to south soon knew Samuel Adams, Thomas Paine, and Patrick Henry.

Lesson Objectives

- Identify Sam Adams and Patrick Henry as opposition leaders.
- Analyze Patrick Henry's speech.

PREPARE

Approximate lesson time is 60 minutes.

Materials

For the Student

Patrick Henry: Give Me Liberty or Give Me Death

Some Detective Work

A History of US (Concise Edition), Volume A (Prehistory to 1800) by Joy Hakim

History Journal

LEARN
Activity 1: Liberty or Death *(Offline)*

Instructions
Check Your Reading (Chapter 57, pages 265–270)

Discuss Chapter 57 with an adult, using the following questions:

1. How did firebrands such as Sam Adams help speed the flow of ideas?
2. What special talents helped make Sam Adams, Thomas Paine, and Patrick Henry effective firebrands?
3. What did Thomas Paine help make clear to colonists in his pamphlet *Common Sense*?
4. What did Patrick Henry mean when he said, "The war is actually begun"?

Complete the Some Detective Work sheet.

Use What You Know

- Read Patrick Henry's "Give Me Liberty or Give Me Death" speech.
- Imagine you are a newspaper reporter from the *Virginia Gazette* and were in the church that night listening to Patrick Henry's speech. Write a newspaper story in your History Journal based on what you saw and heard that night. Be sure to include sounds and sights, not only from Patrick Henry, but from the crowd as well.

Read On

Massacre or tragic accident? Either way, citizens of Boston were killed by British soldiers on a cold March evening in 1770. Who would defend the soldiers in court? Would you have the courage to take the case when your neighbors are looking for revenge? And what should the colonies do as the situation worsenes?

Read Chapter 58, pages 271–275.

Vocabulary

You'll see these words as you read. Write a brief definition for each word in your History Journal.

- Patriot
- quarter
- Loyalist
- congress
- redcoat

Name _____   Date _____

Some Detective Work

The year is 1770. The tension is rising between Britain and the American colonies. You have heard rumors that a revolution is in the works. The quotes below clue you in to the crisis at hand. Can you connect each quote with its speaker?

William Pitt Thomas Paine Benjamin Franklin

Sir William Johnson Patrick Henry

1. "If England is to become a great nation, she must go to school with the Iroquois."

   _____

2. "We have an old mother that peevish has grown,
   She snubs us like children that scarce walk alone,
   She forgets we're grown up and have sense of our own."

   _____

3. "I know not what course others may take, but as for me, give me liberty, or give me death!"

   _____

4. "This is the mother country, they are the children; they must obey, and we prescribe."

   _____

5. "Common Sense, Addressed to the Inhabitants of America..."

   _____

Thinking Cap Question! When Britain tried to enforce the Stamp Act, colonists let the world know that they hated the new tax, crying "No Taxation Without Representation." They even tarred and feathered commissioners for trying to collect the taxes. If Americans felt they were being unfairly taxed today, do you think they would protest? How?

Adapted from *A History of US*

Name _____ Date _____

Patrick Henry: Give Me Liberty or Give Me Death

Patrick Henry, March 23, 1775

… I shall speak forth my sentiments freely and without reserve. This is no time for ceremony. The question before the House is one of awful moment to this country. For my own part, I consider it as nothing less than a question of freedom or slavery…

… I know of no way of judging of the future but by the past. And judging by the past, I wish to know what there has been in the conduct of the British ministry for the last ten years to justify those hopes with which gentlemen have been pleased to solace themselves… Are fleets and armies necessary to a work of love and reconciliation? Have we shown ourselves so unwilling to be reconciled that force must be called in to win back our love? Let us not deceive ourselves, sir. These are the implements of war and subjugation; the last arguments to which kings resort.

… If we wish to be free… we must fight! I repeat it, sir, we must fight! An appeal to arms and to the God of hosts is all that is left us!

… They tell us, sir, that we are weak; unable to cope with so formidable an adversary. But when shall we be stronger? Will it be the next week, or the next year? Will it be when we are totally disarmed, and when a British guard shall be stationed in every house?… Sir, we are not weak if we make a proper use of those means which the God of nature hath placed in our power. The millions of people, armed in the holy cause of liberty, and in such a country as that which we possess, are invincible by any force which our enemy can send against us.

There is no retreat but in submission and slavery! Our chains are forged! Their clanking may be heard on the plains of Boston! The war is inevitable—and let it come! I repeat it, sir, let it come.

… Gentlemen may cry, Peace, Peace—but there is no peace. The war is actually begun! The next gale that sweeps from the north will bring to our ears the clash of resounding arms! Our brethren are already in the field! Why stand we here idle? What is it that gentlemen wish? What would they have? Is life so dear, or peace so sweet, as to be purchased at the price of chains and slavery? Forbid it, Almighty God! I know not what course others may take; but as for me, give me liberty or give me death!

Student Guide
Lesson 7: The Boston Massacre

The Boston Massacre brought into sharp focus the colonists' growing frustration with British soldiers in America. The trial that followed highlighted John Adams's commitment to the belief that everyone deserves a fair trial. The debates in the First Continental Congress showed the quality of the leaders who would soon shape a new nation.

Lesson Objectives

- Demonstrate mastery of important knowledge and skills taught in previous lessons.
- Analyze an artist's representation of the Boston Massacre.
- Identify John Adams as a Boston lawyer who defended the British soldiers after the Boston Massacre.
- Identify *Quartering Act* and *redcoat*.
- Identify George III as the king of England in the mid-eighteenth century.
- Identify and describe the Stamp Act.
- Identify Sam Adams and Patrick Henry as opposition leaders.
- Analyze Patrick Henry's speech.

PREPARE

Approximate lesson time is 60 minutes.

Materials

For the Student

The Midnight Rider

A History of US (Concise Edition), Volume A (Prehistory to 1800) by Joy Hakim

History Journal

LEARN
Activity 1: Massacre in Boston *(Offline)*
Instructions
Check Your Reading (Chapter 58, pages 271–275)

Review Chapter 58.

Answer the following questions in complete sentences in your History Journal.

1. Why do you think the colonists didn't like the Quartering Act?
2. How did most of the British soldiers feel about being in America?
3. Who were the redcoats and why did John Adams take their case?
4. Did all of the representatives at the Continental Congress agree on what they should do about England? Explain.

Use What You Know

Complete the Midnight Rider sheet.

ASSESS

Lesson Assessment: The Boston Massacre (*Online*)

You will complete an online assessment covering the main points of this lesson. Your assessment will be scored by the computer.

Name 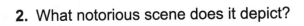   Date

The Midnight Rider

Answer the questions by recalling information from your reading.

1. What famous horseback rider carved this engraving? _____

2. What notorious scene does it depict?

   _____

   _____

3. Who are the soldiers? Who are the civilians?

   _____

   _____

   _____

4. How is the engraving misleading?

   _____

   _____

   _____

5. Look up the word propaganda in the dictionary. In your own words, explain what

   propaganda is. _____

   _____

   _____

6. Was this engraving used as propaganda? By whom, and for what purpose?

   _____

   _____

   _____

   _____

Student Guide
Lesson 8: The Shot Heard Round the World

Fighting in Lexington and Concord between the redcoats and colonists pushed the colonies toward war and on the road to nationhood.

Lesson Objectives

- Summarize the events at Lexington and Concord and explain the phrase "the shot heard round the world."
- Use a map to understand the battles of Lexington and Concord.

PREPARE

Approximate lesson time is 60 minutes.

Materials

For the Student

Fight for Independence

A History of US (Concise Edition), Volume A (Prehistory to 1800) by Joy Hakim

History Journal

LEARN
Activity 1: Fight for Independence *(Offline)*
Instructions
Read

Conflict turned to war when the minutemen and redcoats scuffled at Lexington and Concord. The march toward nationhood had begun.

Read Chapter 59, pages 276–282, to learn about Paul Revere's ride and how it helped warn the colonists of a British attack.

Discuss the following questions with an adult:

1. What triggered the British march on Concord?
2. Why were Samuel Adams and John Hancock hiding in Lexington?
3. Why did the poet Ralph Waldo Emerson call the first bullet fired in Lexington "the shot heard round the world"?
4. What did the battles of Concord and Lexington prove about the colonists?

Use What You Know

- Go back online and select the links to the Archiving Early America website to see two movies: *Paul Revere* (http://earlyamerica.com/paul_revere.htm) and *The Shot Heard Round the World* (http://earlyamerica.com/shot_heard.htm).
- Complete the Fight for Independence sheet using information from your book and the two online movies.

Name _____   Date _____

Fight for Independence

Write a brief description in each box of what happened at that location on the night of April 18, 1775. Use what you learned from your reading and from the movie clips at the Archiving Early America website to help you. Use the map key and draw the routes of Paul Revere, William Dawes, and Dr. Samuel Prescott on that famous night.

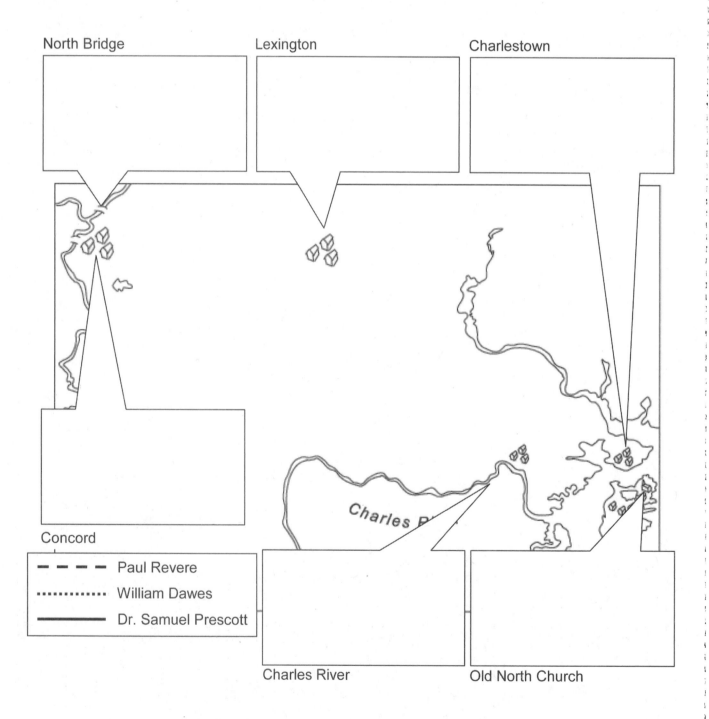

Student Guide
Lesson 9: Map Skills

In 1763, King George III issued a proclamation to keep the colonists east of the Appalachian Mountains. That same year, the French colony of New Orleans was given to the Spanish Empire. This port would play an important role in the coming war between the colonies and England.

Learn about the physical changes that have occurred in New Orleans over the past 200 years. Then read on to learn about the Second Continental Congress.

Lesson Objectives

- Compare maps and tables to assess change over time.
- Define *elevation* as height above sea level.
- Identify major landforms in the United States.
- Use landform maps and relief maps to locate physical features.

PREPARE

Approximate lesson time is 60 minutes.

Materials

For the Student

A History of US (Concise Edition), Volume A (Prehistory to 1800) by Joy Hakim

Understanding Geography: Map Skills and Our World (Level 5)

History Journal

LEARN
Activity 1: Mapping Change (Offline)
Instructions
Learn from Maps

Places change over time. New Orleans has changed dramatically over the past 200 years. People and the forces of nature have modified it. To learn about landforms and compare maps of New Orleans at different times:

- Complete Activity 5, "Landforms" (pages 20–23), and Activity 10, "Change Over Time: The Example of New Orleans" (pages 40–43), in *Understanding Geography*.
- Answer Questions 1–9 and 13–15 of Activity 5 in your History Journal. (Questions 10–12 and 16–19 are optional.)
- Answer Questions 1–12 of Activity 10 in your History Journal. (Questions 13–14 are optional.)
- If you have time, you may want to answer the Skill Builder Questions on pages 23 and 43. They are optional.
- After you have finished, compare your answers with the ones in the Learning Coach Guide.

ASSESS

Lesson Assessment: Map Skills (*Online*)

Answer the online geography questions for this assessment. Your assessment will be scored by the computer.

Student Guide
Lesson 10: A Continental Congress

When delegates to the Second Continental Congress met in Philadelphia, it became clear that they needed to choose a general to turn the raggedy militia into a powerful army. George Washington was the man for the job.

Lesson Objectives

- Explain the purpose of the Second Continental Congress and describe the kinds of men who attended the Second Continental Congress as mostly educated, wealthy and prominent.
- Explain the reasons for choosing George Washington to command the Continental Army, including his experience and character.

PREPARE

Approximate lesson time is 60 minutes.

Materials

> For the Student
>> Who's Who at the Second Continental Congress
>> A History of US (Concise Edition), Volume A (Prehistory to 1800) by Joy Hakim
>> History Journal

LEARN
Activity 1: The Second Continental Congress (Offline)
Instructions
Read

Few of the delegates who traveled to Philadelphia in 1775 wanted to rush headlong into revolution. However, with musket balls flying in Boston, most wondered how long they could continue to call themselves English subjects. How did they make such a difficult decision?

The delegates assigned the task of shaping a raggedy militia into a Continental Army to George Washington. When King George III rejected the Olive Branch Petition, Washington knew the war would go on. But could he have imagined he would not go home for nearly eight years?

Read Chapter 60, pages 283–289, and Chapter 61, pages 290–292. As you read, complete the Who's Who at the Second Continental Congress sheet.

Name _____   Date _____

Who's Who at the Second Continental Congress

For each delegate at the Second Continental Congress, fill in the colony he represented and any important facts that tell you what kind of man he was. For example, was the delegate rich or poor? What kind of education did he have? Was he well known in the colony he came from? What accomplishments was he best known for?

Delegate	Colony	Important Facts
George Washington		
Richard Henry Lee		
Phillip Livingston		
Joseph Hewes		
Stephen Hopkins		
Benjamin Franklin		
John Adams		
John Hancock		
Thomas Jefferson		

Student Guide
Lesson 11: The Fighting Begins

As the delegates to the Second Continental Congress were meeting in Philadelphia, the first major battle occurred at Breed's Hill and Bunker Hill.

Lesson Objectives

- Describe the battle at Breed's Hill and Bunker Hill and explain its significance as demonstrating the colonists' ability to fight.

PREPARE

Approximate lesson time is 60 minutes.

Materials

For the Student

Who? What? When? Where? Why?

A History of US (Concise Edition), Volume A (Prehistory to 1800) by Joy Hakim

History Journal

LEARN
Activity 1: The Revolution Begins *(Offline)*

Instructions
Read

Read Chapter 62, pages 293–297. (Do not read the feature on the Age of Enlightenment; you will read that in the next lesson.) Then complete the Who? What? When? Where? Why? sheet.

Name _____   Date _____

Who? What? When? Where? Why?

Can you summon up the answers to these questions?

1. **WHO?** They were asleep on that June night in 1775 as Massachusetts soldiers dug in fortifications on Breed's Hill. Who were they?

_____

2. **WHAT?** What river did the British cross to get from Boston to Charlestown?

_____

3. **WHERE?** A famous battle took place in this lady's hairdo! What were the names of the hills on which the fighting took place?

_____

4. **WHEN?** What were the American soldiers instructed to hold fire until they saw?

_____

5. **WHY?** Why did they hold fire until the last minute?

_____

Thinking Cap Question! Imagine you were one of the soldiers who fought in the battle pictured above. Write a diary entry describing what happened to you that day.

Adapted from *A History of US*

Student Guide
Lesson 12: Will You Sign?

The Declaration of Independence introduced the world to the American idea of representative government. Its focus on equality and natural rights has guided generations of Americans.

Lesson Objectives

- Demonstrate mastery of important knowledge and skills in previous lessons.
- Summarize Thomas Paine's arguments for independence.
- Explain how Thomas Jefferson was chosen to write the Declaration of Independence.
- Recognize the Enlightenment ideas Jefferson used in the Declaration of Independence.
- Summarize the events at Lexington and Concord and explain the phrase "the shot heard round the world."
- Explain the reasons for choosing George Washington to command the Continental Army, including his experience and character.
- Describe the battle at Breed's Hill and Bunker Hill and explain its significance as demonstrating the colonists' ability to fight.

PREPARE

Approximate lesson time is 60 minutes.

Materials

For the Student

Age of Enlightenment

A History of US (Concise Edition), Volume A (Prehistory to 1800) by Joy Hakim

History Journal

LEARN
Activity 1: Declaring Independence (Offline)
Instructions
Discuss

Do you remember when you read about the "firebrands"? One of those firebrands, Thomas Paine, made his mark around this time. Paine came to America from England and helped the colonists say what was really in their hearts. Paine's pamphlet, *Common Sense*, stated clearly that the colonies must be free from England. In its first three months, *Common Sense* sold 120,000 copies in the colonies. It stressed three points:

1. Monarchy was a poor form of government, and the colonies would be better off without it.
2. Great Britain was hurting the colonies' economy with taxes and trade restrictions.
3. It was foolish for a small island 3,000 miles away to try to rule a whole continent.

Discuss Thomas Paine's arguments for independence with an adult.

Read

Read the feature in Chapter 62 titled, "How the New World Changed the Old, and Vice Versa," and complete the Age of Enlightenment sheet.

Read Chapter 63, pages 298–302, and answer the following questions in your History Journal.

1. What was the goal of the people who signed the Declaration of Independence?
2. Why was Thomas Jefferson chosen to write the Declaration of Independence?
3. What three things did the delegates want Jefferson to accomplish in the Declaration?
4. The author wants to know: What does *equal* mean?
5. What Enlightenment ideas did Jefferson use in the Declaration of Independence?

Look Back

Go back online and review previous lessons with the flash cards to prepare for the assessment.

ASSESS

Mid-Unit Assessment: Will You Sign? *(Online)*

You will complete an online assessment covering the main points of this unit. Your assessment will be scored by the computer.

Name _____   Date _____

The Age of Enlightenment

Fill in the blanks with terms from the word bank below. Some terms may be used more than once. Refer to the feature in Chapter 62, partially quoted below, if you need help.

Enlightenment	John Locke	Jean-Jacques Rousseau
people	rulers	House of Burgesses
democratic government	natural rights	Isaac Newton
governments	superstition	assemblies	raw materials

Lights were being lit in the eighteenth century—so many lights that it would come to be

called a time of _____. The lights were going on in the minds of the

thinking people. Some of the electricity for those lights had come from a scientist named

_____. He had shown that the universe was not as full of mystery as

people had supposed. It could be understood with study and observation and by people

using their brains. That was an astonishing thought in a world that had often been guided

by _____ and fear. Suddenly there seemed to be all kinds of brilliant

thinkers who were using their minds and encouraging others to do the same thing.

An Englishman named _____ and a Frenchman named

_____ were two of the most important Enlightenment thinkers.

They thought about politics and the way _____ were run . . . .

_____ wrote about _____. He said

that governments should be run for the _____, not for their

_____. He made people think about democracy . . . .

The colonists knew something else: they knew they could govern themselves. They didn't need kings or nobles to make decisions for them. Americans had been running their own _____ for years. There was the General Court in Massachusetts, the _____ in Virginia, and lawmaking bodies in each colony. Nowhere in Europe did people have that kind of experience in self-government . . . .

Americans were sending _____ to England—like lumber and tobacco—and getting them sent back as finished goods—furniture and cigars. Well, another raw material got sent back and forth across the sea: the idea of freedom and _____ .

Student Guide
Lesson 13: Life, Liberty, and the Pursuit of Happiness

The Declaration of Independence stated clearly that colonists were breaking away from England. It was a very bold statement. Fifty-six men signed the document.

Lesson Objectives

- Read and analyze the Declaration of Independence to gain understanding of its meaning.

PREPARE

Approximate lesson time is 60 minutes.

Materials

> For the Student
>
> > Guided Reading: Declaration of Independence
> >
> > A History of US (Concise Edition), Volume A (Prehistory to 1800) by Joy Hakim
> >
> > History Journal

LEARN
Activity 1: Understanding the Declaration *(Offline)*
Instructions
Read

Follow the instructions on the Guided Reading: Declaration of Independence sheet as you read sections of the Declaration of Independence in the book's appendix.

Optional: Beyond the Lesson
See what went on in Philadelphia during the summer of 1776. Visit Archiving Early America: Declaring Independence (http://earlyamerica.com/independence.htm).

Activity 2. Optional: The Summer of 1776 *(Online)*

Name _____   Date _____

Guided Reading: The Declaration of Independence

Complete this sheet as you read sections 1–4 of the Declaration of Independence. It is located in the book's appendix.

I.   Preamble

Read the first paragraph of the Declaration of Independence.

1. This long first sentence is called the Preamble, which means "introduction." What country does Thomas Jefferson say the people of the colonies must break away from?

_____

2. When Jefferson says Americans "should declare the causes which impel them to the Separation," he means they should state to the world why they are forced to become independent. Why do you think he says that they should explain this to the whole world?

_____

_____

II. Philosophy

Read the first sentence of the second paragraph that begins with "We hold..."

3. What does Jefferson say about human beings? _____

_____

4. What rights does the Declaration of Independence say that all people are born with?

_____

_____

_____

Read the next sentence that begins with "That to secure..."

5. According to the Declaration, governments exist in order to do what? _____

_____

6. Where do governments get their power? _____

7. What should the people do when a government does not protect their rights?

_____

III. Grievances

8. Jefferson lists the destructive things King George III has done to the colonies. You don't need to read them unless you would like to, but you might find it interesting to count them and see how many crimes are mentioned. Start with the sentence beginning, "He has refused his assent…" Count every paragraph that begins with the word "he" or "for" and see how many you find by the time you see the one that begins, "He has excited domestic

Insurrections…" How many complaints are there? _____

IV. Declaration

Read the paragraph that begins with "We, therefore…"

9. Jefferson wrote, "these United Colonies are, and by Right ought to be, FREE AND INDEPENDENT STATES; that they are absolved from all Allegiance to the British Crown…" Rewrite that sentence in your own words.

_____

_____

10. What did the signers promise to each other? What does it mean in your own words?

_____

_____

11. Who was the first person to sign the Declaration of Independence?

_____

Student Guide
Lesson 14: Unit Review

You've completed Unit 5, Road to Revolution. It's time to review what you've learned. You'll take the Unit Assessment in the next lesson.

(This review might refer to topics presented in optional lessons in this unit.)

Lesson Objectives
- Summarize the ideas and events leading to the American Revolution.

PREPARE

Approximate lesson time is 60 minutes.

Materials

> For the Student
>
>> A History of US (Concise Edition), Volume A (Prehistory to 1800) by Joy Hakim
>>
>> History Journal

LEARN
Activity 1: A Look Back *(Offline)*
Instructions
Online Review

Use the following to review this unit online:

- The Big Picture
- Time Line
- Flash Cards

History Journal Review

Review more by going through your History Journal. Look at the worksheets you completed for this unit. Review your vocabulary words. If you completed writing assignments, read them. Don't rush through; take your time. Your History Journal is a great resource for a unit review.

Student Guide
Lesson 15: Unit Assessment

You've finished this unit! Take the unit assessment. Then read on for the next lesson.

Lesson Objectives

- Analyze the wisdom of Benjamin Franklin and apply it to today.
- Explain the causes of the French and Indian War as competition between France and England for land and power.
- Identify George Washington as a soldier in the British Army during the French and Indian War.
- Describe the problems the British government faced after 1763 in trying to limit westward migration and why many Americans wanted to go west.
- Locate the Appalachian Mountains on a map and explain that the British did not want migration across them for reasons of economics and security.
- Explain the significance of Magna Carta and the "rights of Englishmen."
- Identify and describe the Stamp Act.
- Analyze Patrick Henry's speech.
- Identify John Adams as a Boston lawyer who defended the British soldiers after the Boston Massacre.
- Summarize the events at Lexington and Concord and explain the phrase "the shot heard round the world."
- Explain the purpose of the Second Continental Congress and describe the kinds of men who attended the Second Continental Congress as mostly educated, wealthy and prominent.
- Explain the reasons for choosing George Washington to command the Continental Army, including his experience and character.
- Summarize Thomas Paine's arguments for independence.
- Explain how Thomas Jefferson was chosen to write the Declaration of Independence.
- Recognize the Enlightenment ideas Jefferson used in the Declaration of Independence.
- Read and analyze the Declaration of Independence to gain understanding of its meaning.
- Identify the Boston Massacre as a clash between colonists and British soldiers.

PREPARE

Approximate lesson time is 60 minutes.

Materials

For the Student

A History of US (Concise Edition), Volume A (Prehistory to 1800) by Joy Hakim

History Journal

ASSESS

Unit Assessment: Road to Revolution, Part 1 *(Online)*

Complete the computer-scored portion of the Unit Assessment. When you have finished, complete the teacher-scored portion of the assessment and submit it to your teacher.

Unit Assessment: Road to Revolution, Part 2 *(Offline)*

Complete the teacher-scored portion of the Unit Assessment and submit it to your teacher.

LEARN

Activity 1: Chapters 64 and 65 *(Offline)*

Instructions

Read On

Read Chapter 64, pages 303–305, and Chapter 65, pages 306–310. Prepare to explain what effect the signing of the Declaration of Independence had on many of the colonists. Also prepare to describe the roles of women during the Revolution.

Student Guide
Lesson 1: John and Abigail Adams

How did a loosely knit group of colonies defeat the most powerful military in the world? Or did they? One biography of Washington gives him the credit for making the cost of a British victory too high. How? And what social and political changes occurred as a result of the war?

John Adams never gave up on independence. His hard work and the words of the Declaration of Independence finally convinced people to unify and fight for liberty. The men who fought were not alone. Women played an important part in the American Revolution, too. They served on the home front and on the battlefront. Their experiences during the war got them thinking about equality and liberty.

Lesson Objectives
- Recognize John Adams's role in declaring independence as one of early and persistent support.
- Explain the significance of the Declaration of Independence in unifying people for the war effort.
- Describe the roles of women during the Revolution, including maintaining farms and businesses, assisting in the war effort, fighting, and being politically vocal.

PREPARE

Approximate lesson time is 60 minutes.

Materials
For the Student

Mail Bag!

A History of US (Concise Edition), Volume A (Prehistory to 1800) by Joy Hakim

History Journal

LEARN
Activity 1: Revolutionary Women and Children (Offline)
Instructions
Check Your Reading (Chapter 64, pages 303–305, and Chapter 65, pages 306–310)

- Go over what you learned in Chapters 64 and 65.
- Complete the Mail Bag sheet. Have an adult check your answers.

Discuss

John Adams played an important role in getting the delegates to sign the Declaration of Independence. He was an early and persistent supporter of independence. He stood up for what he believed, even though he knew it could mean his life.

Have you ever believed strongly in something? Did you stand up for what you believed in? How far would you go in defending your beliefs?

Discuss the idea of standing up for what you believe with an adult.

Use What You Know

Write a list of "did you know" questions about women in the Revolution in your History Journal. Include the interesting, sometimes little-known facts mentioned in the book. For example: Did you know that women ran the family farms when their husbands went off to fight?

When you have finished, quiz your friends and family.

Read On

Would slaves fight in a revolution for a nation that allowed slavery? Would they side with the British? Would either side allow slaves to fight at all?

Read Chapter 66, pages 311–315, and Chapter 67, pages 316–317. Prepare to discuss how a black person or a woman of 1776 might have interpreted this phrase from the Declaration of Independence: "All men are created equal."

Optional: Beyond the Lesson

Join the signers in an interactive activity at the National Archives website (www.archives.gov/exhibit_hall/charters_of_freedom/declaration/join_the_signers/join_the_signers.html)

Activity 2. Optional: Signers of the Declaration of Independence *(Online)*

Name _____ Date _____

Mail Bag!

TO MR. JOHN ADAMS:

"In the new code of laws... I desire you remember the ladies... if particular care and attention are not paid to the ladies we are determined to foment a rebellion and will not hold ourselves bound to obey any laws in which we have no voice or representation."

1. Who wrote this angry letter to John Adams? _____

2. What were women left in charge of when their husbands went to war? _____

   _____

3. What were some of the things women did during the war? _____

   _____

   _____

4. Did any women fight on the battlefields of the Revolution? How? _____

   _____

5. Do you think women started to become politically vocal during the war? Why or why not?

   _____

   _____

6. What is the name of the woman in the picture above? (Hint: She was famous for bringing

   water to thirsty patriot soldiers.) _____

Use the Benjamin Banneker to Thomas Jefferson feature in Chapter 64 to answer the following questions.

7. How were Benjamin Banneker and Thomas Jefferson alike? _____

   _____

8. In your own words, what does Benjamin Banneker hope Thomas Jefferson will do?

   _____

   _____

Adapted from *A History of US*

Student Guide
Lesson 2: Decisions

People of African ancestry in the colonies understood very well the limits on equality. Some accepted offers of freedom from the British. Others fought to plant the seeds of racial freedom in their own land. And in Virginia, people had to choose to rebel or support the king when the royal governor proclaimed that "all indentured servants, Negroes, and others" were free if they were willing to defend the crown.

Lesson Objectives

- Summarize the dilemma many blacks faced in taking sides during the Revolution.
- Describe the roles of blacks on both sides of the conflict.

PREPARE

Approximate lesson time is 60 minutes.

Materials

For the Student

More Mail

A History of US (Concise Edition), Volume A (Prehistory to 1800) by Joy Hakim

History Journal

LEARN
Activity 1: Liberty for All? *(Offline)*
Instructions
Check Your Reading (Chapter 66, pages 311–315, and Chapter 67, pages 316–317)

- Go over what you learned in Chapters 66 and 67.
- Complete the More Mail sheet. Have an adult check your answers.

Discuss

The Declaration of Independence and the American Revolution influenced attitudes in the United States. They changed people's ideas of equality in ways that the Continental Congress did not intend. Discuss some of these changes with an adult.

184

Use What You Know

Choose one of the following activities to complete.

- Write a short newspaper article that explains the roles of blacks on both sides of the Revolutionary War.
- Imagine you are an African American or a woman in 1776. Write a letter to the editor of a newspaper expressing your interpretation of the Declaration of Independence.

Discuss your writing with an adult.

Read On

American colonists were not the only ones to fight for independence in the Continental Army. Many foreign soldiers came to America to help the colonies in their war with Britain. What were some of the reasons these men took part in the Revolution?

Read Chapter 68, pages 318–321. Be prepared to name two soldiers who fought on the side of the colonists, but were from another country.

Optional: Beyond the Lesson

Follow the directions online to learn more about James Forten.

Activity 2. Optional: James Forten *(Online)*

Name _____   Date _____

More Mail

TO GOVERNOR GAGE OF MASSACHUSETTS:

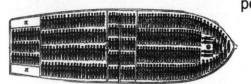

"We have in common with all other men a natural right to our freedoms... we are a freeborn people and have never forfeited this blessing by any compact or agreement whatever. But we were unjustly dragged by the cruel hand of power from our dearest friends and some of us stolen from... our tender parents and from a populous, pleasant and plentiful country and brought hither to be made slaves for life."

1. What did the authors of this letter claim to have in common with other men? _____

_____

2. How were slaves collected and brought to America? _____

_____

3. Many African-American men fought in the Revolutionary War. Why did this frighten many

white Southerners? _____

_____

4. What happened to Thomas Jefferson's slaves after they were carried off by British

troops? _____

_____

5. What did the African-American patriot soldier James Forten refuse to do for the British

captain? _____

_____

6. Why was the idea of equality radical in the 1770s? _____

_____

Adapted from *A History of US*

Student Guide
Lesson 3: Best Friends

People from many nations were drawn into the conflict between Britain and the newly formed United States. These people contributed many things to the colonists' fight for liberty and independence: leadership, money, and even their lives.

Lesson Objectives

- Demonstrate mastery of important knowledge and skills taught in previous lessons.
- Identify individuals who came from Europe to aid the American cause, including the Marquis de Lafayette, Baron Friedrich von Steuben, and Haym Salomon.
- Use research skills to gain information on one of the people mentioned in this lesson.
- Recognize John Adams's role in declaring independence as one of early and persistent support.
- Explain the significance of the Declaration of Independence in unifying people for the war effort.
- Describe the roles of women during the Revolution, including maintaining farms and businesses, assisting in the war effort, fighting, and being politically vocal.
- Summarize the dilemma many blacks faced in taking sides during the Revolution.

PREPARE

Approximate lesson time is 60 minutes.

Materials

For the Student

A History of US (Concise Edition), Volume A (Prehistory to 1800) by Joy Hakim

History Journal

LEARN
Activity 1: Soldiers from Everywhere (Offline)
Instructions
Check Your Reading (Chapter 68, pages 318–321)

Discuss Chapter 68 with an adult. Then, play the "Who Is It?" game.

1. Using information from Chapter 68, fill four index cards with information about the following people, one card per person:

- Marquis de Lafayette
- Baron Friedrich von Steuben
- Haym Salomon
- Robert Morris

---

2. Ask an adult to read each card to you and see if you can remember who each person is. Here's an example:

"This man wrote the Declaration of Independence. He was one of the youngest members of the Continental Congress. He was tall and shy with red hair. He lived in Virginia. Who is it?" (Thomas Jefferson)

Use What You Know

Research one of the people you read about:

- Marquis de Lafayette
- Baron Friedrich von Steuben
- Haym Salomon
- Robert Morris

Use nonfiction books, encyclopedias (in print or online), and websites. Take notes during your research.

Use the information you gathered to write a commendation for the person you selected. In this sense, a *commendation* is a piece of writing that praises something, or many things, the person has done.

Read On

Now that the colonies had declared their independence, they had a war to fight. And unless they won, the Declaration of Independence would mean nothing. General Washington would face many problems. And although things didn't go well in the beginning, one major victory would turn things around for the Americans.

Read Chapter 69, pages 322–328. Be prepared to describe the difficulties George Washington faced as commander of the Continental Army, and name the battle that was a turning point in the war.

Vocabulary

You'll see the following terms as you read. Write a brief definition for each in your History Journal.

- Hessian
- mercenary

_____

ASSESS

Mid-Unit Assessment: Best Friends *(Online)*
You will complete an online assessment covering the main points of this unit. Your assessment will be scored by the computer.

Student Guide
Lesson 4: Challenges for the Continental Army

The opening battles of the Revolutionary War went badly for George Washington. He was sometimes forced to focus more on avoiding capture than on victory. But victories did come. The American victory at Saratoga changed the course of the war. Seeing the possibility of victory, the French joined the conflict on the side of the Americans.

Lesson Objectives

- Define *Hessian* and *mercenary.*
- Identify Sir William Howe as the commander in charge of all the British forces in America.
- Describe the difficulties George Washington faced as commander of the Continental Army, including a small, unstable army, lack of supplies, and need to use retreat as a way to save the army.
- Analyze a painting, *Washington Crossing the Delaware,* to assess historical accuracy and bias.
- Explain the significance of the battles of Trenton and Saratoga (one boosted American morale; the other was a turning point in the war).

PREPARE

Approximate lesson time is 60 minutes.

Materials

For the Student

A History of US (Concise Edition), Volume A (Prehistory to 1800) by Joy Hakim

History Journal

LEARN
Activity 1: A Shaky Start, Then Victory (Offline)

Instructions

Check Your Reading (Chapter 69, pages 322–328)

Use the flash cards to review your reading. Then discuss the following with an adult.

1. What hardships did soldiers face early in the war?
2. What was Washington's strategy in the early battles waged in New York?
3. Who were the Hessians, and why did their use by the British anger many Americans?
4. Why were each of the following battles important to the American cause: the Battle of Trenton, the Battle of Princeton, and the Battle of Saratoga?

Use What You Know

Imagine you're George Washington. It's 1776. In your History Journal:

- Make a list of the problems you are having as you try to fight the war.
- Make a list of the kinds of help you would like to get from France.

When you've finished, go back to the lesson online and click the link to view the painting *Washington Crossing the Delaware.*

- Look closely at the painting. Is it historically accurate? See if you can find any inaccuracies. There are five errors that are often observed.
- Do you see any bias in the way the painter shows this event? In other words, do you think the painter was influenced by his feelings and emotions toward the subject of his painting? If so, in what ways? How did this come out in the painting?

Read On

In 1777, the British captured Philadelphia. Before that, General Washington lost two battles in Pennsylvania. Things weren't going well for the Americans. But things were about to change. Although no battles were fought at Valley Forge, and there was terrible suffering, something very good happened there. What was it?

Read Chapter 70, pages 329–335. Be prepared to name two important American military leaders of the Revolution, not including George Washington.

Student Guide
Lesson 5: Turning Points

The hardships of war gave Washington a battle-tested army. After Valley Forge, these troops began a campaign to sweep the British and their mercenaries off the continent.

Lesson Objectives

- Locate the following places on a map: Saratoga, Philadelphia, Valley Forge, and Vincennes.
- Identify Martha Washington as providing moral support and Nathaniel Greene and George Rogers Clark as significant military leaders of the Revolution.
- Describe conditions at Valley Forge and summarize the significance of the winter there.
- Explain the reasons for the warfare on the frontier and the effect of the Revolution on Native Americans.
- Identify George Washington as providing example, dignity and determination to his army.

PREPARE

Approximate lesson time is 60 minutes.

Materials

For the Student

Map of the Revolutionary War

Revolutionary War: People and Places

A History of US (Concise Edition), Volume A (Prehistory to 1800) by Joy Hakim

History Journal

LEARN
Activity 1: Valley Forge to Vincennes (Offline)
Instructions
Check Your Reading (Chapter 70, pages 329–335)

Go over Chapter 70 with an adult. Then complete the map activity and the descriptions of the first four people on page 2 of the Revolutionary War: People and Places sheet. Refer to the map of the Revolutionary War online to complete the map activity.

You will complete more activities on the sheet in the next lesson.

Discuss

Discuss the following two questions with an adult:

- Although no battles were fought at Valley Forge, it is considered a major American triumph. Why?
- What was all the fighting in the West about?

Use What You Know

Write a letter about Valley Forge in your History Journal:

- Reread the letter from Dr. Albigence Waldo in Chapter 70.
- Imagine you are Dr. Waldo and it's now spring. You have survived the terrible winter.
- Write a letter describing the changes that have taken place in the troops and in your morale.

Read On

As the war dragged on, it became more and more unpopular in England. But time did not diminish the Americans' belief in their cause. This gave the colonists an advantage over their English cousins. Soon the war in the northern colonies became a stalemate. Sir William Howe resigned. The new British commander shifted his attention to the southern colonies. How would the Patriots react in Georgia and South Carolina? Would Washington get the help he desperately needed from the French?

Read Chapter 71, pages 336–343. Be prepared to explain the roles geography and the French played in Cornwallis's defeat at Yorktown.

Optional: Beyond the Lesson

Explore the Valley Forge National Historic Park online. The site contains many images of Revolutionary War-era artifacts.

Activity 2. Optional: Valley Forge *(Online)*

Name _____   Date _____

Revolutionary War: People and Places

Add the following to the map below: Saratoga, Philadelphia, Valley Forge, and Vincennes.

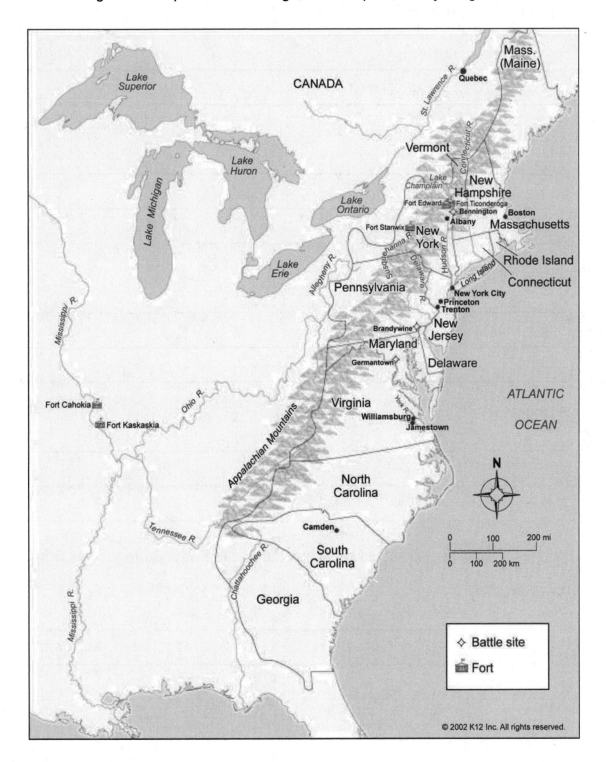

Write a brief description of each person. Include any information you've learned that you believe is important and/or interesting.

1. George Washington

_____

_____

_____

2. Martha Washington

_____

_____

_____

3. Nathanael Greene

_____

_____

_____

4. George Rogers Clark

_____

_____

_____

The descriptions for these people should be written during the Sweet Surrender lesson.

5. Alexander Hamilton

_____

_____

_____

6. General Henry Clinton

_____

_____

_____

7. Lord Charles Cornwallis

_____

_____

_____

8. Comte de Grasse

_____

_____

_____

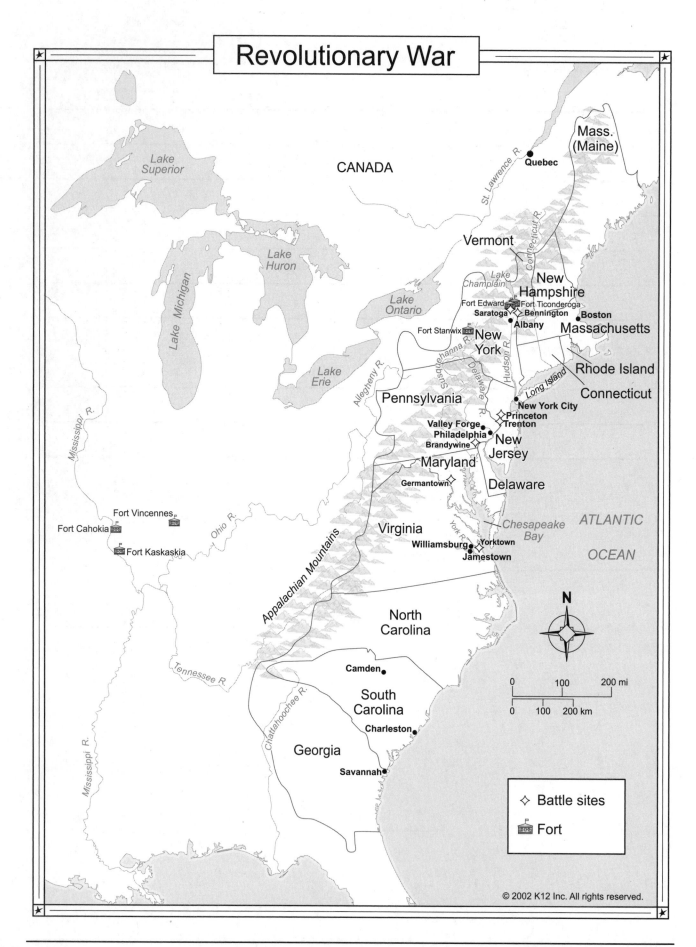

Revolutionary War

Lake Superior

CANADA

Mass. (Maine)

Quebec

Lake Huron

Lake Michigan

Lake Ontario

Vermont

Lake Champlain

New Hampshire

Fort Edward Fort Ticonderoga

Saratoga Bennington Boston

Fort Stanwix Albany

New York Massachusetts

Lake Erie

Rhode Island

Allegheny R.

Susquehanna R.

Delaware R.

Hudson R.

Long Island Connecticut

Pennsylvania

New York City

Mississippi R.

Princeton
Valley Forge Trenton
Philadelphia
Brandywine New Jersey

Maryland Delaware

Germantown

Fort Vincennes

Fort Cahokia

Ohio R.

Virginia

Chesapeake Bay

ATLANTIC

Fort Kaskaskia

York R.

Williamsburg Yorktown
Jamestown

OCEAN

Appalachian Mountains

N

Tennessee R.

North Carolina

200 mi

Camden

0   100   200 km

South Carolina

Chattahoochee R.

Charleston

Georgia

Savannah

◇ Battle sites

🏰 Fort

Student Guide
Lesson 6: Sweet Surrender

With the help of France, the Americans finally backed the British into a corner at Yorktown. The fife and drum played a tune that summed up American victory: "The World Turned Upside Down."

Lesson Objectives

- Demonstrate mastery of important knowledge and skills taught in previous lessons.
- Locate the following places on a map: Savannah, Charleston, Chesapeake Bay, and Yorktown, and U.S. boundaries in 1783.
- Identify Cornwallis as the leader of the British forces and Alexander Hamilton as aide to George Washington.
- Explain the role of geography and the French in Cornwallis's defeat at Yorktown.
- Analyze art of the Revolution to determine the values it promotes.
- Explain the significance of the Declaration of Independence in unifying people for the war effort.
- Describe the roles of women during the Revolution, including maintaining farms and businesses, assisting in the war effort, fighting, and being politically vocal.
- Define *Hessian* and *mercenary.*
- Identify Sir William Howe as the commander in charge of all the British forces in America.
- Describe the difficulties George Washington faced as commander of the Continental Army, including a small, unstable army, lack of supplies, and need to use retreat as a way to save the army.
- Explain the significance of the battles of Trenton and Saratoga (one boosted American morale; the other was a turning point in the war).
- Locate the following places on a map: Saratoga, Philadelphia, Valley Forge, and Vincennes.
- Identify Martha Washington as providing moral support and Nathaniel Greene and George Rogers Clark as significant military leaders of the Revolution.
- Describe conditions at Valley Forge and summarize the significance of the winter there.
- Explain the reasons for the warfare on the frontier and the effect of the Revolution on Native Americans.

PREPARE

Approximate lesson time is 60 minutes.

Materials

For the Student

Map of the Revolutionary War

A History of US (Concise Edition), Volume A (Prehistory to 1800) by Joy Hakim

History Journal

LEARN
Activity 1: The World Turned Upside Down (Offline)
Instructions
Check Your Reading (Chapter 71, pages 336–343)

Refer to the Revolutionary War map to add these places to the map on page 1 of the Revolutionary War: People and Places sheet:

- Savannah
- Charleston
- Chesapeake Bay
- Yorktown

Show the boundaries of the United States in 1783 using boundary lines or shading. (Use the map of North America in 1783 in Chapter 71 as a reference.)

Now add a description for each of the following people on the same sheet:

- Alexander Hamilton
- General Henry Clinton
- Lord Charles Cornwallis
- Comte de Grasse

Discuss

1. How did the geography at Yorktown help the Americans defeat the British?
2. What role did the French play in the British defeat at Yorktown?
3. Why do you think the tune "The World Turned Upside Down" was a fitting way to end the Revolution?

Analyze Art of the Revolution

Go back to the lesson online and analyze a painting about the Revolutionary War. Discuss these questions with an adult:

1. In *The Spirit of '76,* by Archibald Willard, two men and a boy play music while leading a parade of soldiers. Did the artist paint a realistic and orderly scene or an emotional scene to get you to experience what he's showing in the painting? What details tell you that?
2. Do you think the artist valued freedom and liberty? Why or why not?
3. Why do you think the artist included a flag in the painting? What is the flag a symbol of? How do you feel when you look at your country's flag?
4. Do you think the artist created a painting to influence the way people feel? If so, do you think he succeeded? How did he do this?

ASSESS
Mid-Unit Assessment: The American Revolution *(Online)*

You will complete an online assessment covering the main points of this unit. Your assessment will be scored by the computer.

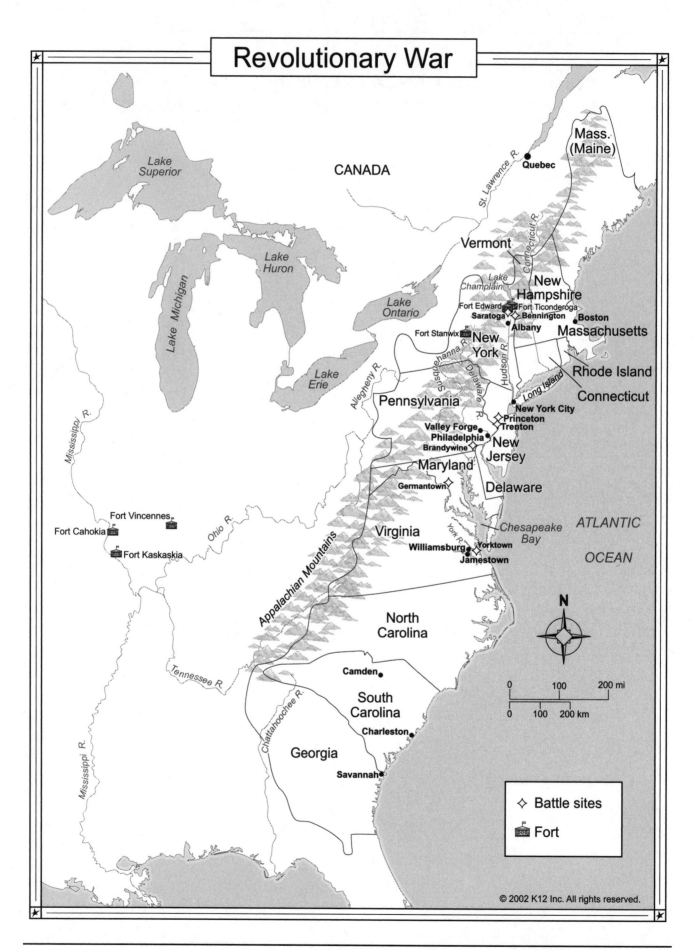

Revolutionary War

CANADA

Mass. (Maine)

Quebec

Lake Superior

Lake Huron

Lake Michigan

Lake Ontario

Lake Erie

Vermont

Lake Champlain

New Hampshire

Fort Edward   Fort Ticonderoga
Saratoga   Bennington   Boston
Fort Stanwix   Albany   Massachusetts

New York

Rhode Island

Long Island   Connecticut

Pennsylvania

New York City

Allegheny R.   Princeton
Trenton
Valley Forge
Philadelphia   New Jersey
Brandywine

Maryland

Delaware

Germantown

Fort Vincennes

Fort Cahokia

Ohio R.

Fort Kaskaskia

Chesapeake Bay   ATLANTIC

OCEAN

Virginia

York R.   Yorktown
Williamsburg   Jamestown

Mississippi R.

Appalachian Mountains

Tennessee R.

North Carolina

N

Camden

South Carolina

Chattahoochee R.

Charleston

Georgia

Savannah

0   100   200 mi
0   100   200 km

◇ Battle sites

🏰 Fort

Student Guide
Lesson 7: (Optional) What Did It All Mean?

From the signing of the Declaration to the victory at Yorktown, Americans turned their dreams of liberty into a new nation. The American Revolution was a defining period in American history that brought about many changes.

Lesson Objectives

- Summarize the key events and ideas of the Revolution.
- Analyze the changes that the Revolution brought about.

PREPARE

Approximate lesson time is 60 minutes.

Materials

For the Student

Revolutionary Changes

A History of US (Concise Edition), Volume A (Prehistory to 1800) by Joy Hakim

History Journal

LEARN
Activity 1. Optional: Revolutionary Changes (Offline)
Instructions
Use What You Know

Revolutionary Changes

On the Revolutionary Changes sheet, examine the list of changes that came about as a result of the Revolution. Decide whether each change supported or conflicted with the values of the Revolution.

Liberty! The American Revolution

Go back online to explore the PBS website Liberty! The American Revolution. This site has many interesting sections. You may be especially interested in these two:

- The Road to Revolution Game
- Chronicles of the Revolution

Name _____   Date _____

Revolutionary Changes

Read the following list of changes that came about as a result of the American Revolution. For each change, indicate whether you believe the change supported or conflicted with the values of the Revolution.

1. Men no longer tipped their hats to those of a higher class.

   SUPPORTED or CONFLICTED

2. A number of planters and others freed their slaves.

   SUPPORTED or CONFLICTED

3. George Washington resigned his commission in the army and returned to being a farmer.

   SUPPORTED or CONFLICTED

4. Academies for women were established.

   SUPPORTED or CONFLICTED

5. Men stopped wearing wigs and powdering their hair in the English fashion.

   SUPPORTED or CONFLICTED

6. About 100,000 Loyalists left the country for their own physical or political security.

   SUPPORTED or CONFLICTED

7. Laws requiring a man to leave his entire estate to his eldest son and not split it up were taken off the books.

   SUPPORTED or CONFLICTED

8. The first representative government for a large nation in modern history was formed.

   SUPPORTED or CONFLICTED

Merriam-Webster's Collegiate Dictionary defines revolution as "a sudden, radical, or complete change." Many historians argue that the American Revolution was really a war for independence, rather than a revolution. What do you think?

Student Guide
Lesson 8: Unit Review

You've completed Unit 6, The American Revolution. It's time to review what you've learned. You'll take the unit assessment in the next lesson.

Lesson Objectives
- Demonstrate mastery of important knowledge and skills taught in previous lessons.
- Make quilt squares that represent the major events, people, and ideas from the American Revolution.

PREPARE

Approximate lesson time is 60 minutes.

Materials

For the Student

A History of US (Concise Edition), Volume A (Prehistory to 1800) by Joy Hakim

History Journal

LEARN
Activity 1: A Look Back *(Offline)*
Instructions
History Journal Review

Review the unit by going through your History Journal. You should:

- Look at worksheets you have completed for this unit.
- Review unit vocabulary words.
- Read through any writing assignments you did during the unit.
- Review the two assessments you took.

Online Review

Go online and use the following to review this unit:

- The Big Picture
- Flash Cards
- Time Line
- *Liberty! The American Revolution*
- Map of Revolutionary War

Beyond the Lesson

Create squares for a quilt that symbolizes the major events, people, and ideas from the American Revolution.

Activity 2: Revolutionary Quilt *(Offline)*

Student Guide
Lesson 9: Unit Assessment

You've finished this unit! Take the Unit Assessment. Then look at today's reading assignment.

Lesson Objectives

- Recognize John Adams's role in declaring independence as one of early and persistent support.
- Explain the significance of the Declaration of Independence in unifying people for the war effort.
- Summarize the dilemma many blacks faced in taking sides during the Revolution.
- Describe the roles of blacks on both sides of the conflict.
- Identify individuals who came from Europe to aid the American cause, including the Marquis de Lafayette, Baron Friedrich von Steuben, and Haym Salomon.
- Define *Hessian* and *mercenary*.
- Explain the significance of the battles of Trenton and Saratoga (one boosted American morale; the other was a turning point in the war).
- Identify Martha Washington as providing moral support and Nathaniel Greene and George Rogers Clark as significant military leaders of the Revolution.
- Describe conditions at Valley Forge and summarize the significance of the winter there.
- Explain the reasons for the warfare on the frontier and the effect of the Revolution on Native Americans.
- Identify Cornwallis as the leader of the British forces and Alexander Hamilton as aide to George Washington.
- Explain the role of geography and the French in Cornwallis's defeat at Yorktown.
- Identify George Washington as providing example, dignity and determination to his army.
- Identify Abigail Adams as a delegate's wife who wrote letters to her husband about the unequal treatment of women and blacks.

PREPARE

Approximate lesson time is 60 minutes.

Materials

For the Student

A History of US (Concise Edition), Volume A (Prehistory to 1800) by Joy Hakim

History Journal

ASSESS

Unit Assessment: The American Revolution, Part 1 *(Online)*

Complete the computer-scored portion of the Unit Assessment. When you have finished, complete the teacher-scored portion of the assessment and submit it to your teacher.

Unit Assessment: The American Revolution, Part 2 *(Offline)*

Complete the teacher-scored portion of the Unit Assessment and submit it to your teacher.

LEARN

Activity 1: Chapters 72 and 73 *(Offline)*

Instructions

After they had won their independence, American citizens saw themselves more as a collection of 13 states than as one strong nation. In fact, it might have been more accurate to call them the "Disunited States of America."

You will learn about successes and failures in the first attempt to form a government. You will also learn how those successes and failures set the stage for the creation of a strong U.S. Constitution.

Read Chapter 72, pages 344–346, and Chapter 73, pages 347–349. Be prepared to discuss these concepts:

- constitutional convention
- separation of powers
- bill of rights
- freedom of religion
- Articles of Confederation

Student Guide
Lesson 1: Confederation and Constitutions

The government that came to power in 1789 was an experiment, established by the first enduring written constitution in history. Success and failure under the Articles of Confederation set the stage for a new plan of government. Hard work, compromise, and the genius of men like James Madison and Alexander Hamilton made the Constitution a reality.

After they won their independence, American citizens saw themselves more as a collection of 13 states than as one strong nation. Fortunately, each state had written its own state constitution. Unfortunately, people were so wary of a strong national government that they created a weak one. The lessons learned from these two actions paved the way for the creation of the U.S. Constitution.

Lesson Objectives
- Explain the need for and significance of state constitutions during the Revolution.
- Define *separation of powers* as the division of political power among branches of government.
- Identify the Articles of Confederation as the first government of the United States and describe its weaknesses, including the lack of an executive and of taxing power.
- Identify traditional English freedoms, such as trial by jury, guaranteed in state constitutions' bills of rights, and identify freedom of religion as a new freedom in state constitutions.

PREPARE

Approximate lesson time is 60 minutes.

Materials
For the Student

Strong Constitutions, Weak Confederation

A History of US (Concise Edition), Volume A (Prehistory to 1800) by Joy Hakim

History Journal

LEARN
Activity 1: The Disunited States of America *(Offline)*
Instructions
Check Your Reading (Chapter 72, pages 344–346, and Chapter 73, pages 347–349)

- Print the Strong Constitutions, Weak Confederation sheet and fill out as much as you can from memory.
- Review Chapters 72 and 73.
- Fill in any missing answers on the Strong Constitutions, Weak Confederation sheet, and check all your answers against the book. When you think you've got them all right, check your answers with an adult.

Use What You Know

Think about what you have read and answer the following questions in your History Journal. Discuss your answers with an adult.

1. Why was it important that each state write a constitution? How was that helpful for the future?
2. What document formed the first government of the newly independent American states? Why was it so weak? What were its two major weaknesses? How was its weakness helpful for the future?

Assessment

There is no assessment in this lesson.

Read On

Read Chapter 74, pages 350–353. Be prepared to discuss the reasons for the Northwest Ordinance and to describe its provisions.

Vocabulary

You'll see these terms as you read. Write a brief definition for each term in your History Journal.

- ordinance
- involuntary servitude

Optional: Beyond the Lesson

Go online to learn about your state's origins and constitution.

Activity 2. Optional: Your State's Constitution (Online)

Name _____ Date _____

Strong Constitutions, Weak Confederation

Fill in the blanks to answer these questions with choices from the answer box on page 3.

1. The colonists knew that they had to come up with a new form of government to replace the British after the war was over. The Continental Congress suggested that each state

   write a _____ .

2. This drawing represents the "tree of government." Label the three branches of this tree. In each label, write a word that describes one branch. At the bottom of the picture, write a caption that describes all three branches of government.

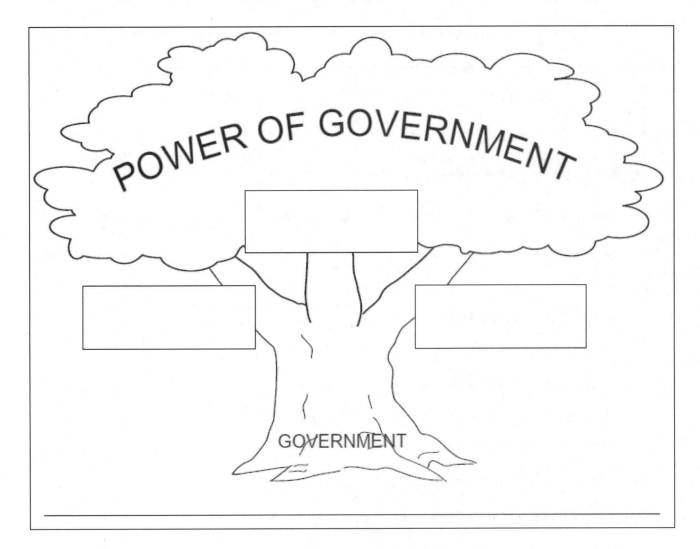

3. In 1780, Massachusetts was the first state to use a particular process to write and adopt its constitution. Identify and describe that process. The name of the process is in the answer box—you have to come up with the description.

_____

_____

_____

4. Identify six things that states discussed including in their constitutions.

_____

_____

_____

_____

_____

5. Every state constitution had a _____. Virginia's, written by George Mason, was a model for many others.

6. Identify five English rights Americans were determined to have in their state constitutions.

_____

_____

_____

_____

_____

7. The Virginia constitution went beyond the rights of Englishmen and added an extra, new right. What was it? _____

8. Under the Articles of Confederation, whom could Congress tax? _____

9. Under the Articles of Confederation, who was responsible for the printing of money?

_____

10. What was the basic problem with the Articles of Confederation? _____

_____

Bonus Question

The answer to this question is not in the answer box. On November 5, 1781, who became the first president of the newly independent American states?

Answer Box

Alert! One of these answers is used twice!

- Constitution
- Separation of powers
- Freedom of religion
- Executive (governor)
- Bill of Rights
- Constitutional Convention
- Freedom of speech and of the press
- It was too weak to do a good job.
- Judicial (courts)
- Free education
- The right of the majority to change the government
- The right of citizens not to be taxed without their consent or that of their representatives
- Nobody
- Free elections
- Each state and the Congress
- Government power derived from the people
- The right to a trial by jury
- Slavery
- Voting rights
- Protection against unreasonable arrest
- Legislative (assembly)

Student Guide
Lesson 2: The Northwest Ordinance

The greatest act of the government under the Articles of Confederation was the passage of the Northwest Ordinance in 1787. This law set the rules for the settlement of the Northwest Territory—the western land claims that Virginia and other states gave up. It included a bill of rights for the settlers. It also provided for the creation of public schools. It established a way for settlements to organize as states and join the rest of the nation.

Lesson Objectives
- Review a map of the new nation and identify the western lands under dispute.
- Summarize the reasons for and major provisions of the Northwest Ordinance.
- Explain the importance of the Northwest Ordinance in terms of future territories and the precedents it set for education and slavery.

PREPARE

Approximate lesson time is 60 minutes.

Materials
> For the Student
>> The Northwest Ordinance
>>
>> A History of US (Concise Edition), Volume A (Prehistory to 1800) by Joy Hakim
>>
>> History Journal

LEARN
Activity 1: Thirteen States and More to Come *(Offline)*
Instructions
Check Your Reading (Chapter 74, pages 350–353)

Review Chapter 74 by completing the Northwest Ordinance sheet. Check your answers with an adult.

Discuss

1. One of the "firsts" in world history was the American plan in the Northwest Ordinance to provide a means for territories to join the Union as states on an equal footing with the other states. Why was this a "first"? Why was it important?
2. Why did Americans feel that it was important to require townships to set aside land for public schools and for the territories to encourage education?

Assessment

There is no assessment in this lesson.

Read On

Thomas Jefferson was fascinated with the Northwest Territory. He valued education and political power for all citizens. Jefferson was a thinker who promoted several important ideas in American government, including the separation of church and state.

Read Chapter 75, pages 354–357. Be prepared to discuss how hard it is to get people to accept new ideas.

Name _____   Date _____

The Northwest Ordinance

You'll find the answers to these questions in Chapter 74. Write your answers in the spaces provided.

1. What happened to Native Americans when Great Britain lost control of the colonies?

   _____

   _____

   _____

2. Five states and a part of a sixth state would eventually form from the Northwest Territory. What are those states? _____

   _____

3. The Confederation Congress passed the Northwest Ordinance in 1787. Under what government did the Confederation Congress exist? _____

4. The new states had until recently been British colonies. How did their memory of that experience affect their view of the western lands? _____

   _____

   _____

   _____

5. What ordinance established a system for dividing land into townships?

   _____

6. What did this system also allow townships to do? _____

   _____

7. The Northwest Ordinance guaranteed three rights for the settlers of the Northwest Territory. What were they? _____

   _____

8. The Northwest Ordinance had a number of "firsts." Two in particular were important to the course of American history. One dealt with slavery and another with education. Describe how these two issues were provided for in the Northwest Territory.

_____

_____

_____

_____

9. What provision did the Northwest Ordinance have for the Indians? Do you think it was

enforced? Give a reason for what you think. _____

_____

_____

10. From Settlement to State

How does a region go from having almost no settlers to becoming a state? The Northwest Ordinance had a plan.

Put the events listed here in correct sequence to describe how settlements could evolve into states. Write the numbers 1 through 4 in the spaces provided with 1 being the earliest event and 4 being the latest.

The chapter does not explicitly describe the order. Use what you have learned and what makes sense to sequence these events in the correct order.

_____ Townships organize into a territory.

_____ Settlers start farms, towns, and businesses.

_____ When territories get a large enough population, they can apply for statehood.

_____ Settlements organize into a township.

Student Guide
Lesson 3: Thomas Jefferson: A Man for All Time

You know Thomas Jefferson as the author of the Declaration of Independence. He was also secretary of state, vice president, and president of the United States. He was an architect, a violinist, a mathematician, an inventor, an experimental farmer, and a natural scientist. He spoke six languages. And there is more.

Lesson Objectives

- Demonstrate knowledge gained in previous lessons.
- Describe Thomas Jefferson as accomplished in areas including philosophy, government, arts, and sciences.
- Use the Internet to gain information on Thomas Jefferson.
- Explain the need for and significance of state constitutions during the Revolution.
- Define *separation of powers* as the division of political power among branches of government.
- Identify the Articles of Confederation as the first government of the United States and describe its weaknesses, including the lack of an executive and of taxing power.
- Review a map of the new nation and identify the western lands under dispute.
- Explain the importance of the Northwest Ordinance in terms of future territories and the precedents it set for education and slavery.
- Identify traditional English freedoms, such as trial by jury, guaranteed in state constitutions' bills of rights, and identify freedom of religion as a new freedom in state constitutions.

PREPARE

Approximate lesson time is 60 minutes.

Materials

For the Student

A History of US (Concise Edition), Volume A (Prehistory to 1800) by Joy Hakim

map, U.S.

History Journal

LEARN
Activity 1: The Renaissance Man of Monticello *(Offline)*
Instructions
Check Your Reading (Chapter 75, pages 354–357)

In your History Journal, write a paragraph expressing your thoughts about Thomas Jefferson and his accomplishments.

Use What You Know

Go online and visit the Monticello website. You may take a quiz on Thomas Jefferson or go on a scavenger hunt about his life. If you finish the quiz, print the Congratulations screen!

Look Back

- Review Lessons 1-3 of Unit 7 (Chapters 72, 73, 74, and 75).
- In your History Journal, look at the activity sheets you completed for these lessons. Review your vocabulary words. If you completed any writing assignments, read them. Don't rush through; take your time. Your History Journal is a great resource for lesson reviews.
- Go online and review the First U.S. Government flash cards.

Assessment

Take the assessment.

Read On

Do you remember all the problems the country was having with its government under the Articles of Confederation? James Madison couldn't stop thinking about them. When delegates met in Philadelphia in the hot summer of 1787, he was ready to make a plan for a whole new government. Why were delegates gathering that summer? What ideas did they have for solving their problems? And why did they decide to keep everything they did a secret?

Read Chapter 76, pages 358–363. Be prepared to discuss James Madison's background and talents and the importance of his work before and during the convention.

Vocabulary

As you read, write a brief definition for each of these terms in your History Journal.

- Virginia Plan
- Framers

ASSESS

Mid-Unit Assessment: Thomas Jefferson: A Man for All Time *(Online)*
You will complete an online assessment covering the main points of this unit. Your assessment will be scored by the computer.

Student Guide
Lesson 4: James Madison and a Philadelphia Summer

James Madison thought the Articles of Confederation had to be abandoned and a new constitution written to take their place. When the Constitutional Convention met in Philadelphia, he came with a plan. As they worked throughout a sweltering summer, the delegates kept their discussions secret. What came out of those meetings was the U.S. Constitution.

Lesson Objectives
- Identify James Madison as the man given the title "Father of the Constitution."
- Summarize the background and talent James Madison brought to the Constitutional Convention, including scholarship and willingness to work hard.
- Explain that the reason for calling the convention in Philadelphia was the need to revise the Articles of Confederation or write a new Constitution.
- Recognize the arguments for and against keeping the convention debates a secret.

PREPARE

Approximate lesson time is 60 minutes.

Materials
For the Student

Convention Secrecy

A History of US (Concise Edition), Volume A (Prehistory to 1800) by Joy Hakim

History Journal

LEARN
Activity 1: Summer in Philadelphia *(Offline)*
Instructions
Check Your Reading (Chapter 76, pages 358–363)

Review Chapter 76 by writing the answers to these questions in complete sentences in your History Journal.

1. What talents did James Madison bring to the Constitutional Convention?
2. How did Thomas Jefferson, Madison's good friend, help him at the Constitutional Convention?
3. Based on what you know about the Articles of Confederation, why do you think James Madison wanted to abandon them?
4. Why did the Framers adopt a secrecy rule?
5. Why has James Madison been called "the Father of the Constitution"?

Use What You Know

Complete the Convention Secrecy sheet on the pros and cons of keeping the convention a secret. Then decide what you think. Explain to an adult why you believe the convention meetings should or should not have been kept secret.

Read On

Many issues divided delegates, but the most explosive one was political power. Some delegates wanted strong state governments; others wanted a strong national government. Out of the debate came a compromise—a federal system in which governments share power.

Another conflict over power erupted when big and little states battled over representation. Roger Sherman settled the matter with a compromise.

Read Chapter 77, pages 364–369.

Vocabulary

You'll see these terms as you read. Write a brief definition for each term in your History Journal.

- confederation
- federation
- Virginia Plan
- New Jersey Plan
- Connecticut Compromise

Name _____   Date _____

Convention Secrecy

Write the reasons for keeping the Constitutional Convention a secret (pros) on one side of the balance scale, and the reasons it should not be kept secret (cons) on the other side.

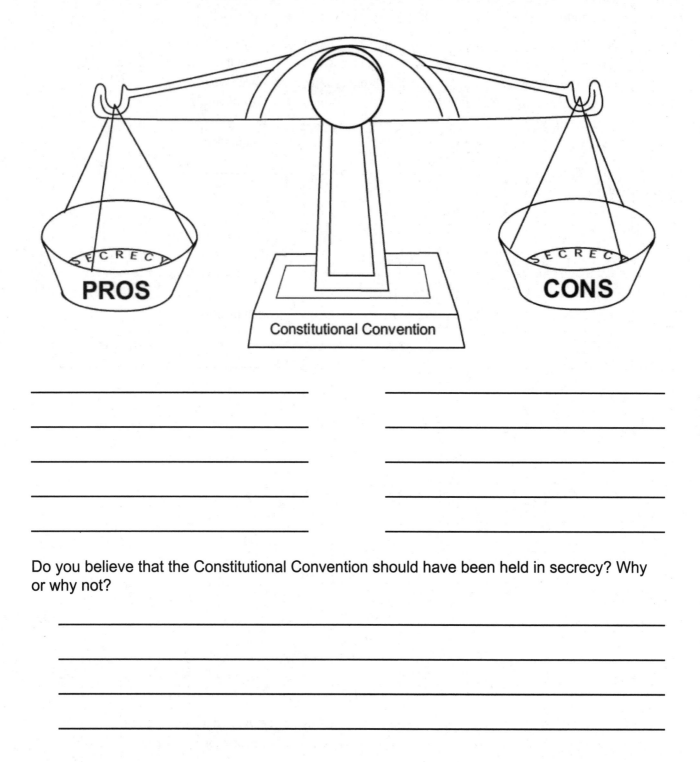

_____   _____

_____   _____

_____   _____

_____   _____

Do you believe that the Constitutional Convention should have been held in secrecy? Why or why not?

_____

_____

_____

_____

Student Guide
Lesson 5: An Important Compromise

The delegates at the Constitutional Convention were divided over many things, but power was the most explosive. They had to reach a compromise over representation. Should each state have one vote in the legislature as it did under the Articles of Confederation? Or should the states with more people have more votes? Roger Sherman came up with a solution to the problem.

Lesson Objectives

- Analyze a political cartoon to gain information on the positions taken at the convention.
- Identify Roger Sherman as the delegate who proposed the compromise we use today.
- Summarize the issues on which the delegates to the Constitutional Convention were divided, including representation and slavery.
- Explain the Virginia Plan and the New Jersey Plan in terms of representation.

PREPARE

Approximate lesson time is 60 minutes.

Materials

For the Student

Compromise

A History of US (Concise Edition), Volume A (Prehistory to 1800) by Joy Hakim

History Journal

LEARN
Activity 1: Compromise (Offline)
Instructions
Check Your Reading (Chapter 77, pages 364–369)

Review Chapter 77 using the following questions.

1. What was the issue involved in the debate between small and large states? How did the New Jersey and Virginia plans reflect this?
2. How did compromise settle the debate over representation?

Use What You Know

Complete the Compromise sheet.

Read On

The powerful words "We the People" began the Constitution. But exactly whom did those words include? Did they include women, blacks, and Native Americans? Americans are still working toward this ideal.

Read Chapter 78, pages 370–374. Think about the following questions for discussion as you read.

1. What is the basic difference between the Declaration of Independence and the Constitution?
2. What is the purpose of the Preamble?
3. On what issues did the Framers have to make compromises in order to complete the Constitution?
4. Do you think the Framers of the Constitution meant all the people when they wrote the words "We the People"?

Name _____ Date _____

Compromise

Fill in the chart with information about the Virginia and New Jersey Plans and the Great Compromise.

Virginia Plan	**New Jersey Plan**
_____	_____
_____	_____
_____	_____
_____	_____
_____	_____
_____	_____

Great Compromise
_____
_____
_____
_____
_____

Student Guide
Lesson 6: We the People

"We the People..." begins the Preamble to the Constitution—the document written to put the ideals of the people of this new country into practice. But just who are "the people"? And what were their ideals for government?

Lesson Objectives

- State the six purposes of the Constitution found in the Preamble.
- Distinguish between the Declaration of Independence and the Constitution.
- Recognize the importance of compromise in writing the Constitution.
- Give concrete examples of the Preamble in practice today.

PREPARE

Approximate lesson time is 60 minutes.

Materials

For the Student

Understanding the Preamble

A History of US (Concise Edition), Volume A (Prehistory to 1800) by Joy Hakim

History Journal

LEARN
Activity 1: Introducing the Constitution *(Offline)*
Instructions
1. Check Your Reading (Chapter 78, pages 370–374)

Say the words "We the People . . .", the first three words of the Constitution, aloud. Think about what the words mean. Now, write a paragraph in your History Journal describing your reaction to these words. Discuss your paragraph with an adult.

Answer the following questions in your History Journal to review Chapter 78.

1. What is the basic difference between the Declaration of Independence and the Constitution?
2. What is the purpose of the Preamble?
3. On what issues did the Framers have to make compromises in order to complete the Constitution?
4. Do you think the Framers of the Constitution meant all the people when they wrote the words "We the People"?

---

2. Use What You Know

Complete the Understanding the Preamble sheet. First identify the six goals stated in the Preamble. Then, for each goal, redefine the goal in your own words and provide an example of that goal in practice today. A current newspaper may be useful for finding examples.

3. Read On

Even more compromises were necessary once the Constitution was revealed to the public. People in some states thought too many powers had been given to the federal government. In other states, people thought that important federal powers had been left out.

Read Chapter 79, pages 375–377. Be prepared to discuss the arguments made for and against acceptance of this new Constitution. Write a brief definition for the following term in your History Journal—*ratify*.

Name _____   Date _____

Understanding the Preamble

Fill in the six purposes of the Constitution as outlined in the Preamble. Then define each purpose in your own words and provide an example.

We the People of the United States, in order to form a more perfect union, establish justice, ensure domestic tranquility, provide for the common defense, promote the general welfare, and secure the blessings of liberty to ourselves and our posterity, do ordain and establish this Constitution for the United States of America.

List the goals set in the Preamble.	Explain each goal in your own words.	Provide an example.

Student Guide
Lesson 7: Ratification!

After a long, hot summer of secrecy, arguments, threats, and compromise, the delegates finally presented a Constitution to the states for ratification. Now it was each state's turn to compromise—in order to create "a more perfect union."

Lesson Objectives

- List the major supporters and opponents of ratification in 1787.
- Summarize the arguments for and against the ratification of the Constitution.
- Recognize the difficulties faced by delegates to the Constitutional Convention.
- State the six purposes of the Constitution found in the Preamble.
- Distinguish between the Declaration of Independence and the Constitution.
- Explain that the reason for calling the convention in Philadelphia was the need to revise the Articles of Confederation or write a new Constitution.
- Recognize the arguments for and against keeping the convention debates a secret.
- Identify Roger Sherman as the delegate who proposed the compromise we use today.
- Explain the Virginia Plan and the New Jersey Plan in terms of representation.

PREPARE

Approximate lesson time is 60 minutes.

Materials

For the Student

A History of US (Concise Edition), Volume A (Prehistory to 1800) by Joy Hakim

History Journal

LEARN
Activity 1: For and Against (Offline)
Instructions
Check Your Reading (Chapter 79, pages 375–377)

Review Chapter 79. Answer the following question to review your reading: Why did some people oppose the Constitution?

Use What You Know

In your History Journal, make a chart or list showing who supported and who opposed ratification and why.

Now take on the role of a delegate. Using the information in your chart, deliver a brief speech in which you argue for or against ratification of the Constitution. Explain the difficulty you have had reaching your decision.

Look Back

- Review Unit 7, Lessons 4–7 (Chapters 76–79).
- Review vocabulary words, writing, and worksheets in your History Journal.
- Go online and review the Constitutional Convention Flash Cards.

ASSESS

Mid-Unit Assessment: Ratification! *(Online)*

You will complete an online assessment covering the main points of this unit. Your assessment will be scored by the computer.

Student Guide
Lesson 8. Optional: Mason Makes His Mark

George Mason was a Virginia delegate who helped form Virginia's government, drafting the Virginia Declaration of Rights and the Virginia State Constitution. Mason was concerned primarily with preserving individual rights and was an adamant supporter of the Bill of Rights.

Even though you may skip this lesson, you must complete the **Read On** activity before moving on to the next lesson.

Lesson Objectives
- Demonstrate knowledge gained in previous lessons.
- Use the Internet to gain information on George Mason.
- Evaluate Mason's contributions to the United States as the chief supporter of the Bill of Rights.

PREPARE

Approximate lesson time is 60 minutes.

Materials
> For the Student
>> A History of US (Concise Edition), Volume A (Prehistory to 1800) by Joy Hakim
>>
>> History Journal

LEARN
Activity 1. Optional: George Mason (Offline)
Instructions
Use What You Know
Visit the Gunston Hall website and click "George Mason On-Line" to learn about George Mason and the Constitution. After you explore the site, list three things in your History Journal that you learned about George Mason and his thoughts about the Bill of Rights.

Read On
The delegates who wrote the Constitution intended it to be the supreme law of the land. They also made sure that no part of the government got too powerful. The Constitution is a beautiful document that is written simply, clearly, and very carefully. The Framers provided a way to change it, but they didn't make it easy. Read Chapter 80, pages 378–383. Be prepared to discuss the duties of each of the three branches of government, and to find current newspaper or magazine articles that demonstrate the powers and duties of those three branches.

Vocabulary

You'll see these terms as you read. Write a brief definition for each term in your History Journal.

- checks and balances
- amendment

Student Guide
Lesson 9: The Constitution: Branches and Balances

The Constitution is alive and well today as the supreme law of the United States of America. We still have three separate, balanced branches of government—each with the power to check one another. You won't have to look hard to find current events that either challenge the Constitution or turn to it for guidance.

Lesson Objectives
- Identify the Constitution as the supreme law of the land.
- Identify the three branches of government and summarize the role of each branch, including the concept of checks and balances.
- Define *amendment* and explain the purpose of amendments.

PREPARE

Approximate lesson time is 60 minutes.

Materials
For the Student

Constitutional Branches and Balances

A History of US (Concise Edition), Volume A (Prehistory to 1800) by Joy Hakim

History Journal

LEARN
Activity 1: A Good Constitution Endures *(Offline)*
Instructions
Check Your Reading (Chapter 80, pages 378–383)

- Go over Chapter 80.
- Complete the Constitutional Branches and Balances sheet.
- Check your answers with an adult.

Use What You Know

People use and challenge the Constitution all the time. Newspapers often have articles that demonstrate the powers of the three branches of government. With an adult, review recent newspapers or go online to a major newspaper to find examples of checks and balances in government action. Here are some examples you are likely to find:

- Congress (the legislature) reviews executive or judicial nominations (for example, a cabinet official or a federal judge).
- The Courts (judicial) review executive actions or congressional legislation (for example, ruling a law or executive action unconstitutional).

- Congress approves executive actions in foreign policy (treaties or military activity).
- Executive approves or vetoes congressional legislation.
- State and federal governments share (and sometimes argue over) powers regarding issues such as education or roads.

Identify one or more issues. Then, in your History Journal, write a brief summary of one issue. Identify the branches of government involved, and describe their roles in terms of checks and balances.

Name _____ Date _____

Constitutional Branches and Balances

You'll find the answers to these questions in Chapter 80. Write your answers in the spaces provided.

1. The Constitution is law, but it is no ordinary law. Explain the difference between the Constitution and legislation.

   _____

   _____

   _____

2. According to the author, what has helped make the Constitution long lasting?

   _____

3. What is one of the first things the delegates to the Constitutional Convention decided on?

   _____

4. James Madison's Virginia Plan called for three branches of government. The delegates agreed to build this into the Constitution. Identify the three branches, and write a brief summary of the role each branch plays in government.

   _____

   _____

   _____

5. The delegates were afraid of power. They had already divided the government into three branches. What do we call the system they used to make sure that no one branch of the government gets too much power over the other branches? Can you give one example of this system in practice? Which branches does it involve?

   _____

   _____

   _____

   _____

6. What are two things that all the delegates agreed they wanted in the Constitution?

_____

_____

_____

7. What are the two ways the delegates solved the problem of power?

_____

_____

_____

8. Which part of the government, if any, is allowed to break the rules of the Constitution?

_____

9. What is the term for changes to the Constitution? Describe what must happen for a constitutional change to be accepted.

_____

_____

_____

_____

10. To date, about how many changes have been suggested for the Constitution? How many have been accepted?

_____

Student Guide
Lesson 10: The Constitution: What Does It Say?

One of the nice things about the U.S. Constitution is that it is not very complicated. If you read it carefully, you will understand it. It is that simplicity that has helped make the Constitution so lasting.

Lesson Objectives
- Analyze the Constitution to gain familiarity with its structure.

PREPARE

Approximate lesson time is 60 minutes.

Materials
For the Student

Constitutional Scavenger Hunt

A History of US (Concise Edition), Volume A (Prehistory to 1800) by Joy Hakim

History Journal

LEARN
Activity 1: Getting into the Constitution (Offline)
Instructions
Discuss

The Constitution is made up of a preamble followed by seven articles. How are these two parts different? What is the purpose of the preamble, and what is the purpose of the rest of the document?

Use What You Know

The Constitution is a well-organized document that is not hard to read. Get ready to roll up your sleeves and take a good look at it as you try to find the answers to the Constitutional Scavenger Hunt.

- Discuss with an adult the word *clause* and how it relates to the Constitution.
- Print the Constitutional Scavenger Hunt sheet and follow the instructions.

Read On

The Constitution defined a powerful new federal government. But what about the rights of individual citizens and of the states? The Constitution didn't say much about the freedoms, rights, protections, and powers that the people and the states felt they needed to "secure the blessings of liberty." For this, they needed a Bill of Rights.

Read Chapter 81, pages 384–388. Be prepared to identify the kinds of rights that are protected by the Bill of Rights. Also be prepared to discuss the rights and responsibilities of citizenship in a republic.

Vocabulary

Write a brief definition of the following terms:

- Bill of Rights
- republic

Optional: Beyond the Lesson

Go online to learn more about the U.S. Constitution.

Activity 2. Optional: The Constitution: What Does It Say? *(Online)*

Name _____   Date _____

Constitutional Scavenger Hunt

The text of the United States Constitution is located at the back of your book. You can find the answers to these questions there. Answer the questions aloud or in writing. Work with an adult. When you think you've got the answer to a question, check with an adult. Ask for help if you get stuck. After you answer a question correctly, place a check next to that number and move on to the next one. Good luck, and have fun!

1. Article I gives legislative, or lawmaking, power to _____ . Article II

   gives the president _____ power. Article III gives judicial power to

   _____ and to inferior (lower) courts.

2. Which article of the Constitution addresses the rights of the states?

3. Which article of the Constitution addresses how the Constitution can be amended?

4. Article VI, clause (paragraph) 2, states that judges in every state must go by what the

   Constitution says. It says that the Constitution is the _____ of the land.

5. How many of the 13 states were required to ratify the Constitution before it could go into effect? (Look in the last article of the Constitution.)

Now go back to Article I to find out more about Congress.

6. How old would you have to be to serve in the House of Representatives?

7. To impeach means to formally accuse an official of a crime. Who has the "sole power of impeachment" in the Constitution?

8. How many senators are there from each state?

9. What is the term (number of years) served by a member of the Senate?

10. What is the minimum age for a senator?

11. Only one constitutional responsibility is defined for the vice president. What is it?

Now take a closer look at the executive branch in Article II.

12. What is the minimum age for a president?

13. What oath must the president-elect take before assuming the office of the presidency?

14. Article II, Section 2, clause 2, identifies two powers of the president. What are those powers? (This clause also identifies congressional checks on those powers.)

Find out more about Article III.

15. The only crime defined by the Constitution can be found in Article III, Section 3. What is it? Article IV, you remember, deals with the states.

16. Which section of Article IV tells you that there could be 51 or 52 states someday?

Look at Article V to find out how things change.

17. If two-thirds of the Congress or two-thirds of the states propose an amendment to the

Constitution, it will take effect when _____ of the states ratify it.

Student Guide
Lesson 11: The Bill of Rights

As soon as Americans saw the newly written Constitution, they set out to improve it. They wanted a bill of rights. Some states proposed amendments as they voted to ratify the Constitution. Then James Madison wrote the amendments we call the Bill of Rights. These first 10 amendments to the Constitution still protect Americans' freedom today.

Lesson Objectives
- Demonstrate knowledge gained in previous lessons.
- Identify the major rights guaranteed by the Bill of Rights.
- Discuss the responsibilities of citizens in maintaining democracy.
- State the six purposes of the Constitution found in the Preamble.
- Identify the Constitution as the supreme law of the land.
- Identify the three branches of government and summarize the role of each branch, including the concept of checks and balances.
- Define *amendment* and explain the purpose of amendments.

PREPARE

Approximate lesson time is 60 minutes.

Materials
For the Student

Cover Me, Bill of Rights!

A History of US (Concise Edition), Volume A (Prehistory to 1800) by Joy Hakim

History Journal

LEARN
Activity 1: "To Secure the Blessings of Liberty" *(Offline)*
Instructions
Check Your Reading (Chapter 81, pages 384–388)

Review Chapter 81 by discussing the following with an adult:

1. Why didn't the Framers include a bill of rights in the original Constitution?
2. The Bill of Rights defines many of the rights of citizens. However, with rights come responsibilities. What are the responsibilities of the citizens of a democratic republic?
3. How do many of the rights defined in the Bill of Rights promote responsible citizenship?

Use What You Know

- With an adult, read the Bill of Rights located at the back of the book.
- Complete the Cover Me, Bill of Rights! sheet. Identify which amendment protects you in each of the situations described.
- Check your answers with an adult.

Review

Review online with the flash cards. (Hint: If you can correctly answer all of the questions on the flash cards, you'll do great on the assessment!)

ASSESS
Mid-Unit Assessment: The Bill of Rights, Part 1 *(Online)*
Complete the computer-scored portion of the Mid-Unit Assessment. When you have finished, complete the teacher-scored portion of the assessment and submit it to your teacher.

Mid-Unit Assessment: The Bill of Rights, Part 2 *(Offline)*
Complete the teacher-scored portion of the Mid-Unit Assessment and submit it to your teacher.

Name _____   Date _____

Cover Me, Bill of Rights!

The Bill of Rights is "insurance" that covers you in the form of rights and protections from government abuse. The situations presented here are made up. For each situation, review the explanation of the Bill of Rights in the book, and identify which amendment is involved. You will have to use the Bill of Rights at the back of the book to answer the last two questions. Write the amendment number and which right or protection applies in the spaces provided.

1. You have been arrested for a crime. At your trial, you are forced to answer questions, even though you don't want to.

   Amendment: _____ Right or protection: _____

   _____

2. A local army base doesn't have housing for all its soldiers. You're ordered to provide a room, bed, shower, laundry, and meals for a soldier in your home.

   Amendment: _____ Right or protection: _____

   _____

3. The government establishes an official religion and bans all other religions.

   Amendment: _____ Right or protection: _____

   _____

4. A crime is committed at your workplace. When you get home, you learn the police searched your home and seized your computer while you weren't there.

   Amendment: _____ Right or protection: _____

   _____

5. The government decides that a particular state or any citizen of that state may not own firearms.

   Amendment: _____ Right or protection: _____

   _____

6. The government decides that newspapers and book and magazine publishers can't print any writings that aren't in line with the government's views.

Amendment: _____ Right or protection: _____

_____

7. You are caught stealing a car, tried, and convicted. You are fined ten million dollars and sentenced to life in solitary confinement.

Amendment: _____ Right or protection: _____

_____

8. You are arrested for stealing a new car. The judge does not allow you to have a trial by jury.

Amendment: _____ Right or protection: _____

_____

Student Guide
Lesson 12: Unit Review

You've completed Unit 7, The Constitution. It's time to review what you've learned. You'll take the Unit Assessment in the next lesson.

Lesson Objectives
- Review important knowledge and skills taught in this unit.

PREPARE

Approximate lesson time is 60 minutes.

Materials

For the Student

A History of US (Concise Edition), Volume A (Prehistory to 1800) by Joy Hakim

History Journal

LEARN
Activity 1: A Look Back *(Offline)*
Instructions
Online Review

Go online and use the following to review this unit:

- The Big Picture
- Time Line
- Flash Cards

History Journal Review

Review some more by going through your History Journal. Look at the worksheets you completed for this unit. Review your vocabulary words. If you completed any writing assignments, read them. Don't rush through; take your time. Your History Journal is a great resource for a unit review.

Student Guide
Lesson 13: Unit Assessment

You've finished this unit! Now take the Unit Assessment.

Lesson Objectives

- Demonstrate mastery of important knowledge and skills in this unit.
- Explain the need for and significance of state constitutions during the Revolution.
- Explain the importance of the Northwest Ordinance in terms of future territories and the precedents it set for education and slavery.
- Summarize the arguments for and against the ratification of the Constitution.
- Identify the three branches of government and summarize the role of each branch, including the concept of checks and balances.
- Define *amendment* and explain the purpose of amendments.
- Identify the major rights guaranteed by the Bill of Rights.
- Identify James Madison as the man given the title "Father of the Constitution."
- Explain that the reason for calling the convention in Philadelphia was the need to revise the Articles of Confederation or write a new Constitution.
- Summarize the issues on which the delegates to the Constitutional Convention were divided, including representation and slavery.
- Evaluate Mason's contributions to the United States as the chief supporter of the Bill of Rights.

PREPARE

Approximate lesson time is 60 minutes.

ASSESS

Unit Assessment: The Constitution, Part 1 *(Online)*
Complete the computer-scored portion of the Unit Assessment. When you have finished, complete the teacher-scored portion of the assessment and submit it to your teacher.

Unit Assessment: The Constitution, Part 2 *(Offline)*
Complete the teacher-scored portion of the Unit Assessment and submit it to your teacher.

Student Guide
Lesson 14: Semester Review

You've completed the first semester. It's time to review what you've learned.

The next two lessons are optional and can be used to further review for the Semester Assessment.

Lesson Objectives
- Prepare for the assessment by reviewing content and skills presented in this semester.

PREPARE

Approximate lesson time is 60 minutes.

Materials

    For the Student

        A History of US (Concise Edition), Volume A (Prehistory to 1800) by Joy Hakim

        History Journal

LEARN
Activity 1: A Look Back *(Offline)*
Instructions
History Journal Review

Review the first semester by going through your History Journal. You should review:

- Completed work
- Maps
- Vocabulary
- Assessments

Online Review

Go online and use the following to review the first semester:

- Flash cards
- Big Pictures

The following Unit Review lessons have a Big Picture:

- Unit 1, Lesson 11
- Unit 2, Lesson 10
- Unit 3, Lesson 9
- Unit 4, Lesson 12
- Unit 5, Lesson 14
- Unit 6, Lesson 8
- Unit 7, Lesson 12

As you review the Big Pictures, write an assessment item for each unit that you think should be included on the first semester assessment. You can use multiple choice, fill-in-the-blank, and matching. Include the correct answer.

Do this work on notebook paper. Have an adult check your work, and then put it in your History Journal.

Student Guide
Lesson 15: (Optional) Semester Review

Use this OPTIONAL lesson to prepare for the Semester Assessment.

Lesson Objectives
- Prepare for the assessment by reviewing content and skills presented in this semester.

PREPARE

Approximate lesson time is 60 minutes.

Student Guide
Lesson 16: (Optional) Semester Review

Use this OPTIONAL lesson to prepare for the Semester Assessment.

Lesson Objectives

- Prepare for the assessment by reviewing content and skills presented in this semester.

PREPARE

Approximate lesson time is 60 minutes.

Student Guide
Lesson 17: Semester Assessment

You have finished the first semester. Take the Semester Assessment. Then prepare for the next lesson.

Lesson Objectives

- Demonstrate mastery of important knowledge and skills in this unit.
- Identify geographic reasons for diversity among Native American groups.
- Explain the reasons for European desire to go to Asia, including an interest in learning and the desire for power, wealth, and goods.
- Explain the reason for the introduction of African slavery into the Americas as a way to fill the need for field workers.
- Explain the causes of the French and Indian War as competition between France and England for land and power.
- Identify and describe the Stamp Act.
- Explain the importance of the Northwest Ordinance in terms of future territories and the precedents it set for education and slavery.
- Identify the three branches of government and summarize the role of each branch, including the concept of checks and balances.
- Identify the major rights guaranteed by the Bill of Rights.
- Describe three changes that occurred as a result of the Spanish introduction of the horse to North America.
- Identify the House of Burgesses as the first representative assembly in the European colonies.
- Describe the factors in England that pushed people to come to America, including poverty and a growing population.
- Explain the reasons for conflict between English settlers and Native Americans as racism and the disagreement over land use and ownership.
- Identify James Madison as the man given the title "Father of the Constitution."

PREPARE

Approximate lesson time is 60 minutes.

Materials

For the Student

George Washington

A History of US (Concise Edition), Volume B (1790-1877) by Joy Hakim

History Journal

ASSESS

Semester Assessment: MS American History Before 1865, Semester 1 *(Online)*

You will complete an online assessment covering the main points of this semester. Your assessment will be scored by the computer.

LEARN

Activity 1: Chapters 1 and 2 *(Offline)*

Instructions

Read On

The new Constitution called for an elected president. Do you know who the first president was? He was also called "the father of our country." His name is George Washington, and he was an impressive man. He left his beloved home to serve his country as the first president in 1789. No one had been president before, so he had a lot to do. You will read about some of the things he did as the nation was just beginning.

Read Chapter 1, pages 2–5, and Chapter 2, pages 6–8, in *A History of US (Concise Edition),* Volume B (1790-1877). Complete the "What I Know" and "What I Want to Know" columns of the George Washington sheet. Review your answers with an adult.

Name _____   Date _____

George Washington

Think about what you already know and what you want to
know about George Washington. Complete the first two
columns of the chart below. Then read Chapter 1 in *A History
of US (Concise Edition)*, Volume B. After you finish reading,
complete the last column.

What I Know	What I Wanted to Know	What I Learned

Student Guide
Lesson 1: The Father of His Country and Ours

The early years of the Constitution were a time of learning and growth. Washington set an example presidents follow even today. Jefferson doubled the size of the nation with the Louisiana Purchase and sent men to explore it. The War of 1812 proved the United States was a real nation. None of this was easy, and there were mistakes and arguments along the way.

When you do something for the first time and set a standard for others to follow, you set a precedent. George Washington set a lot of precedents. From being elected unanimously as the first president of the United States to creating the first cabinet (group of advisers), he did many things that no one had ever done before. By working hard and setting many new standards, Washington earned the title "Father of Our Country."

Lesson Objectives
- Define *precedent*.
- Recognize the significance of George Washington's unanimous election.
- Summarize the challenges Washington faced, including debt and lack of precedent.
- Identify the advisors Washington chose, including Jefferson and Hamilton.

PREPARE

Approximate lesson time is 60 minutes.

Materials
For the Student

A History of US (Concise Edition), Volume B (1790-1877) by Joy Hakim

History Journal

LEARN
Activity 1: Washington's Presidency (Offline)
Check Your Reading (Chapter 1, pages 2–5, and Chapter 2, pages 6–8)

Review Chapters 1 and 2 and complete the "What I Learned" column of the George Washington sheet. Go over your answers with an adult.

Discuss

1. What was unique about the outcome of George Washington's election in 1789? Why was that so important?
2. How did George Washington feel about leaving Mount Vernon and becoming president of the United States? How would you feel if you had to leave your home to lead your nation?
3. How did the American people treat George Washington on his trip to New York for the inauguration? How did George Washington react?

4. What sorts of challenges did George Washington face when he took office?
5. What sort of impression do you think George Washington made on people? Why was this important?
6. What is a cabinet in government? List the titles and names of the first cabinet members.
7. Compare George Washington's view of political parties with James Madison's view.

Use What You Know

People in America were excited about George Washington leading their new nation. Unlike England, the United States would have no king or queen. This was a radical idea for people around the world. It made some people excited and others nervous.

Imagine that you are part of the parade that greets George Washington on his journey to New York for his inauguration. In your History Journal, write a letter to your 10-year-old cousin in England explaining why you are excited about the new president. Explain why America does not want a king.

Optional: Beyond the Lesson

Visit Grolier's online *Presidency of the United State*s site to compare Washington's cabinet positions of today. Discuss why you think the number of positions has changed.

Activity 2. Optional: The Cabinet *(Online)*

Student Guide
Lesson 2: The Well Resorted Tavern

As the first president, George Washington set many precedents. He established the role of the president as an important and respected figure. After two terms, he retired to Mount Vernon. It was a popular place! He had so many visitors that he called Mount Vernon a "well resorted tavern."

Lesson Objectives
- Identify the precedents set by George Washington.
- Use the Internet to gain information about George Washington.

PREPARE

Approximate lesson time is 60 minutes.

Materials
For the Student

Precedents for the President

A History of US (Concise Edition), Volume B (1790-1877) by Joy Hakim

History Journal

LEARN
Activity 1: Precedents and the Presidency *(Offline)*
Use What You Know

Use the information in Chapters 1 and 2 to complete the Precedents for the President sheet. Review your answers with an adult.

Mount Vernon

Mount Vernon is a lovely place to visit. So lovely, in fact, that George and Martha Washington rarely ate a meal without having guests at the table. Find out why so many people enjoyed the Washingtons' hospitality. Spend some time online visiting Mount Vernon (http://www.mountvernon.org/learn/index.cfm/). You may take a tour of the mansion and grounds, learn interesting facts about George Washington, and even take a quiz to see how much you know about the first president.

Read On

Where's the party? The political party, that is. The Republican Party and the Democratic Party didn't always exist. When Thomas Jefferson and Alexander Hamilton disagreed about who should control the power in the government, their followers created what became political parties.

Read Chapter 3, pages 9–13. Be prepared to discuss the creation of political parties in the United States.

Vocabulary

Write a brief definition for *masses* in your History Journal.

Name _____   Date _____

Precedents for the President

Read each paragraph and choose the precedent that it describes. Write the precedent on the line after the description. Then, answer the question at the end of the worksheet.

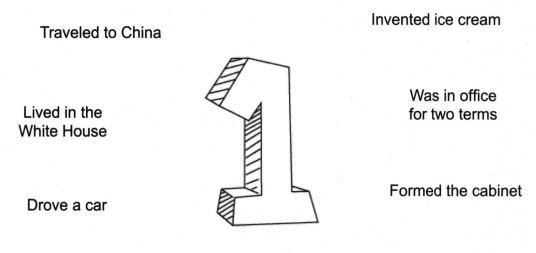

Traveled to China

Invented ice cream

Lived in the White House

Was in office for two terms

Drove a car

Formed the cabinet

Wore civilian (non-military) clothes and promoted dignity in office

1. As president, George Washington was head of the executive branch of our three-part government. Washington knew he couldn't possibly make all the hundreds of decisions by himself, so he appointed advisers. Washington appointed his advisers carefully and made sure they answered only to the president. Most of those helpers were called secretaries: secretary of the treasury, secretary of war, secretary of state. His advisers also included an attorney general.

    _____

2. George Washington was a popular president. He served two terms in office. The American people wanted him to be president again, but he said no. He didn't think the president should be in office until he died, like a king.

    _____

3. George Washington didn't want the president to be like the English king, but he did think it was important that the president be grand. He wanted people to look up to the president and respect and admire him. "When President Washington held official receptions he wore velvet knee breeches, yellow gloves, silver buckles, and a sword strapped to his waist."

    _____

4. Why were these precedents important to future presidents? _____

_____

_____

_____

_____

Student Guide
Lesson 3: Parties and Change

Disagreements aren't always bad. In American history, disagreements have often led to new ideas and ways of doing things. Thomas Jefferson and Alexander Hamilton argued about how to run the new government and who should control the power. Their arguments led to the formation of the first political parties. America's political party system was born to allow people to voice their opinions in an effective, organized way.

Lesson Objectives
- Demonstrate knowledge gained in previous lessons.
- Define *faction*, *Federalist*, and *Democratic-Republican*.
- Compare and contrast the views of Hamilton and Jefferson on the power of government, the power of the people, and the economy of the nation.
- Define *precedent*.
- Recognize the significance of George Washington's unanimous election.
- Identify the precedents set by George Washington.

PREPARE

Approximate lesson time is 60 minutes.

Materials
For the Student

Party and Money Vocabulary

Talking Heads: Jefferson and Hamilton

A History of US (Concise Edition), Volume B (1790-1877) by Joy Hakim

History Journal

LEARN
Activity 1: Party, Anyone? *(Offline)*
Check Your Reading (Chapter 3, pages 9–13)

Review Chapter 3 by discussing the following questions with an adult:

1. Why did Jefferson fear powerful government?
2. Why did Hamilton fear the masses or common people?
3. Which political party was the parent of today's Democratic Party?
4. How did Hamilton and Jefferson disagree about the debts of the old Congress of the Articles of Confederation?

Use What You Know

Thomas Jefferson and Alexander Hamilton were both good men who happened to disagree on a lot of important issues. Jefferson was considered a liberal, and Hamilton a conservative. Neither one is better than the other. Liberals and conservatives just have different ways of looking at issues.

Compare Thomas Jefferson and Alexander Hamilton's political views on the Talking Heads: Jefferson and Hamilton sheet. Then complete the Party and Money Vocabulary sheet. Review your work with an adult.

Optional: Beyond the Lesson

Go online to learn about the history of American currency.

ASSESS

Mid-Unit Assessment: Parties and Change *(Online)*

You will complete an online assessment covering the main points of this unit. Your assessment will be scored by the computer.

LEARN

Activity 2. Optional: History of American Currency *(Online)*

Name _____   Date _____

Talking Heads: Jefferson and Hamilton

These two heads represent Thomas Jefferson and Alexander Hamilton. In each head, write the words or phrases that describe that man's political views.

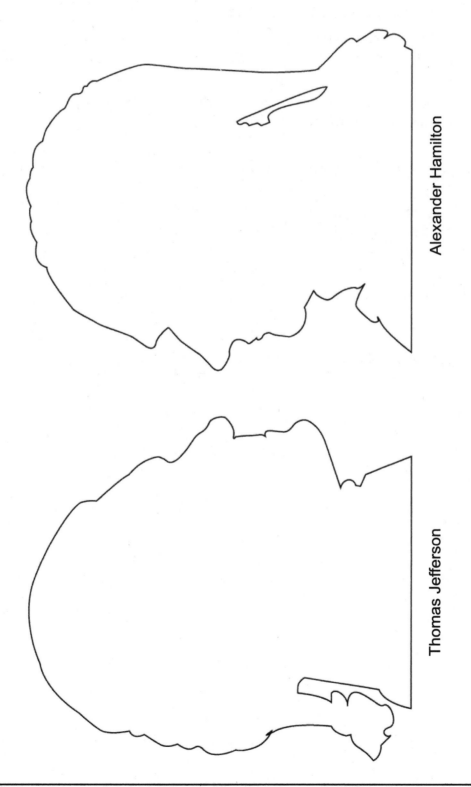

Alexander Hamilton

Thomas Jefferson

Name _____ Date _____

Party and Money Vocabulary

Match each word to its correct definition.

1. _____ Thomas Jefferson's political party

2. _____ The ordinary, common people

3. _____ Money, or any assets or goods that can be turned into money

4. _____ Alexander Hamilton's political party

5. _____ A small group of people who disagree with a larger group or party

6. _____ A form of capitalism in which there are a minimum of government rules

A. faction

B. Democratic-Republican

C. capital

D. masses

E. free enterprise

F. precedent

G. Federalist

Student Guide
Lesson 4: Capital Ideas

A new capital? What a capital idea! Where should it be and what should it look like? To avoid jealousy among the competing states, George Washington picked a central location that would not be part of any state, an area on the Potomac River between Virginia and Maryland. Once the site had been chosen, the planning started on our beautiful new capital city.

Lesson Objectives
- Explain how Washington, D.C., became the nation's capital.
- Identify Benjamin Banneker as the surveyor of the nation's capital.
- Recognize major federal buildings and national monuments including the Capitol, White House, Washington Monument, and Lincoln and Jefferson memorials.

PREPARE

Approximate lesson time is 60 minutes.

Materials
For the Student
A History of US (Concise Edition), Volume B (1790-1877) by Joy Hakim
Understanding Geography: Map Skills and Our World (Level 5)
History Journal

LEARN
Activity 1: Building a Capital *(Offline)*
Read

Read Chapter 4, pages 14–17.
Discuss

1. Why was the site on the Potomac River chosen for the new capital?
2. What was another name for the capital?
3. What were some of Benjamin Banneker's accomplishments?
4. How were the designers for the White House and the Capitol chosen?

Use What You Know

Benjamin Banneker was an impressive man who accomplished a lot during his lifetime. Imagine that you were a good friend of his and were asked to write his eulogy after his death in 1806. A eulogy is a speech honoring someone's life. Write the eulogy in your History Journal. Be sure to describe at least three of his amazing accomplishments.

Learn from Maps

1. Read Activity 13, "Our Nation's Capital" (pages 52–55), in *Understanding Geography*.
2. Answer Questions 1–15 in your History Journal.
3. If you have time, you may want to answer the Skill Builder Questions on page 55.
4. After you have finished, compare your answers with the ones in the Learning Coach Guide.

Read On

As the new Federal City was being built, President John Adams and his wife, Abigail, moved in. They were the first to live in the White House. It wasn't quite as grand as it is today. As they adjusted to their new home, tragedy struck the nation.

Read Chapter 5, pages 18–19, and Chapter 6, pages 20–21. Be prepared to discuss the challenges that John Adams faced as the second president.

Activity 2: Landmarks in the Nation's Capital *(Online)*

Instructions

Take a virtual tour by visiting the National Park Service website. Click the different areas of the map to learn about well-known sites in Washington, D.C. Look for the Capitol, White House, Washington Monument, Jefferson Memorial, and Lincoln Memorial.

Student Guide
Lesson 5: Adams Takes the Helm

Shortly after John Adams and his administration settled into the new capital, George Washington died. The news of his death plunged the nation into grief. It wasn't easy for the second president to fill Washington's big shoes. Adams succeeded in keeping the United States out of war, but he failed to stop the political fighting between the parties.

Lesson Objectives
- Identify John Adams as the second president.
- Describe the strengths and weaknesses of John Adams as president.
- Summarize the difficulties Adams faced as president, including the possibility of war and loss of popularity.

PREPARE

Approximate lesson time is 60 minutes.

Materials
> For the Student
>> A History of US (Concise Edition), Volume B (1790-1877) by Joy Hakim
>>
>> History Journal

LEARN
Activity 1: Adams as President *(Offline)*
Check Your Reading (Chapter 5, pages 18–19, and Chapter 6, pages 20–21)

Review Chapters 5 and 6 by discussing the following questions with an adult:

1. Why was the unfinished Federal City named Washington?
2. What were John Adams's strengths and weaknesses as president?
3. What difficulties did Adams face during his presidency?

Use What You Know

Abigail Adams was a strong and smart woman who frequently advised her husband. He asked her opinion about a lot of issues that he faced as president. How do we know this? They wrote many letters back and forth, discussing the issues of the day.

One of the major issues John Adams faced was whether or not to go to war with France. England was fighting France, and both countries wanted the support of the United States. John Adams was a Federalist. The Federalists wanted to go to war, but Adams didn't. He wanted to follow George Washington's advice and remain neutral (not choose sides).

Write a conversation between John and Abigail Adams in your History Journal. Start with the following question from John:

"Abigail, I am not sure what to do! Should I support my party and go to war against France? Or should I follow Washington's advice and keep our country out of war?"

Read On

Now the Federalists began to fear that French influence and Democratic-Republicans were a threat to the republic. What could they do? Would we do the same thing today? There was also a need for a stronger judicial system, one that could check the laws passed by Congress. Who would meet this need?

Read Chapter 7, pages 22–24, and Chapter 8, pages 25–27. Be prepared to discuss the Alien and Sedition Acts.

Vocabulary

Write a brief definition for each of these terms in your History Journal:

- checks and balances
- judicial review

Optional: Beyond the Lesson

Visit the White House website to learn more about the history of the president's house.

Activity 2. Optional: The White House *(Online)*

Student Guide
Lesson 6: Who Will Decide?

Thinking the French and the Democratic-Republicans were a threat to the country, the Federalists in Congress began passing laws that today we would consider unconstitutional. President John Adams signed the laws, making many people believe that he thought he was King of America. Today, the Supreme Court could review those laws and declare them unconstitutional. Congress would have to go along. We owe that process, judicial review, to John Marshall.

Lesson Objectives

- Assess the possible outcome of the Virginia and Kentucky Resolves as the end of the Union.
- Explain the role of John Marshall as the chief justice who established the role of the Supreme Court in judicial review.
- Analyze a quote and describe Jefferson's view of freedom of the press.

PREPARE

Approximate lesson time is 60 minutes.

Materials

For the Student

Freedom of the Press

A History of US (Concise Edition), Volume B (1790-1877) by Joy Hakim

History Journal

LEARN
Activity 1: A Judicial Decision *(Offline)*
Check Your Reading (Chapter 7, pages 22–24, and Chapter 8, pages 25–27)

Review Chapters 7 and 8 by answering the following questions.

1. What was the purpose of the Alien Acts?
2. What did the Sedition Act outlaw?
3. Why did many people object to these laws?
4. What actions were taken in Virginia and Kentucky against the Alien and Sedition acts?

Discuss

1. What could happen to the country if each state could choose which federal laws to follow and which to ignore?
2. How did John Marshall give the federal government, particularly the Supreme Court, more power?

Use What You Know

Reread the sidebar titled "A Free Press?" to get an understanding of Thomas Jefferson's commitment to freedom of the press.

Thomas Jefferson believed in freedom of the press. One day Baron Alexander von Humboldt, a German scientist, was visiting Jefferson in his presidential office. The scientist's eyes landed on a newspaper article that attacked the president. Von Humboldt couldn't believe it! He thought Jefferson should have the editor arrested or fined immediately.

In your History Journal describe how Jefferson reacted.

Here are a few points you may want to consider:

- Did Jefferson get angry? Why or why not?
- Why did Jefferson give the article to Alexander von Humboldt?
- What do you think Jefferson's actions proved?

Weigh the advantages and disadvantages of a free press by completing the Freedom of the Press sheet.

Read On

The election of Thomas Jefferson marked the end of the Federalist era and the beginning of a quarter-century of Democratic-Republicanism.

Read Chapter 9, pages 28–31. Be prepared to describe Jefferson's character and explain how he changed the size of the country.

Name _____ Date _____

Freedom of the Press

Amendment 1 of the Bill of Rights guaranteed freedom of the press. The Sedition Act made it a crime to criticize the government.

What are the advantages and the disadvantages of allowing the press to criticize the government freely? Write the advantages (pros) and disadvantages (cons) on the scale below. Then write your conclusions about freedom of the press at the bottom of the page.

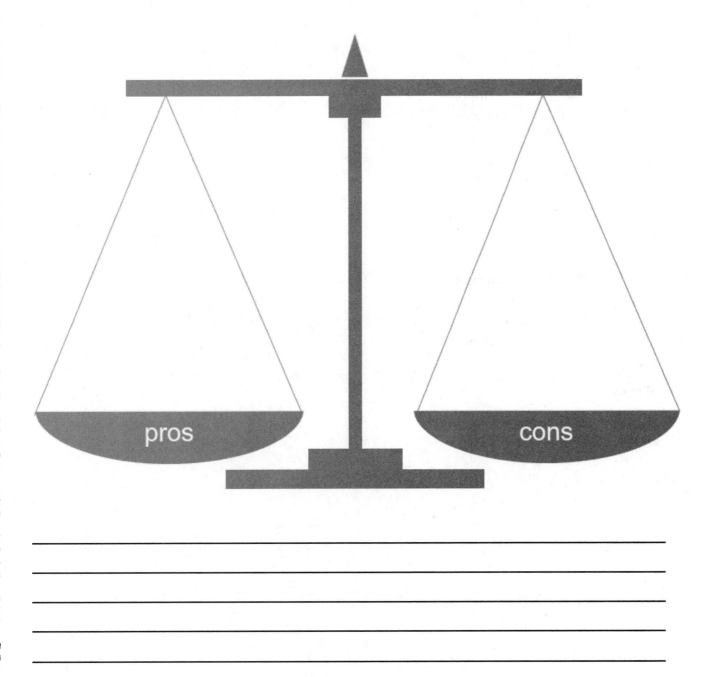

_____

_____

_____

_____

_____

Student Guide
Lesson 7: The Louisiana Purchase and More

The election of Thomas Jefferson ended the real power of the Federalist Party and ushered in a quarter-century of Democratic-Republicanism. One of Jefferson's legacies was the Louisiana Purchase. When he bought the Louisiana Territory from France, Thomas Jefferson doubled the size of the United States.

Lesson Objectives
- Identify Thomas Jefferson as the third president.
- Recognize the significance of the Louisiana Purchase as doubling the size of the country.
- Explain how Washington, D.C., became the nation's capital.
- Identify John Adams as the second president.
- Summarize the difficulties Adams faced as president, including the possibility of war and loss of popularity.
- Assess the possible outcome of the Virginia and Kentucky Resolves as the end of the Union.
- Explain the role of John Marshall as the chief justice who established the role of the Supreme Court in judicial review.

PREPARE

Approximate lesson time is 60 minutes.

Materials
For the Student
  Jefferson: A Man of the People
  Map of the United States, 1804 (b/w)
A History of US (Concise Edition), Volume B (1790-1877) by Joy Hakim
History Journal

LEARN
Activity 1: Meet Mr. Jefferson *(Offline)*
Check Your Reading (Chapter 9, pages 28–31)

Go over Chapter 9 with an adult by answer the following questions:

1. How would you describe Thomas Jefferson?
2. How did Jefferson's beliefs and personality show in his presidency? Give some examples.

Return to the lesson online and view the color version of the map of the United States, 1804. On the black and white version of this map, color the Louisiana Territory red.

Use What You Know

Complete the Jefferson: A Man of the People sheet.

Read On

When the Louisiana Territory was purchased from France in 1803, the United States doubled its size. Some thought the land was not needed and that it was worthless. Were they right? No one could be sure. People had many questions. Just how big was the new territory? What was it like? What kinds of plants and animals existed there? Thomas Jefferson had wanted answers to those questions even before the United States bought the land. There was only one way to find out!

Read Chapter 10, pages 32–39. Be prepared to identify at least three major physical features of the Louisiana Territory.

Vocabulary

Write a brief definition in the History Journal for *piedmont*.

Optional: Beyond the Lesson

Learn more about Thomas Jefferson online at the American President website.

ASSESS
Mid-Unit Assessment: The Louisiana Purchase and More (*Online*)
You will complete an online assessment covering the main points of this unit. Your assessment will be scored by the computer.

LEARN
Activity 2. Optional: Thomas Jefferson (*Online*)

Name _____   Date _____

Jefferson: A Man of the People

Thomas Jefferson considered himself a democratic president and a man of the people. His beliefs and personality shone through in the way he acted as president. For each statement below, circle YES if it describes something he would have said. Otherwise, circle NO.

1. "Make sure you seat the important French and Spanish ambassadors close to me at the dinner tonight. Put the visiting merchants from Boston at the far end of the table."

   YES   NO

2. "We should raise taxes so that the federal government will have a lot of money in case we go to war."

   YES   NO

3. "I think the government should stay out of the affairs of its citizens as much as possible."

   YES   NO

4. "I want large, formal parties at the White House."

   YES   NO

5. "Let's open up the White House on certain days and allow citizens to visit and discuss their concerns with me."

   YES   NO

6. "Just because a man is educated doesn't mean he's fit for public office. Only the aristocracy should be allowed in the government."

   YES   NO

7. In 1803, Thomas Jefferson did something that drastically changed the United States. What did he do, and how did this event change the United States?

   _____

   _____

   _____

   _____

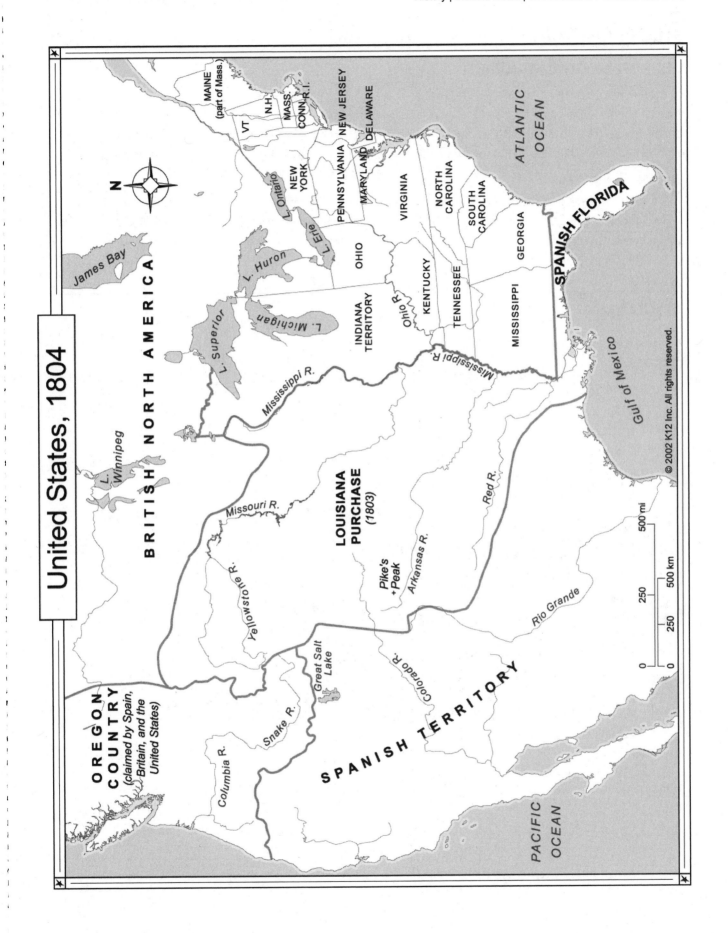

United States, 1804

Student Guide
Lesson 8: An Expedition

When Thomas Jefferson purchased the Louisiana Territory from France in 1803 he doubled the size of the United States. The physical features and plant and animal life of the new territory, however, were virtually unknown to Americans. But Jefferson had a plan—one that involved his new secretary, Meriwether Lewis.

Lesson Objectives

- Identify Lewis and Clark as leaders of the expedition that explored the Louisiana Territory.
- Identify major physical features of the Louisiana Territory including the Mississippi and Missouri rivers; Rocky Mountains, and recognize states made from it.
- Identify the states created from the Louisiana Territory.

PREPARE

Approximate lesson time is 60 minutes.

Materials

For the Student

Lewis and Clark

Map of the Louisiana Purchase (b/w)

A History of US (Concise Edition), Volume B (1790-1877) by Joy Hakim

History Journal

LEARN
Activity 1: Lewis and Clark's Expedition *(Offline)*
Check Your Reading (Chapter 10, pages 32–39)

Review Chapter 10 with an adult.

1. Name at least three major physical features of the Louisiana Territory.
2. Who were the two leaders of the expedition that Thomas Jefferson sent to explore the newly purchased Louisiana Territory?
3. Do you think Jefferson made a wise choice in naming Lewis and Clark as the leaders of the expedition? Why or why not?

Return to the lesson online and view the color version of the map of the Louisiana Purchase. On the black and white version of the map, label the following physical features of the Louisiana Territory:

- Mississippi River
- Missouri River
- Columbia River
- Pacific Ocean

Add mountain symbols to the map to represent the Rocky Mountains. Label them.

Highlight the names of all the states that were once a part of the Louisiana Territory. You should have highlighted 15 states. Keep the map. You will need it again.

Use What You Know

Use the "Lewis and Clark" website to complete the Lewis and Clark sheet. To complete this sheet:

1. Read the introductory section of "Circa 1803" and the first paragraph of "Living in America."
2. Complete the chart on the Lewis and Clark sheet.
3. Use the map of the Louisiana Purchase and your place mat map of the United States to help answer Questions 2–5 on the Lewis and Clark sheet.
4. Click "The Archive" in the left navigation menu. Then click "The Journals" in the submenu.
5. Scroll down to the search form on the Journals page. In Step 2, search entries created on July 28, 1805. (Click "By single day," select "July," enter 28, and select "1805.") Click "Submit."
6. Read Meriwether Lewis's journal entry for that day, Then answer Questions 6 and 7 on the sheet.

Read On

This Read On activity is for Lesson 10: Another War! Note that Lesson 9: A Powerful Orator and the Great Tekamthi, the next lesson, is an OPTIONAL lesson.

In his Farewell Address, George Washington had warned Americans to stay out of European wars. But in 1812, it was getting hard to stay out. Britain was at war with France. Both countries were capturing American ships and taking American sailors as prisoners. Americans were also angry at the British because they were still holding territory west of the Appalachian Mountains. Would America's new leaders get the country mixed up in the war?

Read Chapter 12, pages 44–53. Do not read the feature titled "Our National Anthem: The Star-Spangled Banner." You will read this in another lesson. Be prepared to list three reasons for the War of 1812.

Vocabulary

In your History Journal, write a brief definition for the term *war hawks*.

Beyond the Lesson

There is much more to the Lewis and Clark website than you sampled during the Use What You Know activity. Explore the website to learn more about this fascinating episode in American history.

Activity 2. Optional: Lewis and Clark *(Online)*

Name _____ Date _____

Lewis and Clark

Refer to the Student Guide to complete this sheet.

1. Complete the following chart:

Mythical Animals, People, and Plants of the West	
Geographical Speculations About the West	
The United States in 1803	Population: Boundaries: Where Most People Lived:

2. What rivers did the Lewis and Clark expedition travel on?

   _____

3. What mountain ranges did they cross?

   _____

4. What modern-day states did they go through? _____

_____

_____

5. What modern-day towns did they go through? _____

_____

6. What did Lewis name the three forks of the river they discovered that day? Why do you think he did that? _____

_____

_____

7. If you had been alive in 1804, would you have wanted to go with Lewis and Clark? Why or why not? _____

_____

_____

_____

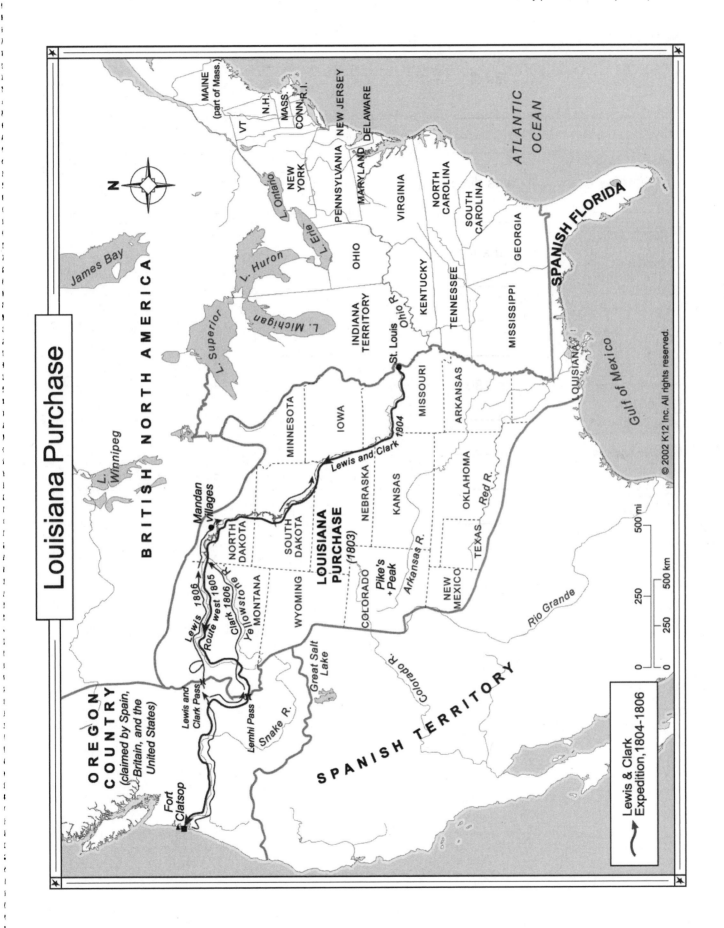

Louisiana Purchase

Lewis & Clark
Expedition, 1804–1806

Student Guide
Lesson 9: (Optional) A Powerful Orator and the Great Tekamthi

Learn how two American Indian leaders—Sagoyewatha of the Iroquois and Tekamthi of the Shawnee—reacted as the United States continued to expand.

Lesson Objectives

- Identify Sagoyewatha and Tekamthi as American Indian leaders of the early nineteenth century.

PREPARE

Approximate lesson time is 60 minutes.

Materials

For the Student

A History of US (Concise Edition), Volume B (1790-1877) by Joy Hakim

History Journal

LEARN
Activity 1. Optional: Sagoyewatha and Tekamthi *(Offline)*
Instructions

You can read Chapter 11, pages 40–43, to learn about two important American Indian leaders of the early nineteenth century.

Student Guide
Lesson 10: Another War!

Once again, the young United States had serious disagreements with Great Britain. Americans in some parts of the nation wanted war. Americans elsewhere opposed war. Finally, a group called the War Hawks carried the day, and the ill-prepared fledgling nation entered into a second war with England.

Lesson Objectives
- Identify *war hawks* as congressmen who supported war with England and James Madison as president during the War of 1812.
- Describe three reasons for the War of 1812 and identify the sections of the country that supported or opposed the war.
- Summarize the major events of the War of 1812, including the attacks on Washington, D.C., and Baltimore, and the role Dolley Madison played in saving national treasures.

PREPARE

Approximate lesson time is 60 minutes.

Materials
For the Student
War of 1812: Pros and Cons sheet
A History of US (Concise Edition), Volume B (1790-1877) by Joy Hakim
History Journal

LEARN
Activity 1: Another War with England *(Offline)*
Instructions
Check Your Reading (Chapter 12, pages 44–53)

Check your understanding of Chapter 12 by completing the following activity.

A storyboard is a panel, or series of panels, in which a set of sketches shows a series of events in order. Filmmakers and animators use storyboards to plan out movies and cartoons.

Storyboard the main events covered in Chapter 12.

1. Fold two, unlined, 8 1/2" × 11" sheets of paper into four sections. Trace over the fold lines with a marker so you end up with four panels on each sheet.
2. In the upper left-hand corner, number the panels 1 through 8.

---

3. Review Chapter 12 and select eight key events.
4. Storyboard these events in chronological order by drawing simple sketches in the eight panels. Imagine you are storyboarding these events for a movie. Your sketches should be very simple, but someone looking at them should be able to understand what happened in the War of 1812.

Use What You Know

Complete the War of 1812: Pros and Cons sheet.

Imagine you're a member of Congress in 1812. Congress is thinking about declaring war against Britain. Write a speech that states your position—be sure to include any information or arguments that support your opinion.

Read On

What do the words to the "Star-Spangled Banner" mean? Are they all literal—do they mean exactly what they say—or are some symbolic?

Read the feature in Chapter 12 titled "Our National Anthem: The Star-Spangled Banner."

Vocabulary

Write a brief definition for the following terms in your History Journal.

- ramparts
- foe
- perilous

Name _____   Date _____

War of 1812: Pros and Cons

The decision to go to war with another nation is not one made lightly. The young, fledgling United States faced this decision in 1812. There were reasons to avoid war and reasons to go to war. On the scale below, write as many pros (reasons to go to war) on the left-hand side of the scale as you can think of. Write all the cons (reasons not to go to war) you can think of on the right-hand side. Review Chapter 12 if you're having trouble deciding what to write.

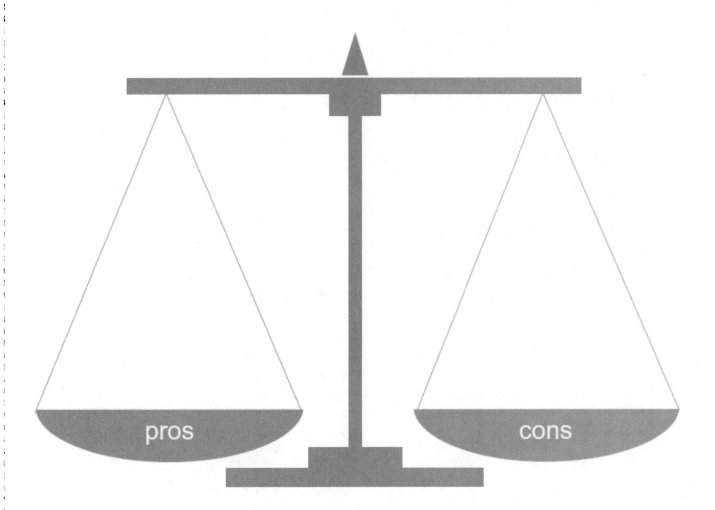

Student Guide
Lesson 11: By the Dawn's Early Light

Francis Scott Key's beautiful poem "The Defense of Fort McHenry" became the national anthem of the United States.

Lesson Objectives
- Describe the significance of the War of 1812.
- Demonstrate understanding of the meaning of the words of the national anthem.

PREPARE

Approximate lesson time is 60 minutes.

Materials
For the Student

Document Analysis: The Star-Spangled Banner

A History of US (Concise Edition), Volume B (1790-1877) by Joy Hakim

History Journal

LEARN
Activity 1: The Star-Spangled Banner (Offline)
Discuss

Discuss the following statements about the War of 1812 with an adult. Decide whether each statement is true or false.

1. After the war, the British believed there was still a chance they could regain control of the colonies.
2. After the war, the British had more respect for the United States.
3. After the war, Americans continued to think about colonizing Canada.
4. The war made the United States grow up and it made Americans feel proud.

Use What You Know

Complete the Document Analysis: "The Star-Spangled Banner" sheet.

Read On

When James Monroe became the fifth president of the United States, he was called the "last of the Revolutionary farmers." What did it mean?

During his presidency, the United States bought some land from Spain. Where was it and why did Spain sell it?

What did Monroe say to the U.S. Congress in a speech that later became known as the "Monroe Doctrine"?

Read Chapter 13, pages 54–57. Be prepared to summarize the major message of the Monroe Doctrine.

Vocabulary

Write a brief definition for each of the following terms in your History Journal.

- reservation
- doctrine

Beyond the Lesson

Learn more about the actual flag that inspired the national anthem. Find out how it is being repaired and restored at the National Museum of American History at *The Star-Spangled Banner* website.

Activity 2. Optional: The Flag *(Online)*

Name _____   Date _____

Document Analysis: "The Star-Spangled Banner"

Francis Scott Key's poetic words did more than give the American flag a name, "the star-spangled banner." They also changed the way Americans looked at their flag. In the early 1800s, most people considered a national flag simply a military emblem. Today the flag is the primary symbol of American patriotism.

The Star-Spangled Banner

Oh! say can you see, by the dawn's early light,
What so proudly we hailed at the twilight's last gleaming?
Whose broad stripes and bright stars, through the perilous fight,
O'er the ramparts we watched were so gallantly streaming.
And the rockets' red glare, the bombs bursting in air,
Gave proof through the night that our flag was still there.
Oh! say, does that star-spangled banner yet wave
O'er the land of the free and the home of the brave?

1. Which of the above words would you consider to be old-fashioned words that aren't often used anymore?

    _____

    _____

2. Read a transcript of a primary source document that describes the bombardment of Fort McHenry (http://americanhistory.si.edu/starspangledbanner/).

    • Go to the online lesson and visit the Smithsonian's Star-Spangled Banner website.
    • Click "War" and then "Baltimore in the Balance."
    • Click the image, "A View of the Bombardment of Fort McHenry."
    • Click the image, "Account of the Bombardment of Fort McHenry."
    • Open the PDF of Major George Armistead's report to James Monroe.
    • Read the letter.

    Using information from the primary source document you just read, what happened on Tuesday, September 13, and Wednesday, September 14, 1814?

    _____

    _____

    What is the only line from the first stanza that describes something that is mentioned in Major Armistead's report?

    _____

3. For each of the following pairs of lines, write in your own words what they mean.

Oh! say can you see, by the dawn's early light,
What so proudly we hailed at the twilight's last gleaming?

_____

_____

Whose broad stripes and bright stars, through the perilous fight,
O'er the ramparts we watched were so gallantly streaming.

_____

_____

And the rockets' red glare, the bombs bursting in air,
Gave proof through the night that our flag was still there.

_____

_____

4. Which two lines do not refer to some actual event or occurrence? Why do you think Francis Scott Key included these lines?

_____

_____

_____

_____

_____

Student Guide
Lesson 12: The Monroe Doctrine

Victory in the War of 1812 brought renewed confidence. The nation turned its back on Europe and looked toward its own hemisphere for its identity and destiny.

Lesson Objectives

- Demonstrate mastery of important knowledge and skills taught in previous lessons.
- Identify the boundary changes that occurred between 1812 and 1821, including the purchase of Florida and the addition of seven states.
- Summarize the major message of the Monroe Doctrine as the closing of the Americas to European colonization.
- Explain the phrases "last of the Revolutionary farmers" and "era of good feelings."
- Identify *war hawks* as congressmen who supported war with England and James Madison as president during the War of 1812.
- Describe three reasons for the War of 1812 and identify the sections of the country that supported or opposed the war.
- Describe the significance of the War of 1812.

PREPARE

Approximate lesson time is 60 minutes.

Materials

For the Student

    U.S. Border Changes, 1812-1821

    A History of US (Concise Edition), Volume B (1790-1877) by Joy Hakim

    History Journal

LEARN
Activity 1: Last of the Revolutionary Farmers *(Offline)*
Check Your Reading (Chapter 13, pages 54–57)

Go over Chapter 13 with an adult. Answer this question in your History Journal: If you were a Seminole, would you prefer to live in a Spanish colony or in the United States? Why?

Discuss

Discuss these questions with an adult.

1. What does the phrase "last of the Revolutionary farmers" mean?
2. Why are the years that Monroe was president referred to as the "era of good feelings"?
3. What was the main message of the Monroe Doctrine?
4. What are some of the factors that led to the Monroe Doctrine?

Use What You Know

- Make a campaign poster for James Monroe's second election in 1820. The poster should show that you understand the meaning of these two phrases: "last of the Revolutionary farmers" and "era of good feelings."
- Complete the U.S. Border Changes, 1812–1821 sheet.

ASSESS

Mid-Unit Assessment: The Monroe Doctrine (*Online*)

You will complete an online assessment covering the main points of this unit. Your assessment will be scored by the computer.

Name _____   Date _____

U.S. Border Changes, 1812–1821

Growth didn't stop with the Louisiana Purchase. The borders of the United States changed significantly between 1812 and 1821.

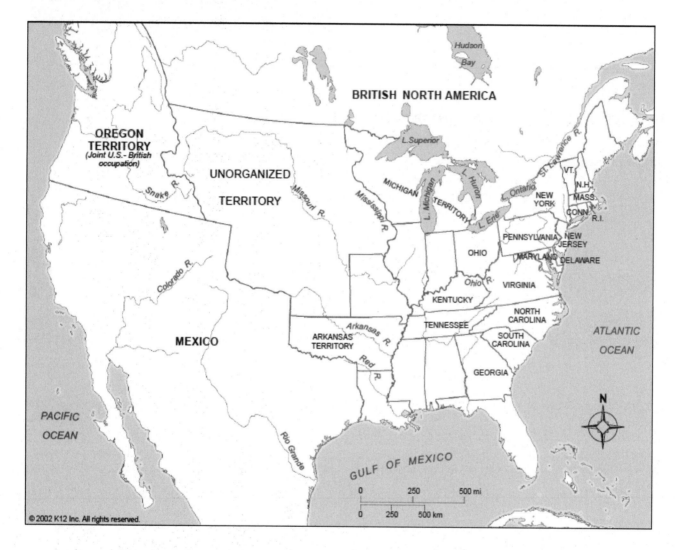

1. What territory did the United States purchase from Spain during Monroe's presidency? Label the territory on the map. Use a colored pencil to lightly color it orange.

2. Seven states were admitted into the Union in the years between 1812 and 1821. They are:

- Louisiana (1812)
- Indiana (1816)
- Mississippi (1817)
- Illinois (1818)
- Alabama (1819)
- Maine (1820)
- Missouri (1821)

Label each state on the map. Put the year it was admitted in parentheses under the name of the state. Lightly color all seven states green with colored pencil.

Student Guide
Lesson 13: Andrew Jackson: An Uncommon Man

Andrew Jackson's election as president set a precedent for "government by the people." The power of the president was no longer held by an aristocrat.

Lesson Objectives

- Identify Andrew Jackson as the first common man elected president.
- Explain the significance of Jackson's election as an example of expansion in the political process.
- Describe the ways in which Jackson represented new ideas and people who had not had political power before, including those with little wealth and those in the West.
- Identify groups who did not have political power in 1828, including blacks and women.

PREPARE

Approximate lesson time is 60 minutes.

Materials

For the Student

Andrew Jackson: Old Hickory

A History of US (Concise Edition), Volume B (1790-1877) by Joy Hakim

History Journal

LEARN
Activity 1: Old Hickory (Offline)
Read

Read Chapter 14, pages 58–64.

Vocabulary

Define these terms in your History Journal as you read:

- Scotch-Irish
- Old Hickory

Woodrow Wilson said that Jackson "came into national party politics like a cyclone from off the western prairies." Find Tennessee on a map and explain why this state was considered part of the West.

Check Your Reading (Chapter 14, pages 58–64)

Complete the Andrew Jackson: Old Hickory sheet. Have an adult check your answers.

Discuss

1. Why do you think John Quincy Adams was outraged that Harvard gave Jackson an honorary degree?
2. Why do you think Harvard made this decision?

Beyond the Lesson

Discover more about Andrew Jackson's life and presidency by viewing the website *American Presidents: Andrew Jackson.*

Activity 2. Optional: Andrew Jackson *(Online)*

Name _____   Date _____

Andrew Jackson: Old Hickory

1. How did the election of Andrew Jackson set a precedent?

   _____

   _____

   _____

   _____

2. In what way did Andrew Jackson change the definition of democracy for the United States?

   _____

   _____

   _____

3. What groups were not included in the democratic process in 1829?

   _____

4. Why do you think Jackson's inauguration was so different from earlier inaugurations?

   _____

   _____

   _____

Student Guide
Lesson 14: (Optional) Our Early Presidents

The American presidency started as an experiment in 1789 when George Washington was unanimously elected president of the United States. By the time John Quincy Adams's term ended 40 years later, the new nation had been led by six presidents.

Lesson Objectives
- Demonstrate an understanding of time and sequence as they apply to the first six U.S. presidents.

PREPARE

Approximate lesson time is 60 minutes.

Materials
> For the Student
>> John Quincy Adams Time Line
>>
>> Presidential Time Line
>>
>> A History of US (Concise Edition), Volume B (1790-1877) by Joy Hakim
>>
>> History Journal

LEARN
Activity 1. Optional: From Washington to Buchanan (Offline)
Complete ONE of the following activities:

Presidential Time Line: The First Six

Follow the directions below to create a time line of the first six presidential administrations.

1. You will need the Presidential Time Line: John Quincy Adams sheet and five copies of the Presidential Time Line sheet.
2. Add information for the first five presidents on the blank Presidential Time Line sheets. Review your history book for information about these presidents: George Washington, John Adams, Thomas Jefferson, James Madison, and James Monroe. Information for John Quincy Adams has been provided—use this as a model when adding information to the other sheets. *Note:* You may not be able to find all the time line information in the history book. If you wish, you may go online to the website listed in the Beyond the Lesson activity to search for information not given in the book.
3. Have an adult check your time lines.
4. Mount each Presidential Time Line sheet on a piece of construction paper to create a border (vary the colors). Then display them in order.

Presidents Eight Through Fifteen

Read the feature in Chapter 14 titled "Naming Presidents." In this feature, the author briefly describes the eight presidents who served after Andrew Jackson. She says these eight presidents were not outstanding. Choose one of these eight presidents. Conduct some research to try and find some information that might make the author change her mind.

Optional: Beyond the Lesson

Visit the *American Presidents* website if you would like to learn more about the first fifteen presidents.

Activity 2. Optional: American Presidents (Online)

Name _____   Date _____

Presidential Time Line: John Quincy Adams

If you can find a picture of this president, attach it here.

Name: John Quincy Adams

Years in Office: 1825–1829

Number of Terms: 1

Vice president: John Calhoun

First Lady: Louisa Catherine Adams

_____Sixth_____ President

The presidency of John Quincy Adams was not marked by any significant events of national importance. He did propose a high tariff that was signed into law in 1828. The "Tariff of Abominations," as it was called, was imposed on imported manufactured goods. John Quincy Adams is one of only two presidents whose father was also a president.

Name _____   Date _____

Presidential Time Line: _____

┌─────────────────────────────────┐
│   │
│   If you can find a picture of this
│   president, attach it here.
│   │
│   │
│   │
│   │
│   │
│   │
│   │
│   │
└─────────────────────────────────┘

Name: _____

Years in Office: _____ – _____

Number of Terms: _____

Vice president: _____

First Lady: _____

_____ President

☆☆☆☆☆☆☆☆☆☆☆☆☆☆☆

_____

_____

_____

_____

_____

_____

_____

_____

_____

Student Guide
Lesson 15: Unit Review

You've completed Unit 8, A New Nation. It's time to review what you've learned. You'll take the Unit Assessment in the next lesson.

Lesson Objectives
- Prepare for the assessment by reviewing content and skills presented in this unit.

PREPARE

Approximate lesson time is 60 minutes.

Materials

> For the Student
>> A History of US (Concise Edition), Volume B (1790-1877) by Joy Hakim
>>
>> History Journal

LEARN
Activity 1: A Look Back *(Offline)*
Use What You Know

George Washington was elected president in 1789. Thirty-five years later, the sixth president, John Quincy Adams, was elected. The United States had changed a lot during that time period.

Discuss with an adult the changes that took place in those 35 years. Focus on two areas: the size of the country and European attitudes toward the United States. Think about the events that triggered the changes during this time period. What adjectives would describe the United States in 1789? in 1824?

History Journal Review

Continue to review by going through your History Journal. You should review:

- Activity sheets completed during the unit
- Unit vocabulary words
- Unit maps
- Your writing assignments from the unit
- Offline lesson and mid-unit assessments

Online Review

Review online, using the following:

- The Big Picture
- Flash Cards
- Time Line

Student Guide
Lesson 16: Unit Assessment

You've finished this unit! Now take the Unit Assessment.

Lesson Objectives

- Demonstrate mastery of important knowledge and skills in this unit.
- Define *precedent*.
- Recognize the significance of George Washington's unanimous election.
- Identify the precedents set by George Washington.
- Explain how Washington, D.C., became the nation's capital.
- Identify Benjamin Banneker as the surveyor of the nation's capital.
- Summarize the difficulties Adams faced as president, including the possibility of war and loss of popularity.
- Identify Lewis and Clark as leaders of the expedition that explored the Louisiana Territory.
- Identify major physical features of the Louisiana Territory including the Mississippi and Missouri rivers; Rocky Mountains, and recognize states made from it.
- Identify *war hawks* as congressmen who supported war with England and James Madison as president during the War of 1812.
- Describe three reasons for the War of 1812 and identify the sections of the country that supported or opposed the war.
- Summarize the major events of the War of 1812, including the attacks on Washington, D.C., and Baltimore, and the role Dolley Madison played in saving national treasures.
- Describe the significance of the War of 1812.
- Identify the boundary changes that occurred between 1812 and 1821, including the purchase of Florida and the addition of seven states.
- Summarize the major message of the Monroe Doctrine as the closing of the Americas to European colonization.
- Identify Andrew Jackson as the first common man elected president.
- Explain the role of John Marshall as the chief justice who established the role of the Supreme Court in judicial review.
- Explain the constitutional conflict over the Alien and Sedition Acts, including the concept of constitutionality.

PREPARE

Approximate lesson time is 60 minutes.

ASSESS

Unit Assessment: A New Nation, Part 1 *(Online)*

Complete the computer-scored portion of the Unit Assessment. When you have finished, complete the teacher-scored portion of the assessment and submit it to your teacher.

Unit Assessment: A New Nation, Part 2 *(Offline)*

Complete the teacher-scored portion of the Unit Assessment and submit it to your teacher.

Student Guide
Lesson 1: Revolutionary Inventions

Andrew Jackson's election in 1828 reflected change in the United States. Democracy was expanding. A revolution in transportation and industry transformed the way people lived, worked, and traveled. Cities grew. Progress seemed more important than politics. But not everyone gained a political voice, and there were problems in the factories, mines, and cities.

England closely guarded its industrial secrets, but the United States was growing and changing and needed those secrets. One man, Samuel Slater, managed to bring the secrets across the ocean. Later, in 1814, as Nathan Appleton watched inventor Francis Lowell start up the first mechanical loom to run in America, he realized it was the birth of the Industrial Revolution on this continent. This revolution would transform jobs, tools, and life in the United States.

Lesson Objectives
- Define *industrial revolution* and *factory system*.
- Identify industrial innovators, including Eli Whitney, Francis Lowell, and Samuel Slater, and their accomplishments.
- Explain why the changes in industry are called a revolution.

PREPARE

Approximate lesson time is 60 minutes.

Materials
> For the Student
>> A History of US (Concise Edition), Volume B (1790-1877) by Joy Hakim
>> History Journal

LEARN
Activity 1: Inventive Minds (Offline)
Read

Read Chapter 15, pages 66–74.

Vocabulary

Write a brief definition for each of the following terms in your History Journal:

- industrial revolution
- factory system

Check Your Reading (Chapter 15, pages 66–74)

Answer the following review questions in your History Journal.

1. Where did the poorer people in colonial times get most of their food and clothing? Where did the wealthy get theirs?

2. What happened to the system of trade between the colonies and Britain during the American Revolution?

3. What was the Industrial Revolution?

4. Who was Samuel Slater, and what did he do to start the Industrial Revolution in America?

5. What did Eli Whitney and Francis Lowell do to improve the production of textiles (fabrics)?

6. Why are the changes that took place in industry around 1800 called a revolution? (You may need to look up the definition of *revolution* before answering this question.)

Use the graph of cotton production in Chapter 15 to answer the following questions:

7. How many bales of cotton does the cotton-bale symbol represent?

8. How many bales of cotton were produced in 1790?

9. Would you rather have been a cotton farmer in 1790 or 1820? Explain your answer.

Use What You Know

How well do you know the inventions and inventors who started America's Industrial Revolution? Go back online to review the flash card questions and answers.

Student Guide
Lesson 2: Transportation and Travel

The North needed the food products that were in the West. The South and West wanted the surplus goods that piled up around the factories and harbors in the North. The whole country needed improved transportation to keep up with the Industrial Revolution.

Lesson Objectives

- Describe transportation before 1800 and explain the need for change.
- Identify four modern innovations in transportation in the early 1800s, including canals, railroads, steamboats, and improved roads.
- Summarize the impact of canals and roads on life and the economy.

PREPARE

Approximate lesson time is 60 minutes.

Materials

For the Student

📇 Document Analysis: The Erie Canal

A History of US (Concise Edition), Volume B (1790-1877) by Joy Hakim

History Journal

LEARN
Activity 1: Modern Transportation (Offline)
Read

Whitney, Slater, and Lowell helped bring the factory system to America. The factory owners had to find faster methods to bring the raw materials to their factories and get their products to the people who wanted to buy them. In the West, farmers wanted to send their grain to eastern markets. How could all this be done?

In today's reading, you will learn about a number of innovations in transportation in the early 1800s that changed life and the economy in the United States.

Read Chapter 16, pages 75–82. Answer the following questions in your History Journal. Go over your answers to the questions with an adult.

1. What was transportation like before 1800, and why was there a need for change?
2. What were the four modern innovations in transportation in the early 1800s?
3. How did the National Road improve trade in America?
4. What changes came about as a result of building the Erie Canal?

Vocabulary

You'll see these words as you read. Write a brief definition in your History Journal for each term as you come to it.

- macadam road
- canal
- lock

Use What You Know

To learn more about the Erie Canal, complete the Document Analysis: The Erie Canal sheet.

Name _____ Date _____

Document Analysis: The Erie Canal

Study two images of the Erie Canal located here: http://www.eriecanal.org/images.html. One image should be a painting, lithograph, or woodcut. The other image should be a photograph of a scene similar to the first image. Form an overall impression of the images. Next, examine the individual items. Divide each image into four equal sections, or quadrants. Study each section closely. Look for details. Answer the following questions.

1. Use the following chart to list people, objects, and activities you notice in the images.

Image	People	Objects	Activities
First image (painting, lithograph, or woodcut)			
Second image (photograph)			

2. Based on what you have observed in the images, list at least two things you might infer from each image. To infer is to draw a conclusion based on facts. For example, if you see a painting of a person wearing lots of jewelry, you could infer that the person likes jewelry.

Image 1:

1. _____

2. _____

Image 2:

1. _____

2. _____

3. What do the images tell you about the environment around the Erie Canal?

_____

_____

_____

_____

4. How are the two images similar?

_____

_____

_____

_____

5. How are the two images different?

_____

_____

_____

_____

Student Guide
Lesson 3: Steaming

Fast-flowing water powered the mills, but it made going up rivers difficult. And in many places there were no rivers. English and American inventors tinkered with steam power. Soon steamships plied the rivers, and railroads crossed the land.

Lesson Objectives

- Demonstrate mastery of important knowledge and skills taught in previous lessons.
- Identify Robert Fulton as a developer of the steamboat.
- Describe the advantages and disadvantages of steam power in boats and trains.
- Describe the advantages of railroads over canals, steamboats, and roads.
- Analyze maps and graphs for information on early transportation.
- Define *industrial revolution* and *factory system*.
- Identify industrial innovators, including Eli Whitney, Francis Lowell, and Samuel Slater, and their accomplishments.
- Identify four modern innovations in transportation in the early 1800s, including canals, railroads, steamboats, and improved roads.

PREPARE

Approximate lesson time is 60 minutes.

Materials

> For the Student
>> Another Revolution
>> Miles of Track
>> A History of US (Concise Edition), Volume B (1790-1877) by Joy Hakim
>> History Journal

LEARN
Activity 1: Teakettle Power *(Offline)*
Read

In today's reading, you will learn how steam power was put to use to create fast and efficient forms of transportation.

Improved roads and new canals were some of the ways people and products could move faster from one place to another. But these forms of transportation had their drawbacks. Canals froze in the winter, and stagecoaches and small horse-drawn trains couldn't carry heavy freight or a lot of people. Horses got tired and needed to be replaced. The United States needed a new source of power. Many inventors blew off a lot of steam just thinking about it. Hmm, steam, now that's an idea . . . .

Read Chapter 17, pages 83–87. Answer the following questions as you read:

1. How fast did Fulton's steamboats travel on the Mississippi River?
2. Before Fulton's steamboats, why did most boats travel downstream on rivers?
3. What were some of the advantages and disadvantages of steam-powered boats and trains?
4. Describe the advantages of railroads over canals, steamboats, and roads.

Discuss your answers with an adult.

Use What You Know

Complete the Miles of Track and Another Revolution activity sheets. Have an adult check your answers. Your work on the Another Revolution sheet will be assessed.

Use the map of Major Transportation Routes, ca.1840, in Chapter 17 to answer the following questions in your History Journal:

1. Based on the map, which region of the country do you think had the greatest number of cargo-carrying riverboats in the 1840s—the Northeast, the Southeast, or the Midwest? Explain your answer.
2. If you wanted to start a manufacturing business in 1840, in which city would you choose to build your factory—Cleveland, Charlotte, or Memphis? Why?

ASSESS

Lesson Assessment: Streaming (Online)
You will complete an online assessment covering the main points of this lesson. Your assessment will be scored by the computer.

Name _____   Date _____

Another Revolution

For questions 1–6, fill in the blanks using the following terms.

Eli Whitney	factory system	Samuel Slater	Industrial Revolution
Francis Cabot Lowell	Peter Cooper	market revolution	Robert Fulton

1. _____ , a New Englander, developed the cotton gin and began making muskets with interchangeable parts.

2. _____ built a successful steamboat called the North River that steamed up the Hudson River.

3. _____ built a small steam-powered railroad locomotive. He called it Tom Thumb.

4. A new system of organizing work, based on new ideas in science, technology, and business, was called the _____ .

5. _____ was an Englishman who brought the Industrial Revolution to America. He built a water-powered cotton-spinning machine in Rhode Island.

6. Lowell built a factory that had machines for both spinning and weaving. He took cotton fibers and turned them into finished cloth, all in the same building. This was an example of a _____ .

In the early 1800s, four modern developments in transportation brought about changes in American life and the economy. Identify the following developments by reading about the changes they caused.

7. I became macadamized and made it easier for Americans to travel, and to buy and sell goods. What am I? _____

8. I am a big man-made ditch filled with water. All kinds of boats, such as passenger boats, flatboats, and rafts, could ride on me. I made the cost of transportation cheaper. Towns grew up around me—as a matter of fact, I helped make New York the country's largest city. DeWitt Clinton was one of my biggest supporters. What am I?

_____

9. I can travel upriver against the current. I am fast, efficient, and fun. I can carry lots of people, goods, and raw materials up and down rivers easily at 10 miles per hour. I helped the cities that live along the river grow into larger cities. What am I?

_____

10. I reduced the time it takes to travel over land. Unlike many other forms of transportation, I can be used year-round and carry heavy loads. What am I? _____

11. The use of steam power really did revolutionize transportation. However, in the beginning, steam power in boats and trains had a few disadvantages. Name two of them.

_____

_____

Name _____ Date _____

Miles of Track

This bar graph shows the growth of railways in the United States between 1800 and 1830. There were no railroad tracks in 1800, but by 1830 there were 13 miles of track.

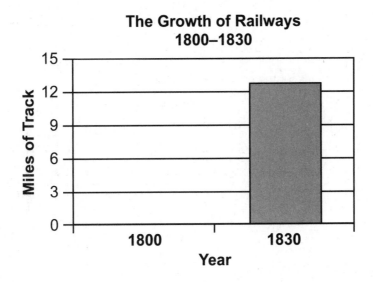

Complete this bar graph to show the growth of railways between 1840 and 1860. Use the information in Chapter 17. Color each bar red.

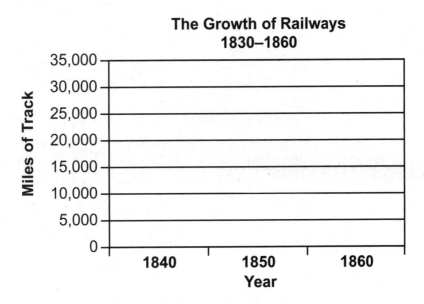

In which decade was the growth of railways in the United States the greatest—the 1840s or the 1850s? _____

Student Guide
Lesson 4: Cities Grow All Around

During the early 1800s, new inventions and new machines led to changes in America. The changes were most evident in the growing cities.

Lesson Objectives

- List at least two examples of the positive and negative characteristics of cities in the early to mid-1800s.
- Locate the cities of New York, Philadelphia, New Orleans, and Boston on a map.
- Discuss the geographic reasons for the growth of cities on rivers.
- Define *urban, suburban*, and *rural.*
- Use population density maps to compare populations over time.

PREPARE

Approximate lesson time is 60 minutes.

Materials

For the Student

📖 Map of the United States, 1850

A History of US (Concise Edition), Volume B (1790-1877) by Joy Hakim

Understanding Geography: Map Skills and Our World (Level 5)

History Journal

LEARN
Activity 1: Cities and Progress *(Offline)*
Read

New and improved roads, railroads, steamships, and canals allowed Americans to move to new areas. Towns and then cities began to spring up where there had been wilderness, and the older cities grew in size. In 1790, only two cities in the United States had 20,000 or more people. By 1860 there were 43 American cities of at least that size. Why did more Americans begin to leave the farms or the rural villages and flock to these cities? In today's reading, you will read about the growth of cities and city life in the early to mid-1800s.

Read Chapter 18, pages 88–94. Answer the following questions in your History Journal. Discuss your answers with an adult.

1. How did American technology and cities change and expand in the early 1800s?
2. List some examples of the positive and negative characteristics of cities in the early and mid-1800s

---

Label the following cities on the map of the United States, 1850. You may use the atlas in the back of your book as a reference.

- New York
- Philadelphia
- New Orleans
- Boston

Write a few sentences in your History Journal expressing your thoughts on what the sites or locations of the cities you labeled have in common and why. Discuss your ideas with an adult.

Use What You Know

In your History Journal, design an advertisement encouraging people to come to the city in 1850.

Learn from Maps

1. Read Activity 9, "Population Maps" (pages 36–39), in *Understanding Geography Level 5*.
2. Answer Questions 1–13 in your History Journal.
3. If you have time, you may want to answer the Skill Builder Questions on page 39.
4. After you have finished, you should compare your answers with the ones in the Learning Coach Guide.

Read On

As the progress of cities and technology increased, so did the need for workers. Men, women, and children all became workers in factories and mills. Women and children often became like slaves to these factories. What do you think it was like to be a child under 10 years of age working in an iron mill, coal mine, or factory?

Read Chapter 19, pages 95–98, and Chapter 20, pages 99–101. Be prepared to describe the problems of workers in the mines and mills of the nineteenth century, and explain why so many women and children worked in mills and mines.
Vocabulary

You'll see these terms as you read. Write a brief definition for each term in your History Journal.

- labor union
- strike

ASSESS

Lesson Assessment: Cities Grow All Around (*Online*)
Answer the online geography questions for this assessment. Your assessment will be covered by the computer.

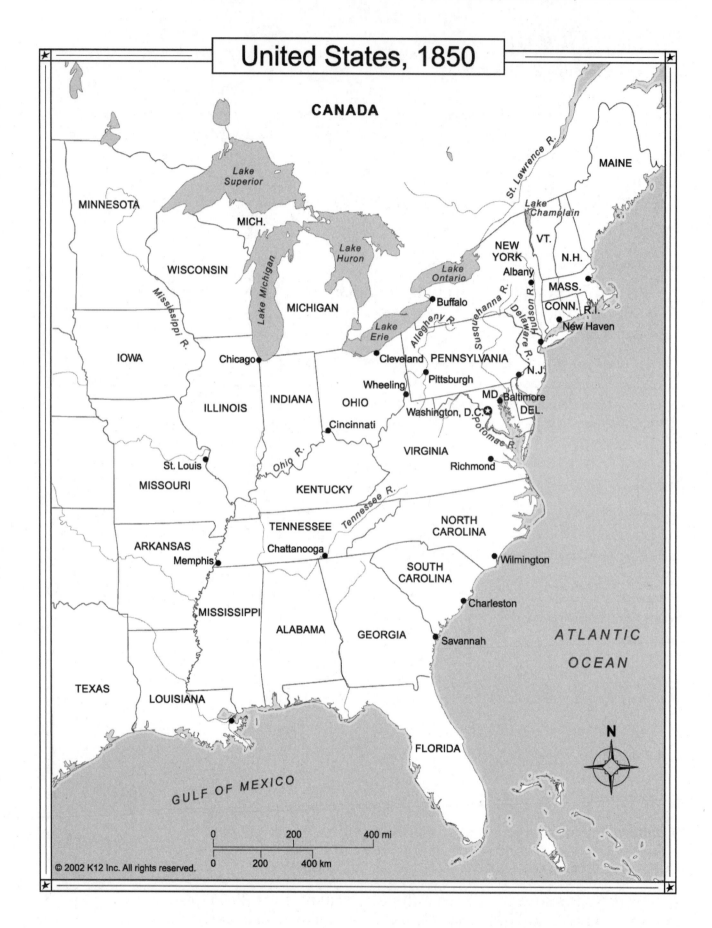

United States, 1850

Student Guide
Lesson 5: Mills and Mines

Industrial growth gave women the opportunity to earn wages for their work. However, those wages were very low. And industrial growth also brought child labor. Women and children became "wage slaves" and endured poor working conditions in the factories, mills, and mines.

Lesson Objectives

- Demonstrate mastery of important knowledge and skills in previous lessons.
- Describe some of the problems of workers in the mines and mills of the nineteenth century, such as low pay and dangerous conditions.
- Explain the geographic reasons for the growth of Pittsburgh and Wheeling as mill towns.
- Explain why so many women and children worked in mills and mines.
- Demonstrate mastery of important knowledge and skills taught in previous lessons.
- Discuss the geographic reasons for the growth of cities on rivers.
- Use population density maps to compare populations over time.

PREPARE

Approximate lesson time is 60 minutes.

Materials

For the Student

Hard Work and Factory Smoke

A History of US (Concise Edition), Volume B (1790-1877) by Joy Hakim

History Journal

LEARN
Activity 1: Life in Mills and Mines *(Offline)*
Check Your Reading (Chapter 19, pages 95–98, and Chapter 20, pages 99–101)

Review Chapters 19 and 20 by completing the Hard Work and Factory Smoke sheet. Have an adult check your answers.

Look Back

Review previous lessons with the flash cards to prepare for the assessment.

ASSESS

Mid-Unit Assessment: Life in Mills and Mines, Part 1 *(Online)*
Complete the computer-scored portion of the Mid-Unit Assessment. When you have finished, complete the teacher-scored portion of the assessment and submit it to your teacher.

Mid-Unit Assessment: Life in Mills and Mines, Part 2 *(Offline)*
Complete the teacher-scored portion of the Mid-Unit Assessment and submit it to your teacher.

Name _____   Date _____

Hard Work and Factory Smoke

Mary Paul worked in a textile mill in Lowell, Massachusetts. In a letter to her father she wrote:

> *"Dear Father, I am well which is one comfort. My life and health are spared while others are cut off. Last week one girl fell down and broke her neck which caused instant death.*
>
> *… Another was nearly killed by falling down and having a bale of cotton fall on him…"*

1. What kinds of working conditions did Mary Paul describe to her father? _____

   _____

2. How did people like Mary Paul put pressure on their employers to pay them higher

   wages and to improve their working conditions? _____

   _____

Herman Melville wrote this about women working in a paper factory.

> *"Not a syllable was breathed. Nothing was heard but the low, steady, overruling hum of the iron animals. The human voice was banished from the spot. Machinery—that vaunted slave of humanity—here stood menially served by human beings… as the slaves serve the sultan. The girls did not so much seem accessory wheels to the general machinery as mere cogs to the wheels."*

3. What was Melville saying about the relationship between people and machinery?

   _____

Rebecca Harding wrote an article called "Life in the Iron Mills" for *Atlantic Magazine*. In it she described:

> *"Masses of men… stooping all night over boiling cauldrons of metal… breathing from infancy to death an air saturated with fog and grease and soot, vileness for soul and body."*

4. How did Harding's article affect Americans? _____

   _____

5. Why were Americans surprised by Harding's descriptions of pollution? _____

   _____

Adapted from *A History of US*

Thinking Cap Question! Write a poem about the children who worked as "wage slaves" in America during the Industrial Revolution.

Student Guide
Lesson 6: Writing a Document-Based Essay, Part 1

You've learned about the changes in transportation and technology that took place in the United States in the early 1800s. Use what you know, along with primary and secondary sources, to answer a question with a well-organized essay. Today you'll complete the first three steps in developing your essay.

Are you ready for the challenge? Don't worry—you'll have help! Kiah (KIY-yah) is writing an essay on a different topic, but she'll show you how to do each step. Let's get started!

Lesson Objectives
- Analyze an essay question to prepare an answer.
- Brainstorm previous knowledge.
- Define *primary source*.

PREPARE

Approximate lesson time is 60 minutes.

Materials

For the Student

    🖳 Guide to Writing an Essay

    🖳 Kiah's Essay

    A History of US (Concise Edition), Volume B (1790-1877) by Joy Hakim

    History Journal

LEARN
Activity 1: Document-Based Writing, Steps 1, 2, and 3 *(Offline)*

Name _____   Date _____

Guide to Writing an Essay

Directions: Read the background information and the essay question below, and then follow the steps to write an essay based on primary and secondary sources that answers the question.

Background Information

There were many changes in transportation and technology in the United States in the early 1800s. These changes influenced the way people lived and worked.

Essay Question

Use the documents (you will analyze them in Step 4), your answers to the document-analysis questions, and your knowledge of the early 1800s to write a well-constructed essay that answers the following question:

> What kinds of changes in transportation and technology took place in the United States in the early 1800s? How did those changes influence the way people lived and worked?

Step 1: Read and Analyze the Question

1. Read the question to yourself and then read it aloud.
2. Highlight the most important words or phrases in the question.

   - Be sure to pay attention to dates, verbs, and adjectives.
   - Check for words that tell you there is more than one side to an issue. They may be words such as "however," "but," and "though."

3. On the list below, circle what the question is asking you to do. You may circle more than one item. Does the question ask you to:

   - compare and contrast?
   - explain?
   - describe?
   - agree or disagree with a statement?
   - prove something?

4. Rewrite the question as a sentence that shows you understand what the question is asking. Start with "I will..."

_____

_____

5. Show your sentence to an adult and discuss your understanding of the question.

Step 2: Record What You Know

1. List everything you know that relates to the topics in the essay question, or create a word web for each topic. Be sure to stay within the time period of the question.

2. Review the following lessons:

   - Lesson 1: Revolutionary Inventions
   - Lesson 2: Transportation and Travel
   - Lesson 3: Steaming
   - Lesson 4: Cities Grow All Around
   - Lesson 5: Mills and Mines

3. Add to your list or word web any additional relevant information you find. Be sure anything you add relates to (fits) the topics. If you would like to see an example of how to complete these steps, see Steps 1 and 2 on the Kiah's Essay sheet.

Step 3: Organize

1. Look back at the question and your sentence of understanding.

2. Sort and organize the information you listed according to the topics in the question. You may need to label the items on your list. There are several ways to do this. You could:

   - highlight each topic in a different color, or
   - number the topics and then number the items in your list to match, or
   - write an abbreviation for the topic in the margin next to each item

If you would like to see an example of how one student organizes information, see Step 3 on the Kiah's Essay sheet.

Step 4: Read and Analyze Documents

1. You will analyze several primary and secondary source documents.

   - Study each document and answer the questions that follow it.
   - Highlight or underline important pieces of the documents you may wish to use.

2. Look back at the essay question, your sentence of understanding, and your organizational topics.

3. Label the documents and your answers to the questions the same way you labeled your list. If you would like to see an example of how one student analyzes and organizes information, see Step 4 on the Kiah's Essay sheet.

Step 5: Write a Thesis Statement

1. Now it is time to answer the question. Go back and read it and your sentence of understanding once more.

2. Look back through the information you gathered from memory, the lesson reviews, and the document analyses.

3. What is your short answer to the question?

   - Write your answer in one or two clear sentences.
   - Use third person (don't use the word "I").
   - You may mention the topics that will appear in the explanation of your answer, or your answer may be more general. Do not include specific information in this short answer. You will add specifics later.

   _____

   _____

   _____

Refer to Step 5 on the Kiah's Essay sheet for an example of a thesis statement.

Step 6: Create an Outline

1. You have organized your information according to topics. Now you will create an outline, organizing the information the way you will use it in your essay.

2. The outline must contain at least two main topics. They are the topics that are listed in the essay question. Put a Roman numeral and a period (I., II.) before each of the main topics of the outline. See the sample on the next page.

3. Decide which category from the essay question you want to write about first, and write it next to the Roman numeral I.

4. Below the first category, write a topic sentence for that section of your essay. Be sure that it tells the reader what this section will be about and how it relates to your thesis statement.

5. Decide which information you will use. In an outline, facts, ideas, or examples are subtopics. Write a capital letter and a period (A., B., C.) before each subtopic. See the sample below.

6. Decide what order the information, or subtopics, should be in. Jot them down in order beneath your topic sentence. Remember to write a capital letter and a period before each subtopic.

7. You can further divide subtopics into specific facts. In an outline, specific facts follow Arabic numerals and periods (1., 2., 3., 4.). Each subtopic or specific fact should contain at least two parts (A. and B., or 1. and 2.) See the sample below.

8. Follow the same procedure for the other section of your essay.

9. Check your information list. You will probably not use all of the information on the list. But be sure you have not left out anything that you think is important. Remember, your outline and your essay should match each other exactly.

If you would like to see an example of how one student creates an outline, see Step 6 on the Kiah's Essay sheet.

Sample Outline:

I. First Main Topic

Topic Sentence

    A. Subtopic

        1. Fact

        2. Fact

    B. Subtopic

        1. Fact

        2. Fact

    C. Subtopic

        1. Fact

        2. Fact

Step 7: Write Your Essay!

Now it is time to write the essay.

1. Use a new sheet of loose-leaf paper for your essay. Keep your notes and outline where you can see them easily.

2. Use your thesis statement as the introduction to your essay. You may add some general information or an explanation before or after it. Do not write more than three or four sentences in the introduction.

3. Using the information you've organized, follow your outline to start writing the body of your essay. Each paragraph in the body should be about one of the topics in the essay question.

4. Write the first section of your essay.

   - Use the topic sentence you have written in your outline. The topic sentence should state the main idea of the paragraph.

   - Explain your topic sentence, using the information from that part of your outline. Be specific (for example: If you wanted to include a wonderful invention in your essay, include the inventor's name, the name of the invention, what it does, and why the invention supports your thesis statement).

   - Write a concluding sentence that connects back to the thesis statement.

5. Write the other section of your essay using the same procedure.

6. Write a concluding paragraph that summarizes the major ideas of your essay and restates your thesis statement in some way.

If you would like to see an example of how one student writes an introduction, body, and conclusion, see Step 8 on the Kiah's Essay sheet.

Step 8: Revise and Refine

1. Read back through the whole essay. Did you answer the essay question? Are all your ideas clearly written? If not, take a moment to reword or rewrite any sections that need to be revised.

2. Correct any spelling, grammar, or punctuation mistakes you see.

3. Now, copy your revised essay onto a new sheet of loose-leaf paper or type it in a word processing program.

4. Have an adult read and review your essay.

Name _____ Date _____

Kiah's Essay

Note: This student sample develops a single paragraph—you will be writing a multi-paragraph essay.

Background Information

The population of the United States grew and changed quite a bit from 1840 to 1860. Immigrants seeking new opportunities moved to America.

Essay Question

Use the documents, your answers to the document-analysis questions, and your knowledge of the years 1840 to 1860 to write a well-constructed essay that answers the following question:

In what ways did the population of the United States change between 1840 and 1860? Describe how many people came, who they were, and their reasons for coming.

Step 1: Read and Analyze the Question

In what ways did the population of the United States change between 1840 and 1860? Describe how many people came, who they were, and their reasons for coming.

- compare and contrast?
- explain?
- describe?
- agree or disagree with a statement?
- prove something?

I will write how the population of the United States changed between the years 1840 and 1860. I will also describe the numbers and kinds of people who came and explain why they came.

Step 2: Record What You Know

As a list:

Events

Potato Famine in Ireland
New factories in Germany
Unemployment in China
Railroads being built in the United
States
Mexican American War
A number of places became states

Migrations

Irish moved to the United States
Germans moved to the United States
Chinese moved to the United States
Chines and other moved to the
western
United States
Americans moved from farms to cities
Americans and new immigrants moved
to
the West

Achievements

Railroads
Mining of Gold
National Road
Cottonn gin
Sewing machine
Water-powered factories
Canals
Ralph Waldo Emerson and Walt
Whitman were authors who wrote
about America—that led to immigrants
moving to certain areas

Whatever

Thousands of Irish immigrants helped
build the Erie Canal
More than 20 thousand Chinese
entered California
The overland stagecoaches reached
California

As a word web:

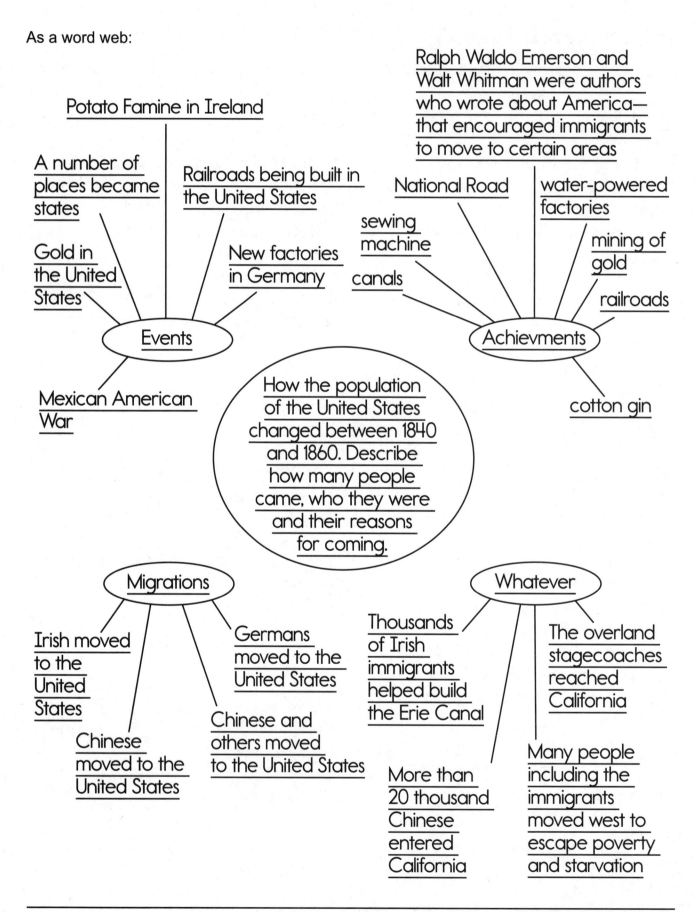

Potato Famine in Ireland

Ralph Waldo Emerson and Walt Whitman were authors who wrote about America— that encouraged immigrants to move to certain areas

A number of places became states

Railroads being built in the United States

National Road

water-powered factories

Gold in the United States

New factories in Germany

sewing machine

mining of gold

canals

railroads

Events

Achievments

Mexican American War

How the population of the United States changed between 1840 and 1860. Describe how many people came, who they were and their reasons for coming.

cotton gin

Migrations

Whatever

Irish moved to the United States

Germans moved to the United States

Thousands of Irish immigrants helped build the Erie Canal

The overland stagecoaches reached California

Chinese moved to the United States

Chinese and others moved to the United States

More than 20 thousand Chinese entered California

Many people including the immigrants moved west to escape poverty and starvation

Step 3: Organize

Population change in the United States between 1840 and 1860

New Factories - Americans move from farms to cities

Railroads - Americans and others go west

Mining of Gold

National Road

Cotton gin

Sewing machine

Water-powered factories

Canals

Ralph Waldo Emerson and Walt Whitman were authors who wrote about

America—that led to immigrants moving to certain areas

Numbers and kinds of people

Irish moved to the United States (about 3 million)

Germans moved to the United States (about 1.5 million)

Chinese move to the United States

Reasons for coming to the United States

Potato famine in Ireland

New factories in Germany

Unemployment in China

Railroads being built in the United States

Gold in the United States

Step 4: Read and Analyze Documents

Document 1: The New Colossus

The New Colossus written by Emma Lazarus, 1883
Not like the brazen giant of Greek fame,
With conquering limbs astride from land to land;
Here at our sea-washed, sunset gates shall stand
A mighty woman with a torch, whose flame
Is the imprisoned lightning, and her name
Mother of Exiles. From her beacon-hand
Glows world-wide welcome; her mild eyes command
The air-bridged harbor that twin cities frame.

"Keep, ancient lands, your storied pomp!" cries she
With silent lips. "Give me your tired, your poor,
Your huddled masses yearning to breathe free,
The wretched refuse of your teeming shore.
Send these, the homeless, tempest-tossed to me.
I lift my lamp beside the golden door."

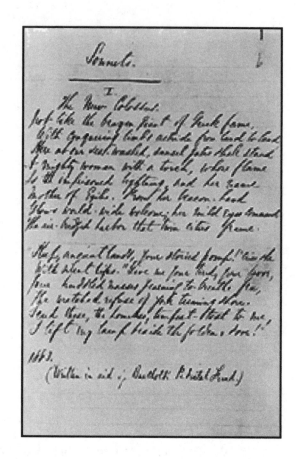

1. Who is the "… mighty woman with a torch, whose flame Is the imprisoned lightning…"?

   She is the Statue of Liberty, standing in New York Harbor.

2. Who does she invite to the United States?

   She invites all people who are unwanted in their own countries or are seeking a better life.

Document 2: Speech

"… We Are Strong and Getting Stronger…"

You intend to shut out the foreigners or naturalized citizens of this country from any benefit that will arise from your plans to get better wages…. You use the word American very often and nothing at all is said about naturalized citizens, but if you think to succeed without the aid of foreigners you will find yourself mistaken; for we are strong and are getting stronger every day, and though we feel the effects of competition from these men who are sent here from the poorhouses of Europe, yet if you don't include us to get better wages by shutting off such men, why, you'd needn't expect our help.

Source: *Champion of American Labor*, April 17, 1847

1. According to the speech, what is the difference between an American and a naturalized citizen?

   According to the speech an American seems to be someone born in the Unites States and a naturalized citizen is someone who was born in another country but has moved to the United States to live and become a United States citizen.

2. What does the author want the reader to understand?

   Immigrants who became citizens of the United States wanted the same benefits that American citizens would get.

Document 3: Graph

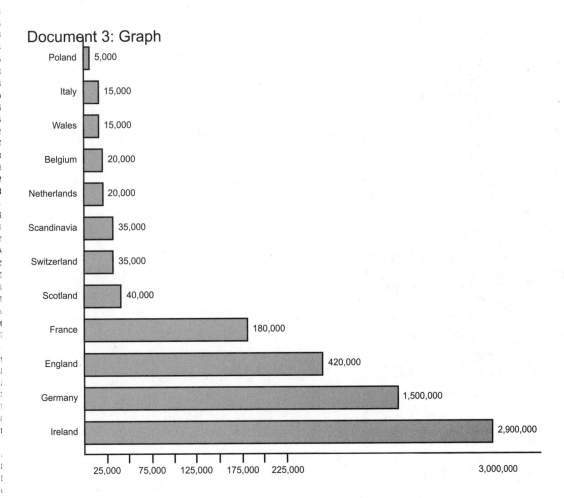

Immigration by Country of Origin, 1841–1860

1. What does the graph show?

The graph shows how many immigrants from each country came to the United States between 1841 and 1860.

2. Where did most immigrants come from?

Most people came from Western Europe. The largest group came from Ireland. The smallest group came from Poland. The second largest group came from Germany. The third largest group came from England.

Document 4: Political Cartoon

The Immigrant, The Stranger at Our Gate

1. What does the cartoon show?

Political Cartoon shows an immigrant and Uncle Sam (US Government).

2. Does this cartoon support immigration? How does this cartoon reflect what the American public thought about open immigration?

The cartoon does not support free immigration. It shows that the American public did not want to allow all people into the United States.

Step 5: Write a Thesis Statement

The population in the United States between the years 1840 and 1860 grew a lot. The cities grew because people moved from farms to the cities. New factories, transportation, and the discovery of gold were some of the reasons people moved to the cities and new areas. Immigrants came to the United States because a lot of things happened such as poverty and lack of work in places like Europe and China.

Step 6: Outline

I. Population growth

The population in the United States between the years 1840 and 1860 grew a lot.

A. Population change in the United States between 1840 and 1860.

1. Many immigrants came to the United States between 1840 and 1860.
2. The population grew mostly in the cities because people moved from farms to the cities.

B. Numbers and kinds of people

1. About 4 million people came mostly from northern and western Europe and China.
2. Most of the people who came to the United States from Europe and China were the Irish, English, Germans, French, Scottish, and Chinese.

C. Reasons for coming to the United States

1. The immigrants came to the United States to escape poverty and to find jobs that pay more money and to find gold.
2. The people from China did not have jobs so they came to the United States to help build railroads. The Chinese also moved to the western United States to find gold. The people in Ireland were starving because of a potato famine. They came to the United States to find work and have a better life. In Germany, the new factories put a lot of people who worked in their homes out of work. The Germans came to the United States to find jobs.

Step 7: Write Your Essay!

Note: This student sample is for a single-paragraph essay. You will write a multi-paragraph essay.

The population of United States between the years 1840 and 1860 grew a lot. The population grew mostly in the cities because people moved from farms to the cities. Most of the people came from Europe and China. The kinds of people who came to the United States migrated from Europe and China. They were the Irish, Germans, English, French, Scottish, and Chinese. The immigrants came to the United States to escape poverty and to find jobs that paid more money and to find gold. People came from China to build railroads in the United States, people came from Ireland because there was a potato famine and they did not have many potatoes, and people came from Germany because new factories were opened and the factories put people out of business.

Step 8: Revise and Refine

The population of the United States grew between the years 1840 and 1860. The population grew mostly in the cities because people moved from farms to the cities. Transportation and new factories also helped cities to grow because with transportation people could move to the cities easily to work in the new factories. Most of the immigrants who came to the United States at this time were from Europe and China. They were the Irish, Germans, English, French, Scottish, and Chinese. The people in China did not have jobs, so they came to the United States to help build railroads and to find gold. The people came from Ireland because there was a potato famine and they were starving. In Germany, new factories were opened and the factories put people who worked in their homes out of business, so they came to the United States to find work. For all these reasons, the population of the United States grew and changed between 1840 and 1860.

Student Guide
Lesson 7: Writing a Document-Based Essay, Part 2

The next step in preparing your essay is to read and analyze source documents. The primary and secondary sources will give you a lot of information. It's up to you to decide how you will use the information to prepare the essay.

Lesson Objectives
- Analyze primary sources.
- Acquire information related to an essay question.
- Organize information.

PREPARE

Approximate lesson time is 60 minutes.

Materials

For the Student

    🖳 Evaluating Primary Sources

    A History of US (Concise Edition), Volume B (1790-1877) by Joy Hakim

    History Journal

LEARN
Activity 1: Document-Based Writing, Step 4 *(Offline)*

Name _____   Date _____

Evaluating Primary Sources

Document 1: Autobiography

Read the document and answer the questions in complete sentences.

In her autobiography, Harriet Hanson Robinson, the wife of a newspaper editor, provided an account of her earlier life as female factory worker (from the age of ten in 1834 to 1848) in the textile Mills of Lowell, Massachusetts.

At the time the Lowell cotton mills were started the caste [social group] of the factory girl was the lowest among the employments of women. . . .The early millgirls were of different ages. Some were not over ten years old; a few were in middle life, but the majority were between the ages of sixteen and twentyfive. The very young girls were called "doffers." They "doffed," or took off, the full bobbins from the spinningframes, and replaced them with empty ones. These mites worked about fifteen minutes every hour and the rest of the time was their own. When the overseer was kind they were allowed to read, knit, or go outside the millyard to play. They were paid two dollars a week. The working hours of all the girls extended from five o'clock in the morning until seven in the evening, with one halfhour each, for breakfast and dinner. Even the doffers were forced to be on duty nearly fourteen hours a day. This was the greatest hardship in the lives of these children. Several years later a tenhour law was passed, but not until long after some of these little doffers were old enough to appear before the legislative committee on the subject, and plead, by their presence, for a reduction of the hours of labor.

Those of the millgirls who had homes generally worked from eight to ten months in the year; the rest of the time was spent with parents or friends. A few taught school during the summer months.

Source: Harriet H. Robinson, "Early Factory Labor in New England," in Massachusetts Bureau of Statistics of Labor, Fourteenth Annual Report (Boston: Wright & Potter, 1883), 38082, 38788, 39192.

---

1. What kind of document is this? When was it produced? Who was the audience?

   _____

   _____

   _____

2. Who were the mill workers? How were they treated?

   _____

   _____

   _____

3. What were the working conditions of the early mill workers?

_____

_____

_____

Document 2: Engraving

Look at the engraving and answer the questions in complete sentences.

Men Working in Coal Mine, engraving, 1840s

1. What kind of document is this? When was it produced? Who was the audience?

_____

_____

_____

_____

2. What does the engraving show?

_____

_____

_____

3. What are the working conditions of the people in the image?

_____

_____

_____

Document 3: Paintings

Study the paintings and answer the questions in complete sentences.

"View of the City of Pittsburgh in 1817" painted by a Mrs. Gibson while on her wedding tour of the West, one year after Pittsburgh became a city. The building with the tower is the first Court House at Market Square. A flatboat is pictured on the left.

1830 view of Pittsburgh shows how steamboats had come to dominate river traffic—the Monongahela wharf is lined with steamers. Note the covered wooden bridge over the Allegheny. Just out of view on the right is the first Smithfield Bridge, the city's first, also built out of wood in 1820.

1. What kind of documents are these? When were they produced? Who was the audience?

_____

_____

_____

2. What do both images show? How many years have passed between the first and second image?

_____

_____

_____

3. How did the scene change over time? Why do you think it changed?

_____

_____

_____

Document 4: Painting

Study the painting and answer the questions in complete sentences.

First American Macadam Road, 1823

1. What kind of document is this? When was it produced? Who was the audience?

   _____

   _____

   _____

2. How do you think the United States was affected by what is happening in the painting?

   _____

   _____

   _____

Student Guide
Lesson 8: Writing a Document-Based Essay, Part 3

Now that you have read and analyzed the primary source documents and organized your information, you are ready to develop a thesis statement and an outline.

Lesson Objectives
- Develop a thesis statement
- Develop an outline of information.

PREPARE

Approximate lesson time is 60 minutes.

Materials

For the Student

A History of US (Concise Edition), Volume B (1790-1877) by Joy Hakim

History Journal

LEARN
Activity 1: Document -Based Writing, Steps 5 and 6 *(Offline)*

Student Guide
Lesson 9: (Optional) Writing a Document-Based Essay, Part 4

Use this OPTIONAL lesson to continue working on your document-based essay. Refer to Steps 1–6 on the Guide to Writing an Essay sheet for specific directions on completing the first six steps.

In the next lesson, you will begin writing your essay.

PREPARE

Approximate lesson time is 60 minutes.

Materials

For the Student

A History of US (Concise Edition), Volume B (1790-1877) by Joy Hakim

History Journal

Student Guide
Lesson 10: Writing a Document-Based Essay, Part 5

You have analyzed primary source documents, organized your information, and written a thesis statement and an outline. Now you're ready to write!

Lesson Objectives

- Write a document-based essay.

PREPARE

Approximate lesson time is 60 minutes.

Materials

For the Student

A History of US (Concise Edition), Volume B (1790-1877) by Joy Hakim

History Journal

LEARN
Activity 1: Document -Based Writing, Steps 7 and 8 *(Offline)*

Student Guide
Lesson 11: Unit Review

You've completed the unit A New Age and New Industries. It's time to review what you've learned. You'll take the Unit Assessment in the next lesson.

Lesson Objectives

- Review important knowledge and skills taught in this unit.

PREPARE

Approximate lesson time is 60 minutes.

Materials

For the Student

A History of US (Concise Edition), Volume B (1790-1877) by Joy Hakim

History Journal

LEARN
Activity 1: A Look Back (Offline)
Online Review

Go online and use the following to review this unit:

- The Big Picture
- Flash cards
- Time line

History Journal Review

Review more by going through your History Journal. Look at the sheets you completed for this unit. Review your vocabulary words. If you completed writing assignments, read them. Don't rush through; take your time. Your History Journal is a great resource for a unit review.

Student Guide
Lesson 12: Unit Assessment

You've finished this unit. Take the Unit Assessment. Then complete the Read On activity.

Lesson Objectives

- Identify Andrew Jackson as the first common man elected president.
- Describe the ways in which Jackson represented new ideas and people who had not had political power before, including those with little wealth and those in the West.
- Identify groups who did not have political power in 1828, including blacks and women.
- Identify the eight presidents between 1832 and 1860.
- Define *industrial revolution* and *factory system.*
- Identify industrial innovators, including Eli Whitney, Francis Lowell, and Samuel Slater, and their accomplishments.
- Identify four modern innovations in transportation in the early 1800s, including canals, railroads, steamboats, and improved roads.
- Summarize the impact of canals and roads on life and the economy.
- Identify Robert Fulton as a developer of the steamboat.
- Discuss the geographic reasons for the growth of cities on rivers.
- Describe some of the problems of workers in the mines and mills of the nineteenth century, such as low pay and dangerous conditions.
- Explain why so many women and children worked in mills and mines.

PREPARE

Approximate lesson time is 60 minutes.

Materials

For the Student

A History of US (Concise Edition), Volume B (1790-1877) by Joy Hakim

History Journal

ASSESS

Unit Assessment: A New Age and New Industries, Part 1 *(Online)*

Complete the computer-scored portion of the Unit Assessment. When you have finished, complete the teacher-scored portion of the assessment and submit it to your teacher.

Unit Assessment: A New Age and New Industries, Part 2 *(Offline)*

Complete the teacher-scored portion of the Unit Assessment and submit it to your teacher.

LEARN
Activity 1: Chapter 21 *(Offline)*

As the pioneers pushed west, their dealings with the native tribes were tense with misunderstandings and conflicting goals—especially with the Cherokee.

Read Chapter 21, pages 102–106.

Student Guide
Lesson 1: Write On, Sequoyah!

Most Americans believed it was God's plan that the United States extend from sea to shining sea. Americans spilled westward and immigrants flooded into the country. New territory was added; Native Americans lost their land and way of life. But the people who searched for a better life left a legacy of determination that still inspires today.

As the population grew, America expanded westward into territory that belonged to the Indians. Most settlers thought of the Indians as uncivilized. One group, the Cherokees, had adopted some of the ways of the white settlers. Convinced that a system of writing was important to preserve their Cherokee traditions, Sequoyah developed a written Cherokee language.

Lesson Objectives
- Describe the ways in which the Cherokee Nation attempted to keep its land, including assimilation and warfare.
- Identify Sequoyah as the Cherokee who invented a written form of the Cherokee language.
- Describe the Indian Removal Act and the economic reasons for it.

PREPARE

Approximate lesson time is 60 minutes.

Materials
For the Student
"Making Words" Word Puzzle
A History of US (Concise Edition), Volume B (1790-1877) by Joy Hakim
History Journal

LEARN
Activity 1: Indian Change (Offline)
Check Your Reading (Chapter 21, pages 102–106)

Review Chapter 21 by completing the "Making Words" Word Puzzle sheet. Have an adult check your answers.

Discuss

Share your answers to the following questions with an adult.

1. The settlers thought the ways of the Indians were strange and uncivilized, even when the Indians had adopted some of the ways of the white settlers. Describe some of the characteristics of the Cherokees that white people of that time would consider "civilized."
2. How did the Cherokees attempt to keep their land?
3. What did the U.S. Congress do to take away the Cherokees' land?

Read On

The new nation still had a lot of growing to do—and it wasn't just physical growth. Americans had to figure out exactly how the national government would work with the state governments and how the government would protect people's rights. The Trail of Tears is just one example of how the new Constitution was tested.

Read Chapter 22, pages 107–111.

Optional: Beyond the Lesson

View the Cherokee Alphabet that Sequoyah developed. Try using their language to write a sentence about the relocation of the Cherokees.

Activity 2. Optional: The Cherokee Alphabet (Online)

Name _____   Date _____

"Making Words" Word Puzzle

Answer the questions below. Then, use the circled letters to fill in the blanks at the bottom of the page to learn what was discovered on Cherokee land in Georgia.

1. Description of life on the frontier:

   ___ ___ ___ (__) ___ ___ ___ ___ ___

2. Person who developed Cherokee system of writing:

   ___ ___ ___ (__) ___ ___ ___

3. Number of symbols in the Cherokee alphabet:

   ___ ___ ___ ___ ___ ___ – ___ ___ ___

4. What the Cherokees called letters:

   ___ ___ ___ ___ ___ ___ ___ (__) ___ ___ ___ ___ ___

5. A word some white people called the Indians:

   ___ ___ ___ ___ ___ ___ ___

6. Where many new immigrants to the United States settled:

   ___ ___ ___ ___

7. What killed many Indians once the settlers arrived:

   ___ ___ ___ ___ ___ ___ ___ ___ and ___ ___ ___ ___ ___ ___ ___

8. Many people wanted the Indians to live west of the

   ___ ___ ___ ___ ___ ___ ___ ___ ___ ___ ___   ___ ___ ___ ___ ___ .

9. Law passed to move Indian tribes west:

   ___ (__) ___ ___ ___   ___ ___ ___ ___ ___ ___ ___   ___ ___ ___

10. What was discovered on Cherokee land in Georgia that forced the Cherokees to relocate? Use the circled letters to spell out the answer.

    ___ ___ ___ ___

Name _____ Date _____

Movement and Migration: Guided Reading

1. In 1821, New Mexico was a territory controlled by _____.

2. Men, and a few women, who traveled the Santa Fe Trail did so to get

   _____, for _____, or to see new

   _____.

3. It took more than a month to travel from _____ to New Mexico along the Santa Fe Trail.

4. James Magoffin was sent to Santa Fe on a _____

   _____ to persuade the governor of New Mexico not to fight the

   U.S. _____ that was coming to capture New Mexico.

5. Following Magoffin's trip, the United States _____ New Mexico, and it

   became a U.S. _____.

6. In 1879, when the _____ reached New Mexico, people stopped using the Santa Fe Trail.

7. In 1846, many immigrants came to the United States from Ireland because

   _____ _____ destroyed the potato crop and people

   were starving. Another reason they came was because small farmers were being

   _____ more than the rich.

8. People in Germany emigrated to the United States to find _____ and

   _____.

9. The Chinese came to America to help build the _____.

10. Briefly describe the people that came to America in the 1800s.

Name _____ Date _____

Reasons for Immigration

People from foreign lands traveled thousands of miles to America— the land of opportunity. They came for many reasons. Look at the list of reasons that people came, and then decide whether each reason is social, political, or economic. Discuss your ideas with an adult if you have trouble deciding which category the reason fits into. Write each reason in the appropriate section on your chart. The first one is done for you. Share your chart with an adult when you have finished.

Categories:
- Social—deals with new ideas and activities; may involve religion
- Political—deals with government and how a country treats its citizens
- Economic—deals with land, money, and jobs

List of Reasons:
- Ireland's potato crop failed.
- "Poor law" taxed Ireland's small farmers.
- New factories in Germany put people out of work.
- A freedom revolution in Germany failed.
- Few jobs existed for workers in China.
- People in some foreign nations were persecuted for their beliefs.
- People searched for adventure.
- A rumor spread in Germany that America would stop immigration.

Social	Political	Economic
		Ireland's potato crop failed

Student Guide
Lesson 4: Westward Ho!

After the 1847 economic depression, many families in the United States lost their farms. People packed up their belongings and headed west. Many people were searching for a better life. Others were looking for adventure. Groups of people banded together, braving rough traveling conditions. While some of the individuals and families found that better life in Oregon or California, others never made it through the long journey.

Lesson Objectives

- Identify the reasons why people chose to go west, including the opportunity to start a new life and to acquire land.
- Analyze photographs and written documents to describe the journey west and its difficulties, including disease, lack of water, and fear of attack.
- Define *prairie schooner, pioneer,* and *wagon train.*

PREPARE

Approximate lesson time is 60 minutes.

Materials

For the Student

New Emigrants

A History of US (Concise Edition), Volume B (1790-1877) by Joy Hakim

History Journal

LEARN
Activity 1: The Oregon Trail *(Offline)*
Read

Read Chapter 24, pages 118–125, and Chapter 25, pages 126–132. Complete the New Emigrants sheet. Have an adult check your answers.

Use What You Know

For a look at more diaries and memoirs of people going west, visit The Oregon Trail website. Choose several entries that interest you and read them. As you read, remember that these were actual people whose experiences were real. In your History Journal, make a list of the positive things about traveling west (such as seeing new places or meeting new friends) and the negative things (such as someone dying or people not having much food). Base the lists on your reading of the diaries and memoirs.

Would you have liked to travel the Oregon Trail as a pioneer? Share your answers with an adult.

Name _____ Date _____

New Emigrants

1. The wooden-wheeled wagons used by the people heading west were called prairie

   _____ .

2. The wagons had to be lightweight so it would be easier for the _____ or

   _____ to pull them.

3. The people heading west called themselves emigrants, but we call them

   _____ .

4. Most of the first pioneers that moved west did so because they wanted to escape an

   economic _____ in the East.

5. Many pioneers headed west to settle on _____ and

   _____ land and for the _____ that seemed to be

   waiting.

6. For most of the emigrants, the journey west began in _____ , where the

   _____ River meets the _____ River.

7. Instead of traveling westward alone, groups joined together and traveled in

   _____ trains.

8. Families who traveled together along the Oregon Trail were like communities; they even

   wrote _____ to help keep order and settle conflicts.

9. The Humboldt River sinks beneath the desert in an area called the Humboldt Sink. From

   there to the Truckee River there is no _____ .

Use the map Trails to the West in Chapter 25 to answer questions 10–12.

10. What did sections of the Santa Fe, California, Oregon, and Mormon trails have in
    common?

11. From which town did three of the trails originate?

_____

12. Based solely on the map, which destination do you think was the easiest to get to—Portland, Sacramento, Salt Lake City, or Santa Fe? Explain your answer.

_____

Student Guide
Lesson 5: Shakers and Movers

The West offered many Americans the opportunity to start a new life. Brigham Young led a group fleeing religious persecution out of Illinois to present-day Utah. The Mormons settled there to build a religious society.

Lesson Objectives

- Demonstrate mastery of important knowledge and skills taught in previous lessons.
- Identify Joseph Smith, Brigham Young, and the Mormons.
- Explain the reasons the Mormons migrated to the West, including persecution and opportunity.
- Use maps to gain familiarity with transportation and migration routes.
- Explain why the Santa Fe Trail fell out of use.
- Describe the "push" and "pull" factors that caused people to leave their home countries and migrate to the United States, including social, political, and economic problems at home and opportunities in the United States.
- Identify the reasons why people chose to go west, including the opportunity to start a new life and to acquire land.
- Define *prairie schooner, pioneer,* and *wagon train.*

PREPARE

Approximate lesson time is 60 minutes.

Materials

For the Student

Guided Reading: Chapter 26

A History of US (Concise Edition), Volume B (1790-1877) by Joy Hakim

Understanding Geography: Map Skills and Our World (Level 5)

History Journal

LEARN
Activity 1: The Mormons Move West *(Offline)*
Read

Read Chapter 26, pages 133–136. As you read, complete the Chapter 26: Guided Reading sheet.

Learn from Maps

- Read Activity 8, "Transportation Maps" (pages 32–35), in *Understanding Geography*.
- Answer Questions 1–19 in your History Journal.
- If you have time, you may want to answer the Skill Builder Questions on page 35.
- After you have finished, compare your answers with the ones in the Learning Coach Guide.
- You will need the *Understanding Geography* book for the online Lesson Assessment.
- Have an adult review your activity sheets from Lessons 3, 4, and 5 for the Mid-Unit Assessment.

ASSESS

Lesson Assessment: Shakers and Movers (*Online*)

Answer the online geography questions for this assessment. Your assessment will be scored by the computer.

Mid-Unit Assessment: Americans Take New Land (*Offline*)

You will complete an offline assessment covering some of the main points of this unit. Your assessment will be scored by the teacher.

Name _____   Date _____

Reading Guide: Chapter 26

1. Who founded the Church of Jesus Christ of Latter-day Saints? _____

2. What did others call the followers of this religion? _____

3. Describe two practices of the church that made others angry. _____

   _____

   _____

4. How were members of this religion treated in Illinois? _____

   _____

5. Who became the Mormon leader after Joseph Smith was murdered? _____

6. Why did this new leader decide to lead his people west? _____

   _____

7. Where did they settle? _____

Student Guide
Lesson 6: (Optional) Don't Forget to Write

Many of the settlers who traveled west along the Santa Fe, Oregon, and California trails kept records of their experiences. Historians have learned a lot about this period of American history from the settlers' diaries. They contain a wealth of information about life along the trail and offer a window into the minds and hearts of their authors.

You must complete the **Read On** activity before moving on to the next lesson.

Lesson Objectives

- Demonstrate understanding of the pioneer experience, including motivation and experience.

PREPARE

Approximate lesson time is 60 minutes.

Materials

    For the Student

        A History of US (Concise Edition), Volume B (1790-1877) by Joy Hakim

        History Journal

LEARN
Activity 1. Optional: From the Trail (Offline)
Use What You Know

People heading west along the Santa Fe, California, and Oregon trails wrote about their experiences on the trail. You've read excerpts from some of their diaries in your book and online. Now it's time to do some writing of your own—but not as yourself!

You will write several diary entries as a young person living in the 1860s. As you write, try not to write as a person living with all the conveniences of the twenty-first century. Put yourself in the place of a boy or girl who actually made a long and dangerous journey out West. Try to feel what they felt and think what they thought; that's not always easy.

Write the entries in your History Journal. Information in Chapters 23–26 will help you.

1. First Diary Entry

Imagine you and your family came to America from another country several years ago. In this diary entry:

Student Guide
Lesson 7: Manifest Destinies

Mexico shook off Spanish rule only to find another foreign power—the United States of America—intent on exerting its dominance over the continent. Richard Henry Dana's narrative of his trip to California whetted America's appetite for all of that desirable land.

Lesson Objectives
- Define *Manifest Destiny*.
- Describe the population of California in 1840 as Native Americans, Spanish-speaking settlers, missionaries, and rancheros.
- Explain why President Polk and other Americans wanted to gain control of California, including its fertile farmlands, excellent harbors, and the idea of Manifest Destiny.

PREPARE

Approximate lesson time is 60 minutes.

Materials
For the Student

California, Mexico?

A History of US (Concise Edition), Volume B (1790-1877) by Joy Hakim

History Journal

LEARN
Activity 1: Coast-to-Coast Destiny *(Offline)*
Check Your Reading (Chapter 27, pages 137–142)

Go over Chapter 27 with an adult by discussing the following:

1. What does *Manifest Destiny* mean?
2. What was the makeup of California's population in the 1840s?
3. What book got Americans interested in, and excited about, California? Who wrote the book?
4. Why did President Polk and other Americans want to gain control of California?

Respond to the following in your History Journal:

You are a Native American living in California in 1840. What do you think about Manifest Destiny? What effect do you think this idea will have on Native Americans living between the Mississippi River and the Pacific Ocean?

Use What You Know

Complete the California, *Mexico*? sheet. Have an adult check your work.

Read On

The Spanish called the land Téjas (TAY-hahs). Americans called it Texas. It was a large territory with a small population of Indians and Spanish Mexicans. Most of the Indians had died from diseases brought by the early gold-seeking Spanish explorers. Spain's hopes that its citizens would settle in Texas went mostly unrealized. But there were people interested in settling there. Who were they? What problems would they face? And what would become of this tempting and beautiful land called Texas?

Read Chapter 28, pages 143–149. Be prepared to explain the causes of the conflicts between Mexicans and Anglo settlers.

Name _____   Date _____

California, *Mexico*?

In 1848, California belonged to Mexico. This land, much larger than the present-day state of California, already had a history hundreds of years old.

1. California, the land controlled by Mexico, included all or part of seven future U.S. states. What states were they? (You'll find them listed at the end of Chapter 27.)

_____ _____

_____ _____

_____ _____

_____

2. There were four distinct groups of people living in California before settlers from the United States started pouring into the territory. Briefly describe each group.

• Native Americans

_____

_____

• Spanish-speaking settlers (Californians)

_____

_____

• Missionaries

_____

_____

• Rancheros

_____

_____

3. The U.S. belief in _____ _____ would eventually lead to California becoming part of the United States.

Student Guide
Lesson 8: Remember More Than the Alamo

Texas has had quite a complicated history. First, Spain took it from the Indians. Then it belonged to Mexico after Mexico gained independence from Spain. Not long after that, Anglos and Tejanos (Mexican Texans) took it from Mexico. For nearly a decade, Texas existed as an independent republic before it became part of the United States.

Lesson Objectives
- Identify Stephen Austin as the leader of American settlers in Texas, Santa Anna as the Mexican dictator, and Sam Houston as the first president of the Republic of Texas.
- Explain the causes of the conflicts between Mexicans and anglo settlers, including the settlers' violations of settlement agreements and Santa Anna's violation of the Mexican Constitution.
- Explain how Texas became an independent country and then a state in the United States.

PREPARE

Approximate lesson time is 60 minutes.

Materials
For the Student

A History of US (Concise Edition), Volume B (1790-1877) by Joy Hakim

History Journal

LEARN
Activity 1: Texas: Tempting and Beautiful (Offline)
Check Your Reading (Chapter 28, pages 143–149)

Use the flash cards to review Chapter 28.

Use What You Know

Create a simple time line that shows a brief history of Texas from 1820 to 1845. Include the following events:

- Sam Houston and his followers defeat Santa Anna at San Jacinto.
- Stephen Austin leads settlers from Missouri to Texas.
- Congress admits Texas into the Union as the 28th state.
- Texas becomes an independent nation—the Republic of Texas.
- Santa Anna defeats a small band of Texas rebels at the Alamo.
- Texas rebels attack San Antonio.

Also include in your time line a very brief description of the following people:

- Stephen Austin
- Santa Anna
- Sam Houston

Activity 2. Optional: The Alamo *(Online)*

Student Guide
Lesson 9: More and More States

In December 1845, Texas became the 28th state to enter the Union. The United States had been steadily growing since the 1780s. By the mid-1850s, the nation had acquired all the land that we now call the contiguous 48 states. But when did the vast territories become states?

Lesson Objectives
- Describe the expansion of the United States from the 1780's to the present.
- Practice identifying the fifty states and their capitals.

PREPARE

Approximate lesson time is 60 minutes.

Materials

For the Student

Fifty States

State Capitals

A History of US (Concise Edition), Volume B (1790-1877) by Joy Hakim

Understanding Geography: Map Skills and Our World (Level 5)

History Journal

LEARN
Activity 1: Growing to Fifty States (Offline)
Learn from Maps

Read Activity 12, "Growing to Fifty States" (pages 48–51), in *Understanding Geography*. Answer Questions 1–17 in your History Journal. Question 10 challenges you to fill in a blank map of the United States. You may use the Fifty States sheet and the State Capitals sheet to practice identifying the states and capitals.

If you have time, you may want to answer the Skill Builder Questions on page 51. After you have finished, you should compare your answers with the ones in the Learning Coach Guide.

You may want to practice identifying states and capitals by going online to take the U.S. State Capitals Quiz or complete the U.S. Map Puzzle. Links to these sites are located in Lesson Resources, under Links.

Read On

Read Chapter 29, pages 150–153. Be prepared to:

- Compare the official cause of the Mexican War with other reasons why people wanted to fight.
- Describe the controversy over the war and list significant Americans who opposed the war.
- Identify on a map the territory gained by the United States as a result of the war.

ASSESS

Lesson Assessment: More and More States (*Online*)

Answer the online geography questions for this assessment. Your assessment will be scored by the computer.

Name _____   Date _____

Fifty States

Write the number of the state on the map next to its name below.

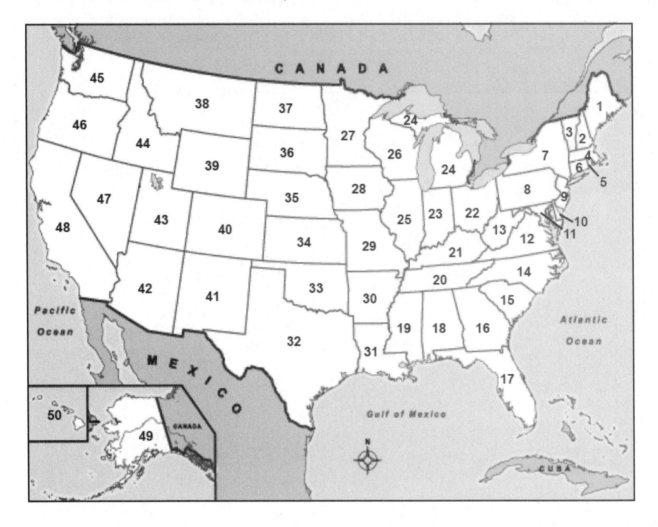

_____ Alabama	_____ Hawaii	_____ Massachusetts	_____ New Hampshire	_____ South Dakota
_____ Alaska	_____ Idaho	_____ Michigan	_____ New Jersey	_____ Tennessee
_____ Arizona	_____ Illinois	_____ Minnesota	_____ New Mexico	_____ Texas
_____ Arkansas	_____ Indiana	_____ Mississippi	_____ New York	_____ Utah
_____ California	_____ Iowa	_____ Missouri	_____ Ohio	_____ Vermont
_____ Colorado	_____ Kansas	_____ Montana	_____ Oklahoma	_____ Virginia
_____ Connecticut	_____ Kentucky	_____ North Carolina	_____ Oregon	_____ Washington
_____ Delaware	_____ Louisiana	_____ North Dakota	_____ Pennsylvania	_____ West Virginia
_____ Florida	_____ Maine	_____ Nebraska	_____ Rhode Island	_____ Wisconsin
_____ Georgia	_____ Maryland	_____ Nevada	_____ South Carolina	_____ Wyoming

Name _____   Date _____

State Capitals

Write the abbreviation of the state on the map next to its capital below.

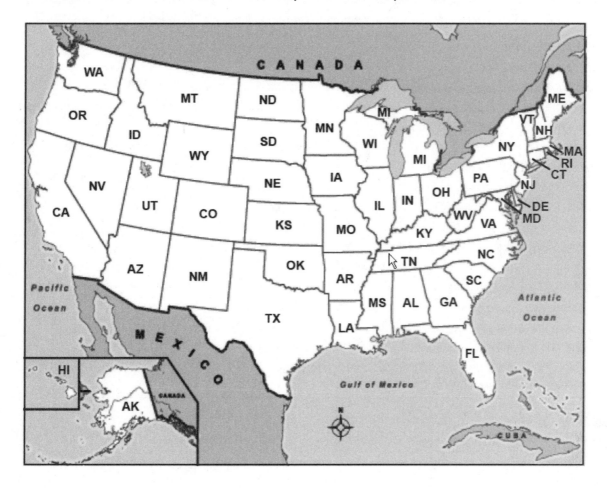

_____ Albany   _____ Charleston   _____ Hartford   _____ Madison   _____ Richmond

_____ Annapolis   _____ Cheyenne   _____ Helena   _____ Montgomery   _____ Sacramento

_____ Atlanta   _____ Columbia   _____ Honolulu   _____ Montpelier   _____ Salem

_____ Augusta   _____ Columbus   _____ Indianapolis   _____ Nashville   _____ Salt Lake City

_____ Austin   _____ Concord   _____ Jackson   _____ Oklahoma City   _____ Santa Fe

_____ Baton Rouge   _____ Denver   _____ Jefferson City   _____ Olympia   _____ Springfield

_____ Bismarck   _____ Des Moines   _____ Juneau   _____ Phoenix   _____ St. Paul

_____ Boise   _____ Dover   _____ Lansing   _____ Pierre   _____ Tallahassee

_____ Boston   _____ Frankfort   _____ Lincoln   _____ Providence   _____ Topeka

_____ Carson City   _____ Harrisburg   _____ Little Rock   _____ Raleigh   _____ Trenton

Student Guide
Lesson 10: The Mexican War

Border disputes between Texas and Mexico had the United States and Mexico itching for war. Although many people protested it, they could not stop the Mexican War. The United States defeated Mexico. The result was new territory not only for Texas but also for the country, extending all the way to the Pacific Ocean.

Lesson Objectives
- Demonstrate knowledge gained in previous lessons.
- Describe the causes of the Mexican War, including border disputes and manifest destiny.
- Describe the controversy over the war and list significant Americans who opposed the war, including Henry David Thoreau and Abraham Lincoln.
- Identify on a map the territory the United States gained as a result of the Mexican War and other territory gained by 1853.
- Define *Manifest Destiny*.
- Describe the population of California in 1840 as Native Americans, Spanish-speaking settlers, missionaries, and rancheros.
- Explain why President Polk and other Americans wanted to gain control of California, including its fertile farmlands, excellent harbors, and the idea of Manifest Destiny.
- Identify Stephen Austin as the leader of American settlers in Texas, Santa Anna as the Mexican dictator, and Sam Houston as the first president of the Republic of Texas.
- Explain the causes of the conflicts between Mexicans and anglo settlers, including the settlers' violations of settlement agreements and Santa Anna's violation of the Mexican Constitution.
- Explain how Texas became an independent country and then a state in the United States.

PREPARE

Approximate lesson time is 60 minutes.

Materials

For the Student

War Fever

A History of US (Concise Edition), Volume B (1790-1877) by Joy Hakim

map, U.S.

History Journal

LEARN
Activity 1: "To The Halls of Montezuma" (Offline)
Check Your Reading (Chapter 29, pages 150–153)

Complete the War Fever sheet. Check your answers with an adult.

Assessment

- Go online and review the flash cards.
- You will be assessed on your ability to answer all the questions on the flash cards correctly.
- You may review the flash cards as many times as you like. Click Shuffle to randomly present the cards.
- If you have difficulty with a question, review the material related to the question in your book or your History Journal.
- Some questions ask you to identify two or three items, even though the answers list more than three correct responses. You only need to know the number of items that you are asked in the question.
- When you think you can answer all the questions correctly, show an adult that you can answer each question correctly before you reveal the answer.

Optional: Beyond the Lesson

A political cartoon shows a point of view on a topic and usually uses symbolism: for example, Uncle Sam is often shown as representing the government, and an eagle as representing the country. Draw a political cartoon expressing a view of the Mexican War, either from the view of a supporter of Manifest Destiny or from the view of an antiwar protester. Show the cartoon to an adult and discuss its meaning.

ASSESS

Mid-Unit Assessment: Americans Take New Land, Part 1 *(Online)*
Complete the computer-scored portion of the Mid-Unit Assessment. When you have finished, complete the teacher-scored portion of the assessment and submit it to your teacher.

Mid-Unit Assessment: Americans Take New Land, Part 2 *(Offline)*
Complete the teacher-scored portion of the Mid-Unit Assessment and submit it to your teacher.

Name _____   Date _____

War Fever

Often people or countries want to go to war and are looking for an excuse to start one.

1. What event triggered the Mexican War? _____

    _____

2. What are three reasons that people in the United States had for wanting to go to war with Mexico?

    _____

    _____

    _____

While most Americans supported the war, many did not. The following people and groups opposed the war. Identify each person or group and what it did to oppose the war in Mexico. The first one is done for you.

3. Frederick Douglass: Frederick Douglass was an abolitionist. He wrote against the war.

4. Henry David Thoreau: _____

    _____

5. Congregationalists, Quakers, and Unitarians: _____

    _____

6. Abraham Lincoln: _____

    _____

7. The House of Representatives: _____

    _____

Use the map in Chapter 29 and a map of the present-day United States to answer the following questions.

8. List the states that are part of the territory the United States gained as a result of the Mexican War (the Mexican Cession):

_____   _____   _____

_____   _____   _____

_____

9. When was the Oregon Territory acquired by the United States? _____

10. List the states that made up the Oregon Territory:

_____   _____   _____

_____   _____

11. What two states were created from territory acquired by the United States after 1853?

_____   _____

Student Guide
Lesson 11: Rushing for Gold

The United States had just won the California territory from Mexico when gold was discovered there. So many people from all around the world scrambled to California to hunt for gold that within two years it was admitted to the Union as the 31st state. People and information were on the move in the mid-1800s, sped along by faster clipper ships, the Pony Express, and the telegraph.

Lesson Objectives

- Define *Gold Rush, forty-niner, Pony Express,* and *telegraph.*
- Explain why people wanted to go to California after 1848 and how they could get there and communicate.
- Recognize the law of supply and demand in effect in California in terms of merchants such as Levi Strauss.
- Describe the results of immigration to California, including statehood and the rise of nativism.

PREPARE

Approximate lesson time is 60 minutes.

Materials

For the Student

Miners, Merchants, Messages, and Movement

A History of US (Concise Edition), Volume B (1790-1877) by Joy Hakim

History Journal

LEARN
Activity 1: California: Gold, Goods, and Getting There *(Offline)*
Read

Read Chapter 30, pages 154–161, and Chapter 31, pages 162–166. Complete the Miners, Merchants, Messages, and Movement sheet as you read. Check your answers with an adult.

Optional: Beyond the Lesson

If you are interested, go online to visit websites about the California Gold Rush and the Pony Express.

Activity 2. Optional: Ponies, Gold, and Clipper Ships *(Online)*

Name _____ Date _____

Miners, Merchants, Messengers, and Movement

1. In the mid-1800s most Americans lived east of the Mississippi. California was very

   far away. When gold was discovered there in _____, people began
   heading west in large numbers by land and by sea. People going to California to look for

   gold were called _____ - _____ . What was the best
   way to get there? To figure it out, fill in the chart below. One section has already been
   filled in for you for each route.

Route	Advantages	Disadvantages
	• A fast route • The easiest route • The safest route	
By sea to Panama, by land to the Pacific Ocean, and then by sea again		
		• The hardest route • The slowest route • Danger of Indian attack • Danger of dying in the desert heat • Danger of freezing or starving in the mountains in winter

2. There wasn't much in California in 1848. No one was prepared for the tens of thousands
   of people who arrived. All of them had needs, or demands, but there wasn't much there.
   When there is less of something that everyone needs, it will cost more. This is part of the

   economic law called _____ and _____ .

3. Most forty-niners never got rich from the California gold rush. What group of people did prosper? _____

4. One merchant got rich making heavy-duty pants from canvas for miners and farmers. His name was _____. His company still exists today. Those pants are called _____.

5. When gold was discovered, people from all over the world rushed to California. They came from Europe, Mexico, South America, and Asia. Who came from Asia in large numbers? _____

6. _____ was a belief that only white Anglo-Saxon Protestants were "real" Americans and that others weren't welcome. Nativists had a political party called the _____ Party, but many called it the _____ Party.

7. Why was California able to become a state quickly, while other western territories took longer to attain statehood? _____

_____

_____

8. California is a long way from the eastern United States. In the mid-1800s, getting messages and mail to California took a long time. Three things helped speed communication. Fill in the blanks below. Some information has been provided for you.

Method of Communication	What it Was or How It Worked	Information Type/Volume/Cost/Time
		• Could carry people, mail, and packages • Slowest of the new methods • Fairly expensive
Pony Express		
	Wires that transmitted coded electric messages	

Student Guide
Lesson 12: Unit Review

You have finished the unit! It's time to review what you've learned. You will take the Unit Assessment in the next lesson.

Lesson Objectives

- Review important knowledge and skills taught in this unit.

PREPARE

Approximate lesson time is 60 minutes.

Materials

For the Student

A History of US (Concise Edition), Volume B (1790-1877) by Joy Hakim

History Journal

LEARN
Activity 1: A Look Back *(Offline)*
History Journal Review

Review what you've learned in this unit by going through your History Journal. You should:

- Look at activity sheets you've completed for this unit.
- Review unit vocabulary words.
- Read through any writing assignments you did during the unit.
- Review the assessments you took.

Don't rush through; take your time. Your History Journal is a great resource for a unit review.

Online Review

Review the following online:

- The Big Picture
- Flash Cards
- Time Line

Student Guide
Lesson 13: Unit Assessment

You've finished this unit! Take the Unit Assessment.

Lesson Objectives

- Identify Joseph Smith, Brigham Young, and the Mormons.
- Define *Manifest Destiny*.
- Describe the population of California in 1840 as Native Americans, Spanish-speaking settlers, missionaries, and rancheros.
- Identify Stephen Austin as the leader of American settlers in Texas, Santa Anna as the Mexican dictator, and Sam Houston as the first president of the Republic of Texas.
- Describe the causes of the Mexican War, including border disputes and manifest destiny.
- Describe the controversy over the war and list significant Americans who opposed the war, including Henry David Thoreau and Abraham Lincoln.
- Identify on a map the territory the United States gained as a result of the Mexican War and other territory gained by 1853.
- Define *Gold Rush, forty-niner, Pony Express,* and *telegraph*.
- Explain why people wanted to go to California after 1848 and how they could get there and communicate.
- Recognize the law of supply and demand in effect in California in terms of merchants such as Levi Strauss.
- Describe the results of immigration to California, including statehood and the rise of nativism.
- Identify Sequoyah as the Cherokee who invented a written form of the Cherokee language.
- Describe the Indian Removal Act and the economic reasons for it.
- Define *Trail of Tears*.
- Describe the significance of *Worcester v. Georgia* and explain why this Supreme Court ruling was not enforced.
- Describe the "push" and "pull" factors that caused people to leave their home countries and migrate to the United States, including social, political, and economic problems at home and opportunities in the United States.
- Identify the reasons why people chose to go west, including the opportunity to start a new life and to acquire land.
- Define *prairie schooner, pioneer,* and *wagon train*.

PREPARE

Approximate lesson time is 60 minutes.

383

ASSESS

Unit Assessment: Americans Take New Land, Part 1 *(Online)*

Complete the computer-scored portion of the Unit Assessment. When you have finished, complete the teacher-scored portion of the assessment and submit it to your teacher.

Unit Assessment: Americans Take New Land, Part 2 *(Offline)*

Complete the teacher-scored portion of the Unit Assessment and submit it to your teacher.

Student Guide
Lesson 1: Reforming a Nation

Between 1800 and 1850, the United States developed an identity all its own. Artists and writers no longer copied European styles and themes. They painted and wrote in American ways about the American people, their land, and their ideas. At the same time, religious revivals and the confidence gained in the War of 1812 encouraged social and educational reform.

As the nation was changing and growing, education was changing as well. Jefferson and Washington said America needed educated voters. Some passionate reformers wanted to give women and black Americans the opportunity to go to college. Others wanted to standardize American textbooks and reform teacher training. This time period also saw the beginning of the modern struggle for women's rights. There were many obstacles to overcome, including the general belief that women were less intelligent because their brains were smaller than men's. Some courageous women didn't agree with that belief, so they set out to change it.

Lesson Objectives

- Give examples of early nineteenth-century education reforms, including public schools, women's colleges, and new books, and the reasons for these reforms, including the need for educated voters.
- Describe the second Great Awakening and its influence on reform movements.
- Identify Sarah and Angelina Grimké as abolitionists and Elizabeth Blackwell as the first woman to attend medical school in the United States.
- Describe women's lives in the United States in the 1800s.

PREPARE

Approximate lesson time is 60 minutes.

Materials

For the Student

    Leaders of Change

    A History of US (Concise Edition), Volume B (1790-1877) by Joy Hakim

    History Journal

LEARN
Activity 1: Education Reform and Women's Rights (Offline)
Read

Read Chapter 32, pages 167–174. After reading the selection, discuss the following questions with an adult.

1. Why did the nation's Founders want everyone to be educated?
2. What was the second Great Awakening?
3. What was the link between the second Great Awakening and the reform movements of the mid-1800s?
4. What were McGuffey Readers and why were they important?
5. Discuss the statement "It's a man's world." In what ways did this saying accurately describe the United States during the years 1800–1860?

Use What You Know

The education reformers of the mid-1800s had quite an influence on American education. Have you ever seen an American dictionary? Before Noah Webster wrote one, it didn't exist. Do American colleges allow women to attend? Before reformers like Sarah Pierce and Mary Lyon, they didn't.

Now that you know some of the challenges women faced in the 1800s, can you imagine standing up to them and overcoming them? Several brave women did just that. They wanted to be considered equal to men, so they did something about it.

Use the information in Chapter 32 to complete the Leaders of Change sheet. Review your answers with an adult.

Now pick one of the reformers mentioned in Chapter 32. Go online to learn more about this reformer. Write a description of this person in your History Journal. You may use a list or a paragraph. If you like, you may also draw a sketch of the person.

Be sure to include:

- The person's background
- What the person did
- The importance of the person's actions on society

Name _____   Date _____

Leaders of Change

Use the chart below to list the names of the reformers mentioned in Chapter 32. For each reformer, list the area of reform and accomplishments.

Reformer	Area of Reform/Accomplishments

Student Guide
Lesson 2: Achieving Their Potential

"All men and women are created equal," stated the Seneca Falls Declaration—the document that started the women's rights movement in the mid-1800s. Many women devoted their lives to women's equality, to ending slavery, and to the rights of prisoners and the mentally ill. Powerful speakers like Susan B. Anthony and Sojourner Truth shook people up and left a deep imprint on American history.

Lesson Objectives

- Demonstrate knowledge gained in previous lessons.
- Describe the accomplishments and reform goals of two of the following: Elizabeth Cady Stanton, Dorothea Dix, Amelia Bloomer, Susan B. Anthony, and Sojourner Truth.
- Define *abolition* and *Seneca Falls Declaration*.
- Give examples of early nineteenth-century education reforms, including public schools, women's colleges, and new books, and the reasons for these reforms, including the need for educated voters.
- Describe women's lives in the United States in the 1800s.
- Describe the Puritan values that influenced people in the 1800s.

PREPARE

Approximate lesson time is 60 minutes.

Materials

For the Student

- A Movement Is Born
- Leaders of Change: Women's Rights

A History of US (Concise Edition), Volume B (1790-1877) by Joy Hakim

History Journal

LEARN
Activity 1: All Men and Women Are Created Equal *(Offline)*
Read

Read Chapter 33, pages 175–179. Then complete the A Movement Is Born sheet. Review your answers with an adult.

Use What You Know

For the first time, women in the United States were organizing to promote their rights. They overcame ridicule and fear to try to make their country a better place for women to live. Many women not only fought for their own rights but also fought for abolition, temperance, prison reform, and children's rights. They really wanted to make a difference in the world.

On the Leaders of Change: Women's Rights chart, list the name, area of reform, and accomplishments of each of the women below. Review your completed chart with an adult.

- Elizabeth Cady Stanton
- Lucretia Mott
- Dorothea Dix
- Amelia Bloomer
- Susan B. Anthony
- Sojourner Truth

Imagine that you are alive in the year 1850. Will you fight for abolition, women's rights, children's rights, temperance, or the rights of disabled and mentally ill people? Which of these causes is most important to you? Explain your choice in your History Journal.

ASSESS

Mid-Unit Assessment: Reform and Reflection, Part 1 *(Online)*

Complete the computer-scored portion of the Mid-Unit Assessment. When you have finished, complete the teacher-scored portion of the assessment and submit it to your teacher.

Mid-Unit Assessment: Reform and Reflection, Part 2 *(Offline)*

Complete the teacher-scored portion of the Mid-Unit Assessment and submit it to your teacher.

Name _____   Date _____

A Movement Is Born

Read each quote before answering the questions below.

> *"No words could express our astonishment on finding, a few days afterward, that what seemed to us so timely, so rational, and so sacred, should be a subject for sarcasm and ridicule to the entire press of the nation."*
>
> — Elizabeth Stanton

1. Complete the first line of the Seneca Falls Declaration: "We hold these truths to be self-evident;_____.

2. How did the national press respond to the Seneca Falls Declaration? _____

   _____

> *"Ain't I a woman? Look at me. Look at my arm. I have ploughed and planted and gathered into barns, and no man could head me! And ain't I a woman? I could work as much and eat as much as a man—when I could get it—and bear the lash as well! And ain't I a woman?"*
>
> — Sojourner _____

3. Who made this speech? Sojourner _____

4. A former slave and young mother, she managed to get back one of her children who had been sold into slavery. How did she do it? _____

   _____

5. After a religious rebirth, what did she do for the next 40 years of her life? _____

   _____

Adapted from *A History of US*

Name _____   Date _____

Leaders of Change: Women's Rights

Use the chart below to list the names of the reformers mentioned in Chapter 33. For each reformer, list the area of reform and accomplishments.

Susan B. Anthony

Reformer	Area of Reform/Accomplishments

Student Guide
Lesson 3: Writing in America

The men and women who founded American literature grew up in the United States as citizens. Therefore, they thought and wrote about national achievements, not colonial achievements. They celebrated events in the United States and the people who made them happen. They turned away from Europe and looked at their own nation with pride. One American writer—Henry David Thoreau—clearly showed the individualism and self-honesty that characterized emerging American literature. His ideas on nonviolent civil disobedience greatly influenced the thinking and actions of many great leaders who followed him.

Lesson Objectives

- Describe the Puritan values that influenced people in the 1800s.
- Identify at least two of the following American writers of the early nineteenth century and their contributions to American literature: Emerson, Thoreau, Alcott, and Longfellow.
- Use the Internet to gain information on one writer.
- Identify Henry David Thoreau as the author of *Civil Disobedience,* and Mohandas Gandhi and Martin Luther King, Jr. as political leaders influenced by this work.

PREPARE

Approximate lesson time is 60 minutes.

Materials

For the Student

🖥 American Writers

A History of US (Concise Edition), Volume B (1790-1877) by Joy Hakim

History Journal

LEARN
Activity 1: The Original American Writers *(Offline)*
Read

Read Chapter 34, pages 180–183. As you read, complete the American Writers sheet.

Discuss

Board our time capsule for a trip to August 1831. Read the prompt and respond to it aloud by answering the questions. Discuss your response.

Prompt: Imagine you are standing in the middle of a crowd at Harvard University. A writer named Ralph Waldo Emerson steps forward to deliver a speech. He says, "We [Americans] will walk on our own feet; we will work with our own hands; we will speak our own minds."

Questions:

1. How would you react to Emerson and his statement?
2. How do Emerson's words express the spirit of the years 1800–1860?

Use What You Know

Review the authors and their contributions by viewing the flash cards online. Then research one writer from this chapter by going to the first screen of the lesson, opening the Lesson Resources tab, and going to Links. You may also use the links on the Beyond the Lesson screen. Select one or more links to read or listen to a selection from the author's works. Then describe in your History Journal how this writer's life and writing reflect the ideas of the new America.

Optional: Beyond the Lesson

To learn more about the writers of Concord, Massachusetts, you can continue exploring the websites:

- The Writers of Concord, Massachusetts
- "Concord Hymn," Ralph Waldo Emerson (text and video reading)
- *Nature,* Chapter 1, Ralph Waldo Emerson
- "A Psalm of Life," Henry Wadsworth Longfellow (text and video reading)
- Louisa May Alcott (biographical information)
- Francis Parkman, author of *The Oregon Trail*
- *The Oregon Trail* (full text and illustrations), Francis Parkman
- Louisa May Alcott

Activity 2: Early American Writers (Online)

Name _____ Date _____

American Writers

1. Puritan values influenced Americans in the 1800s. These values included:

   • A love of _____

   • _____

   • Sense of _____

2. As you read the chapter, complete the following chart.

Writer	Subject or Topic of Writing/Works
Ralph Waldo Emerson	
Louisa May Alcott	
Henry Wadsworth Longfellow	
Henry David Thoreau	

3. Which two political leaders were influenced by Thoreau's *Civil Disobedience*?

Student Guide
Lesson 4: (Optional) Write Every Time

For inspiration, writers of the mid-1800s turned to the growing diversity of the American experience.

Lesson Objectives

- Identify at least three of the following American writers of the mid-1800s and their contributions to American literature: Melville, Poe, Irving, Whitman, Emerson.
- Write a paragraph expressing a reaction to the work of an American author.

PREPARE

Approximate lesson time is 60 minutes.

Materials

For the Student

I Hear America Singing

A History of US (Concise Edition), Volume B (1790-1877) by Joy Hakim

History Journal

LEARN
Activity 1. Optional: New American Writers (Offline)
Read

Read Chapter 35, pages 184–187.

Use What You Know

You will respond to a reading of the Walt Whitman poem "I Hear America Singing." Read on your own, or listen online to, a recording of this poem. Then complete the I Hear America Singing sheet.

In your History Journal, answer the question, "Is America still singing?" What do you hear when you think about America singing today?

Name _____   Date _____

I Hear America Singing

I Hear America Singing by Walt Whitman

I hear America singing, the varied carols I hear,
Those of mechanics, each one singing his as it should be blithe and strong,
The carpenter singing his as he measures his plank or beam,
The mason singing his as he makes ready for work, or leaves off work,
The boatman singing what belongs to him in his boat, the deckhand singing on the steamboat deck,
The shoemaker singing as he sits on his bench, the hatter singing as he stands,
The wood-cutter's song, the ploughboy's on his way in the morning, or at noon intermission or at sundown,
The delicious singing of the mother, or of the young wife at work, or of the girl sewing or washing,
Each singing what belongs to him or her and to none else,
The day what belongs to the day—at night the party of young fellows, robust, friendly,
Singing with open mouths their strong melodious songs.

Write a paragraph in your History Journal expressing your reaction to this poem. Use the following questions to help form your response:

- After reading Whitman's poem, what can you tell about the jobs of Americans in Whitman's time?

- Why are they singing?

- What does this poem say about Americans?

Student Guide
Lesson 5: Art in America

The wilderness and the faces of America became the subject of painters such as John James Audubon, Charles Willson Peale, and George Catlin.

Lesson Objectives
- Identify Audubon and Catlin as two prominent American artists of the early and mid-1800s.
- Describe the contributions of the artists of the early and mid-1800s to American culture.
- Describe how selected works of American art from 1800 to 1850 express the American experience.

PREPARE

Approximate lesson time is 60 minutes.

Materials
For the Student

📖 Who? What? When? Where? Why? How?

A History of US (Concise Edition), Volume B (1790-1877) by Joy Hakim

History Journal

LEARN
Activity 1: New American Painters (Offline)
Read

Read Chapter 36, pages 188–192. Complete the Who? What? When? Where? Why? How? sheet as you read. Review your answers with an adult when you have finished.

Use What You Know

View examples of the painters' works in the Art Gallery online. Using the gallery and the images in the textbook, write a brief response in your History Journal stating how each artist demonstrates his Americanism through his painting. You may reflect on an individual piece or find a theme that connects all the works by a single artist.

Optional: Beyond the Lesson

Visit several websites to learn more about the artists of the American Renaissance.

Activity 2. Optional: Artists of the American Renaissance (Online)

Name _____ Date _____

Who? What? When? Where? Why? How?

1. **WHO?** This self-described "American woodsman" devoted his life to painting birds in the Mississippi Valley. Who was he? _____

2. **WHERE?** He settled in _____ and took up drawing seriously.

3. **WHY?** Why was he in such a hurry to document American birds and animals?

   _____

   _____

4. **WHO?** What important person did Catlin talk to in St. Louis before starting out on his expedition up the Missouri River? _____

5. **WHEN?** George Catlin made his first journey up the Missouri River in _____.

6. **WHAT?** George Catlin painted scenes that showed traditional Indian life including

   _____

7. **HOW?** George Catlin painted Indians with honesty and _____.

8. **WHY?** Why are his portraits valuable to us today? _____

   _____

Student Guide
Lesson 6: (Optional) Made in America

During the years following the War of 1812, Americans wanted their nation to be independent from the rest of the world. New means of transportation increased settlement and travel and helped make the United States economically independent. Educators, artists, writers, and reformers devoted their efforts to American needs and ideas. Their work helped make the United States culturally as well as politically independent from Europe.

Lesson Objectives

- Identify major elements in the development of American culture in the first half of the 19th century, including achievements in reform, literature, and art.
- Explain ways in which the nation expressed its character during the first half of the 19th century.

PREPARE

Approximate lesson time is 60 minutes.

Materials

For the Student

American Renaissance: Reform and Reflection

A History of US (Concise Edition), Volume B (1790-1877) by Joy Hakim

History Journal

LEARN
Activity 1. Optional: An American Renaissance *(Offline)*
Looking Back

Using your textbook and History Journal for reference, complete the American Renaissance: Reform and Reflection sheet. To complete the concept map you should:

- Identify the most important ideas or events in each category of cultural development.
- Identify the people responsible for change in each category.

Name _____   Date _____

American Renaissance: Reform and Reflection

Using what you have learned in this unit, complete the chart below. Identify people and events in each category to help you organize your information and remember some of the things that were going on.

People	Category	Ideas and Events
	ART	
	LITERATURE	
	WOMEN'S RIGHTS	
	EDUCATION REFORM A B C	
	ABOLITION	

Student Guide
Lesson 7: Unit Review

You have finished the Unit 11, Reform and Reflection. It's time to review what you've learned. You will take the Unit Assessment in the next lesson.

Lesson Objectives

- Review the goals, achievements and difficulties of major reform movements before 1860.
- Identify individuals who helped expand the ideals of democracy.
- Review examples of nationalism in American literature and art of the early 19th century.

PREPARE

Approximate lesson time is 60 minutes.

Materials

For the Student

- Outline Map of the United States

A History of US (Concise Edition), Volume B (1790-1877) by Joy Hakim

History Journal

LEARN
Activity 1: A Look Back *(Offline)*
History Journal Review

Review what you've learned in this unit by going through your History Journal. You should:

- Review activity sheets you've completed for this unit.
- Review unit vocabulary words.
- Read through any writing assignments you completed during the unit.
- Review the assessments you took.

Don't rush through; take your time. Your History Journal is a great resource for a unit review.

Online Review

Review the following online:

- The Big Picture
- Flash Cards
- Time Line

This review might refer to topics presented in optional lessons in this unit.

Fifty States

How many states can you name today? Print the Outline Map of the United States and see. You can check your work by comparing it to the political map of the United States in the book's atlas.

The United States

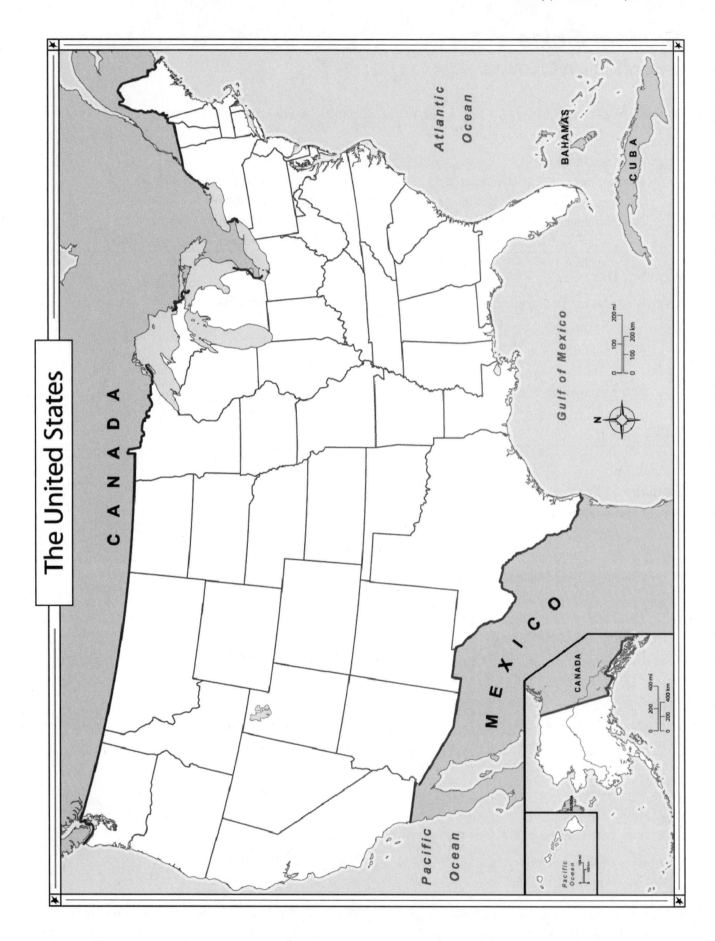

CANADA

Atlantic Ocean

BAHAMAS

CUBA

Gulf of Mexico

MEXICO

Pacific Ocean

CANADA

Pacific Ocean

Student Guide
Lesson 8: Unit Assessment

You've finished this unit! Now take the Unit Assessment, and then read on for the next lesson.

Lesson Objectives

- Demonstrate mastery of important knowledge and skills in this unit.
- Give examples of early nineteenth-century education reforms, including public schools, women's colleges, and new books, and the reasons for these reforms, including the need for educated voters.
- Describe the second Great Awakening and its influence on reform movements.
- Identify Sarah and Angelina Grimké as abolitionists and Elizabeth Blackwell as the first woman to attend medical school in the United States.
- Describe women's lives in the United States in the 1800s.
- Describe the accomplishments and reform goals of two of the following: Elizabeth Cady Stanton, Dorothea Dix, Amelia Bloomer, Susan B. Anthony, and Sojourner Truth.
- Define *abolition* and *Seneca Falls Declaration*.
- Describe the Puritan values that influenced people in the 1800s.
- Define *civil disobedience*.

PREPARE

Approximate lesson time is 60 minutes.

Materials

For the Student

A History of US (Concise Edition), Volume B (1790-1877) by Joy Hakim

History Journal

ASSESS

Unit Assessment: Reform and Reflection, Part 1 *(Online)*

Complete the computer-scored portion of the Unit Assessment. When you have finished, complete the teacher-scored portion of the assessment and submit it to your teacher.

Unit Assessment: Reform and Reflection, Part 2 *(Offline)*

Complete the teacher-scored portion of the Unit Assessment and submit it to your teacher.

LEARN
Activity 1: Chapters 37 and 38 *(Offline)*
Read On

As you know, 1800 to 1860 was an incredible time of accomplishment and growth for the United States. But it was also a time of great struggle as the ideas of America were challenged. You will read about some of the things that challenged our nation and almost tore it apart.

Read Chapter 37, pages 194–197, and Chapter 38, pages 198–202. Be prepared to explain why slavery was a paradox in the United States.

Vocabulary

Write a brief definition for the following term in your History Journal—*paradox.*

Student Guide
Lesson 1: Slavery in a Free Country

Four million people were held as slaves in a country built on the principle that "all men are created equal." And the number of slaves kept increasing as cotton became more and more important. Many people spoke out against the atrocities of slavery but no one seemed to know a way to make it end.

The horror of slavery existed in a country built on the principle that "all men are created equal." And the number of slaves continued to grow as cotton became more and more important. Many people spoke out against the atrocities of slavery, but no one seemed to know how to end it.

Lesson Objectives

- Define *paradox* and explain why slavery was a paradox in the United States, even though slavery had existed for thousands of years in some parts of the world.
- Describe the colonization movement and explain that most blacks did not want to migrate to Africa because they were Americans.
- Give examples of the rights denied to blacks, including personal freedom and political rights.
- Discuss ways in which individuals experienced slavery and fought slavery, and your reactions to them.

PREPARE

Approximate lesson time is 60 minutes.

Materials

For the Student

Reaction and Response

A History of US (Concise Edition), Volume B (1790-1877) by Joy Hakim

History Journal

LEARN
Activity 1: Freedom vs. Slavery *(Offline)*

Instructions
Check Your Reading (Chapter 37, pages 194–197, and Chapter 38, pages 198–202)

Review Chapter 37 by answering the following questions in your History Journal. Ask an adult to check your answers.

1. Slavery had existed around the world for thousands of years. Why does the author call it a paradox in the United States?
2. Why did some well-meaning people start a colonization movement to send blacks to Africa?
3. Why didn't most American blacks want to go to Africa?

Use What You Know

Complete the Reaction and Response sheet.

Read On

The cotton gin turned slavery into the foundation of a new empire in the South. The empire stretched all the way from the Atlantic beyond the Mississippi River into Texas.

Read Chapter 39, pages 203–205. Be prepared to discuss how the invention of the cotton gin led to an increase in slavery.

Name _____   Date _____

Reaction and Response

Refer to Chapter 38 to fill in the chart.

Name	What Happened?	Your reaction (Sad? Angry? Surprised? Inspired? Other reaction?)
Elizabeth Freeman		
Quock Walker		
Paul Cuffe		
James Forten		
Lemuel Haynes		
Richard Allen		

Write two or three sentences to summarize your views of slavery and the African Americans who worked to prove themselves and fight slavery.

_____

_____

_____

_____

_____

Student Guide
Lesson 2: Can a Compromise Work?

King Cotton took control of the South. As settlers moved west and planted cotton, the demand for slaves increased. Although the slave trade had officially ended in 1808, the South continued to rely on slaves to work the fields. At the same time, the North grew more industrialized. Differences between the North and the South grew deeper and the two regions drifted apart.

Lesson Objectives

- Explain with examples the terms *New South* and *Old South* and the role of the cotton gin in transforming them.
- Identify the Missouri Compromise as the 1820 law that maintained the political balance in the Senate and forbade slavery in most of the Lousiana Purchase territory.
- Give examples of the growing differences between North and South after 1820, including changes in population, economy, and political power.
- Identify William Lloyd Garrison as an abolitionist leader.

PREPARE

Approximate lesson time is 60 minutes.

Materials

For the Student

Guided Reading: Chapter 40

A History of US (Concise Edition), Volume B (1790-1877) by Joy Hakim

History Journal

LEARN
Activity 1: Slavery Compromise *(Offline)*
Instructions
Check Your Reading (Chapter 39, pages 203–205)

Eli Whitney invented the cotton gin in 1793. This machine removed seeds quickly and cheaply from a type of cotton called short-staple cotton.

Answer the following question in your History Journal: How did the invention of the cotton gin help create a New South?

Use the graphs of Slavery in the United States, 1800–1860, to answer the following questions in your History Journal:

1. Between what years was the growth of slavery the greatest—1800 to 1820, 1820 to 1840, or 1840 to 1860?
2. By 1860, about how many slaves were there in the United States?
3. In 1860, approximately what percentage (for example, one-fourth, one-half, three-fourths, etc.) of Southerners did not own any slaves?

Read

Complete the Guided Reading: Chapter 40 sheet as you read Chapter 40, pages 206–212.

Name _____ Date _____

Guided Reading: Chapter 40

Answer the following questions as you read Chapter 40.

1. Ben Franklin wrote in a letter that "a disposition to abolish slavery prevails in North America." What did Franklin mean by this statement? In what year did he write this? Was this before or after the American Revolution?

   _____

   _____

2. Why did an illegal slave trade begin after the official African slave trade ended in 1808?

   _____

3. Why did Southern political leaders begin blaming the North for their economic problems?

   _____

   _____

4. Describe the differences between the North and the South in the first half of the nineteenth century. (From the sidebar titled "Two Separate Nations?")

   _____

   _____

   _____

5. The North and South each had the same number of senators in the U.S. Congress. Now Missouri wanted to enter the Union as a slave state. How would this affect the North?

   _____

6. How did the Missouri Compromise keep the peace between the North and the South?

   _____

   _____

7. The Missouri Compromise included a provision that said most of the territory from the

   _____ _____ would remain free.

Use the map of the Missouri Compromise, 1820, to answer questions 8–10.

8. Which two states were admitted into the Union as part of the Missouri Compromise?

_____

9. In 1820, was most of the territory (land not admitted as states) in the United States free or slave? _____

10. What artificial boundary separated parts of the North from parts of the South in the eastern part of the country? _____

11. Did all Southerners agree with slavery? Did all Northerners want to abolish it? Explain your answers.

_____

_____

_____

12. Define secede. _____

13. What did William Lloyd Garrison create to give a voice to abolitionists?

_____

Student Guide
Lesson 3: Frederick Douglass: A Voice Against Slavery

Frederick Douglass bravely spoke of his own experiences as a slave and worked for human rights for all oppressed people.

Lesson Objectives

- Summarize the major hardships the young Frederick Douglass faced and the causes he worked for including abolition, voting rights for blacks and women, fair treatment for Chinese and Indians, and education.
- Use the Internet to gain information on Frederick Douglass.

PREPARE

Approximate lesson time is 60 minutes.

Materials

For the Student

An Interview with Frederick Douglass

A History of US (Concise Edition), Volume B (1790-1877) by Joy Hakim

History Journal

LEARN
Activity 1: Speaking Against Slavery *(Offline)*
Read

Read Chapter 41, pages 213–216. Then complete the An Interview with Frederick Douglass sheet.

Use What You Know

- Visit the American Visionaries: Frederick Douglass website to read more about Frederick Douglass and his achievements.
- Use what you have learned to write a speech honoring Douglass and his many achievements.

Name _____   Date _____

An Interview with Frederick Douglass

Imagine you are Frederick Douglass. You are being interviewed. Try to answer the following questions.

1. Mr. Douglass, in your book you speak of your childhood. Tell our readers, if you would, about your mother.

_____

_____

_____

_____

2. It is illegal to teach slaves to read. How did you learn?

_____

_____

_____

3. You have been touring the nation speaking for the Massachusetts Anti-Slavery Society.

Are there other issues that you speak out on? _____

_____

_____

Thinking Cap Question!
What is the machine in this picture?
What are the men doing to it? Why?

Adapted from *A History of US*

Student Guide
Lesson 4: Clay, Calhoun, and Webster Speak Out

As the conflict over slavery drove a wedge between sections of the nation, three great orators held sway in Congress. One spoke for a divided West, one for the North, and one for the South.

The future of slavery and the nation rested on this question: which was more powerful—federal or state law? The debate between the North and South raged as both sides looked to the West to tip the balance of power.

Lesson Objectives
- Identify Henry Clay, John C. Calhoun, and Daniel Webster as representatives of different parts of the country and identify the sections of the country they represented.
- Recognize the position of each of the three men on slavery and on the Union.
- Define *sectionalism*, *tariff*, *orator*, and *states' rights*.

PREPARE

Approximate lesson time is 60 minutes.

Materials
For the Student

Guided Reading: Chapters 42 and 43

Talking Heads: Clay, Calhoun, Webster

A History of US (Concise Edition), Volume B (1790-1877) by Joy Hakim

History Journal

LEARN
Activity 1: Speaking Up and Out (Offline)
Instructions
Read

Complete the Guided Reading: Chapters 42 and 43 sheet as you read Chapter 42, pages 217–220, and Chapter 43, pages 221–224.

Use What You Know

You have read about three great orators. They all felt very strongly about what was right for their region of the country. Complete the Talking Heads: Clay, Calhoun, Webster sheet with information about each individual and his positions on slavery and the Union (the United States of America).

Name _____   Date _____

Guided Reading: Chapters 42 and 43

1. Define *orator*: _____

_____

2. Fill in the chart with information about the three great speakers.

Speaker	Region Represented	Position on Slavery
Daniel Webster		
Henry Clay		
John C. Calhoun		

3. Define *tariff*: _____

_____

4. What do you think William Seward of New York meant when he said there was a higher law than the Constitution? _____

5. What two gentlemen were involved in the "Great Debate"? _____

_____

6. Define *states' rights*: _____

_____

7. Daniel Webster asks, "What is this government of ours, does it belong to state legislatures or to the people?" How did Webster answer his own question?

_____

_____

8. What was the result of Webster's speech in terms of the West? _____

_____

9. Did President Andrew Jackson provide leadership to the country on the issue of slavery? Explain your answer. _____

_____

10. Why did John C. Calhoun give up his position as vice president? _____

_____

_____

Name _____ Date _____

Talking Heads: Clay, Calhoun, Webster

Fill in each of these great orators' heads with information about them and their positions on slavery and the Union.

Henry Clay

Daniel Webster

John Calhoun

Student Guide
Lesson 5: Another Compromise

Remember the Missouri Compromise of 1820? It was about balancing the number of free and slave states. In 1850, the slavery issue continued to cause problems in the United States. Some people from both Northern and Southern states wanted to end slavery. Others, mainly Southerners, threatened to pull away from the United States and form their own country. Hoping to avoid a showdown that might destroy the country, the government sought another compromise.

Lesson Objectives
- Define *nullify* and *secession*.
- Recognize that there was diversity of opinion on the issue of slavery and secession in 1850.
- Summarize the goals of the Missouri Compromise (Compromise of 1820) and the Compromise of 1850.
- Explain why antislavery people such as Daniel Webster were willing to compromise on the issue of slavery.
- Define *paradox* and explain why slavery was a paradox in the United States, even though slavery had existed for thousands of years in some parts of the world.
- Describe the colonization movement and explain that most blacks did not want to migrate to Africa because they were Americans.
- Identify the Missouri Compromise as the 1820 law that maintained the political balance in the Senate and forbade slavery in most of the Lousiana Purchase territory.
- Give examples of the growing differences between North and South after 1820, including changes in population, economy, and political power.
- Identify Henry Clay, John C. Calhoun, and Daniel Webster as representatives of different parts of the country and identify the sections of the country they represented.
- Define *sectionalism*, *tariff*, *orator*, and *states' rights*.

PREPARE

Approximate lesson time is 60 minutes.

Materials
For the Student

The Compromise of 1850

A History of US (Concise Edition), Volume B (1790-1877) by Joy Hakim

History Journal

LEARN
Activity 1: Let's Make a Deal *(Offline)*
Instructions
Read

Read Chapter 44, pages 225–232. Complete the Compromise of 1850 sheet. Have an adult check your answers.

ASSESS
Mid-Unit Assessment: Slavery, Sectionalism, and the Road to Civil War *(Online)*

You will complete an online assessment covering the main points of this unit. Your assessment will be scored by the computer.

Name _____ Date _____

The Compromise of 1850

Choose the correct words to complete this account of the Compromise of 1850.

Word Bank			
secession	Compromise of 1850	free	Senate
John Calhoun	Daniel Webster	Henry Clay	nullify

Slavery still presented problems to the United States in 1850. Each time a new state entered

the Union, it could throw off the balance of (1) _____ states and
slave states. If California entered as a free state, then the free states would have more votes

in the (2) _____ .

(3) _____ , from South Carolina, spoke out for slavery.
He said that if a state believes a law goes against the Constitution, the state can

(4) _____ , or not recognize, the law. Meanwhile,

(5) _____ had been working on a compromise. Today we

know that compromise as the (6) _____ .

Even though he was against slavery, (7) _____ spoke in the
Senate on behalf of the compromise. Despite his feelings about slavery, he wanted to hold
the Union together. He was willing to see slavery continue rather than risk the

(8) _____ of the Southern states, which would mean that the
states would leave the Union.

Understand: Now that you have read about the Compromise of 1850, what were the goals of
this compromise and of the Missouri Compromise (Compromise of 1820)?

Goals of both compromises: _____

_____

_____

Think: Daniel Webster was against slavery, but he was willing to allow slavery to continue in some parts of the United States. Why would he do that? _____

_____

_____

Student Guide
Lesson 6: Where Is Justice?

The issue of slavery finally came before the Supreme Court. Dred Scott, a slave, thought he should be free because he had lived with his owner in a free territory for several years. What was the Court's decision in this landmark case?

Lesson Objectives

- Explain the argument and decision in the Dred Scott case.

PREPARE

Approximate lesson time is 60 minutes.

Materials

For the Student

Supreme Court Decision

A History of US (Concise Edition), Volume B (1790-1877) by Joy Hakim

History Journal

LEARN
Activity 1: The Supreme Court Decides *(Offline)*
Instructions
Read

Read Chapter 45, pages 233–234. Then complete the Supreme Court Decision sheet. Have an adult check your answers.

Read On

Because slavery was still legal in the United States, some slaves and abolitionists took matters into their own hands.

Read Chapter 46, pages 235–237, OR Chapter 47, pages 238–243. Be prepared to discuss the risks slaves (and those who helped them) took to reach freedom.

Note: You will only read one of these chapters in this lesson. You will read the other one in the next, OPTIONAL lesson.

Name _____   Date _____

Supreme Court Decision

Answer the questions below. Then, use the circled letters to fill in the blanks at the bottom of the page to rediscover the Chief Justice of the Supreme Court at the time of the Dred Scott decision.

1. The big issue in the Dred Scott case was ___ ___ ___ ___ ___ ___ ___.

2. Dred Scott said he should be free because he had lived in Wisconsin, a free

   (○)___ ___ ___ ___ ___ ___ ___ ___.

3. The case went to the ___ ___ ___ ___ ___ ___ ___ Court.

4. The Chief Justice of the Supreme Court wrote that slaves were property, and the

   ___ ___ ___ ___ ___ (○)___ ___ (○)___ ___ ___ ___ protects

   property.

5. The Chief Justice also wrote that the ___ ___ ___ ___ ___ ___ ___ ___

   Compromise that prohibited slavery in the territories was unconstitutional (against the

   Constitution) because it violated slave owners' rights to

   ___ (○)___ ___ (○)___.

6. The Court ruled that blacks had no rights to

   ___ ___ ___ ___ ___ ___ ___ ___ ___ ___ ___ in the United States.

   ┌───┐
   │ The Chief Justice of the Supreme Court when the Dred Scott case was decided: │
   │ Chief Justice ___ ___ ___ ___ ___.   │
   └───┘

Thinking and Evaluating: The picture to the left represents a basic principle of the U.S. judicial system—equal justice under the law. It shows a blindfolded "lady justice" holding scales that are equally balanced.

1. What do you think the blindfold represents?

2. What do you think the balanced scales represent?

3. Was there equal justice under the law in the case of Dred Scott? Explain your answer.

Student Guide
Lesson 7: Not Really a Railroad Underground

Many stories from this time describe the risks slaves took to reach freedom and the risks others took to help them. Some slaves escaped through their own ingenuity, but most traveled the Underground Railroad.

Lesson Objectives
- Describe the Underground Railroad.
- Describe the risks some people took to escape slavery or help others do so.

PREPARE

Approximate lesson time is 60 minutes.

Materials
For the Student

Map of Underground Railroad Routes, 1861; B/W

A History of US (Concise Edition), Volume B (1790-1877) by Joy Hakim

History Journal

LEARN
Activity 1: Escape! *(Offline)*
Instructions
Discuss

You chose to read either Chapter 46, pages 235–237, or Chapter 47, pages 238–243. Both chapters tell stories of daring escapes to freedom. An adult will ask you the following questions about your selected reading. Answer each question aloud and discuss your answers.

Chapter 46

1. How did Ellen and William Craft escape to freedom?
2. What obstacles did they face?
3. What qualities did they have that helped them succeed?
4. Upon arriving in Philadelphia, what was Ellen Craft's opinion of white people?
5. Why do you think slave owners offered big rewards for the capture of fugitive slaves such as the Crafts?

Chapter 47

1. What was the Underground Railroad? Who "ran" it?
2. What obstacles did escaping slaves face on the Underground Railroad?
3. Why was work on the Underground Railroad illegal?
4. Why were the Oberlin Trials big news?

Use What You Know

The routes escaping slaves took were varied. If lucky, a runaway made it to freedom in two months. For others, especially in bad weather, the trek lasted a year. They traveled through open farmlands and dense forests, crossed small streams and wide rivers. The dangers were everywhere, but the chance to reach freedom gave them the courage to continue. Word of successful slave escapes and the Underground Railroad spread like wildfire through the slave cabins of the South.

Go online and use the map of Underground Railroad routes to trace a trail from Alabama to freedom.

Write a dialogue in which you decide to escape and tell two friends, Violet and Franklin, about the "freedom train." Try to convince them to make the journey with you. Include questions that Violet and Franklin might ask before risking their lives.

Consider the following questions as you write:

- What path would you take?
- How far do you think you might travel each day?
- What obstacles would you face?
- How far would you travel before you felt safe enough to end your journey?

Optional: Beyond The Lesson

On the National Geographic Society's Underground Railroad you take on the role of a slave. You have an opportunity to escape on the Underground Railroad—should you go?

Activity 2. Optional: The Underground Railroad *(Online)*

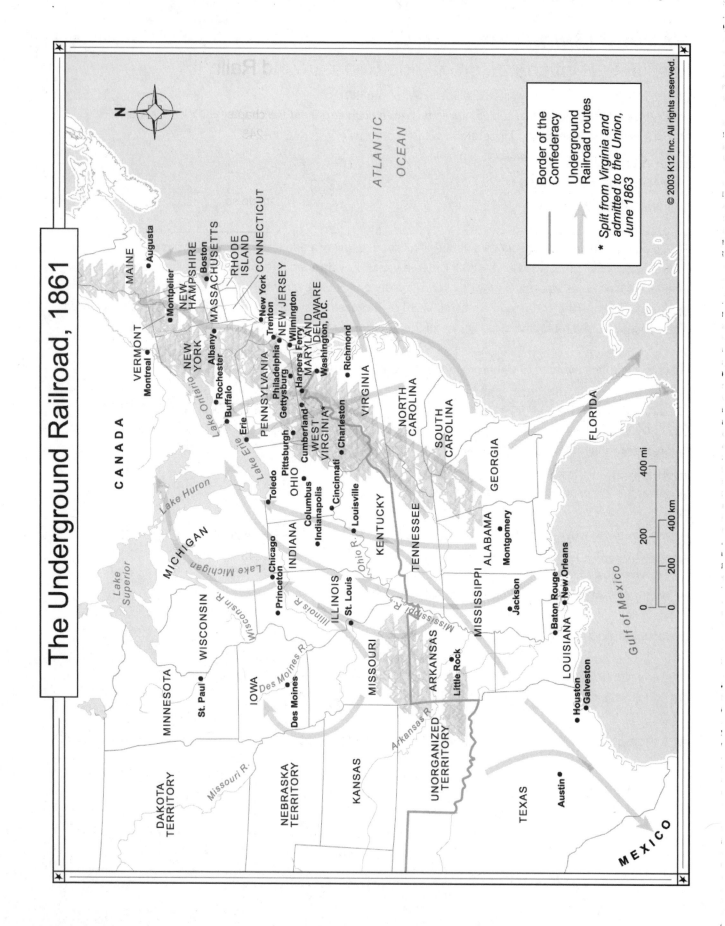

The Underground Railroad, 1861

Legend:
- Border of the Confederacy
- Underground Railroad routes
- * Split from Virginia and admitted to the Union, June 1863

Student Guide
Lesson 8: (Optional) More on the Underground Railroad

Learn more about those who risked their lives to escape slavery. Read the chapter you didn't read in the previous lesson—Chapter 46, pages 235–237, OR Chapter 47, pages 238–243.

Lesson Objectives
- Describe the Underground Railroad.
- Describe the risks some people took to escape slavery or help others do so.

PREPARE

Approximate lesson time is 60 minutes.

Materials
For the Student

A History of US (Concise Edition), Volume B (1790-1877) by Joy Hakim

History Journal

LEARN
Activity 1. Optional: Escaping to Freedom *(Online)*
Instructions
Read

Learn more about those who risked their lives to escape slavery. Read the chapter you didn't read in the previous lesson—Chapter 46, pages 235–237, OR Chapter 47, pages 238–243.

Student Guide
Lesson 9: Is It Ever Okay?

Harriet Tubman, an escaped slave herself, dedicated her life to helping slaves escape to freedom on the Underground Railroad. She, and others who supported her cause, broke laws. They risked imprisonment to help slaves escape and to protest the injustice of slavery. But in a democratic society it's important that citizens respect the law. Is it ever okay to break a law?

Lesson Objectives
- Identify Harriett Tubman as an escaped slave and conductor on the Underground Railroad.
- Identify the reasons, justifications, and consequences of breaking unjust laws.

PREPARE

Approximate lesson time is 60 minutes.

Materials
For the Student

Fighting Injustice

A History of US (Concise Edition), Volume B (1790-1877) by Joy Hakim

History Journal

LEARN
Activity 1: Ethics *(Offline)*
Instructions
Read

Harriet Tubman made it obvious to everyone that the argument that slavery was a positive good was full of holes. By leading hundreds of slaves out of the South, she demonstrated the willingness of enslaved Africans to risk death in pursuit of liberty. Read Chapter 48, pages 244–249, to discover what led Harriet Tubman to her tremendous feats.

Use What You Know

Complete the Fighting Injustice sheet. This sheet focuses primarily on the chapter's feature titled "Breaking the Law—A Discussion of Ethics." Ask an adult to check your answers.

Discuss

In *On Civil Disobedience,* Henry David Thoreau said:

"Thus the state never intentionally confronts a man's sense, intellectual or moral, but only his body, his senses. It is not armed with superior wit or honesty, but with superior physical strength. I was not born to be forced. I will breathe after my own fashion. Let us see who is strongest....They only can force me who obey a higher law than I."

Is it ever okay to break the law? Discuss your thoughts on the question with an adult.

Optional: Beyond the Lesson

People developed codes, passwords, and secret signals for runaways and conductors to use on the Underground Railroad. Since most slaves could not read, many messages were passed on in songs such as "Swing Low Sweet Chariot," "Wade in the Water," "The Gospel Train," and "Follow the Drinking Gourd."

Explore these and other aspects of the Underground Railroad on the website Pathways to Freedom: Maryland and the Underground Railroad.

Activity 2. Optional: Songs of the Underground Railroad *(Online)*

Name _____   Date _____

Fighting Injustice

1. We think of the people who assisted the Underground Railroad as heroes but in their time they were also considered _____.

2. In what ways did some people in the South who opposed slavery violate the laws supporting it? _____

3. What did people have to accept when they decided to break the law? _____

   _____

4. List two other people from history who have made the decision to fight laws they believed to be unjust by breaking them. _____

5. What experiences and characteristics helped shape Harriet Tubman into a fierce opponent of slavery? _____

   _____

   _____

6. How did the Underground Railroad move Northerners toward war? _____

   _____

7. Why was Harriet Tubman called "Moses"? _____

   _____

8. How many people are believed to have been led out of slavery by Harriet Tubman?

   _____

Student Guide
Lesson 10: Against Slavery: Harriet Beecher Stowe

A woman barely five feet tall used a pen to touch the hearts and minds of the nation. Harriet Beecher Stowe—author and abolitionist—gave slavery a human face. In doing so, she inspired many Northerners to embrace the cause of abolition.

Lesson Objectives
- Summarize the way in which Harriett Beecher Stowe worked to end slavery.
- Analyze a primary source to gain understanding of Harriet Beecher Stowe's impact.

PREPARE

Approximate lesson time is 60 minutes.

Materials

For the Student

Guided Reading: Chapter 49

Map of the Underground Railroad, 1861 (B/W)

A History of US (Concise Edition), Volume B (1790-1877) by Joy Hakim

History Journal

LEARN
Activity 1: The Little Woman and the Great War *(Offline)*
Instructions
Read

In 1860, many Northerners had never seen a black person, free or slave. Whatever most Northerners knew about slavery came from what they read or what they heard from others. Harriet Beecher Stowe's writing sparked a tremendous change in the ideas of Northerners about slavery.

Read Chapter 49, pages 250–253, and complete the Guided Reading: Chapter 49 sheet.
Use What You Know

When Abraham Lincoln met Harriet Beecher Stowe during the Civil War, he is said to have remarked, "So this is the little lady who wrote the book that made this great war." She did not really "make" the Civil War, but as Lincoln knew, her work greatly influenced events.

In your History Journal, explain Lincoln's comment. Why did the president of the United States think Stowe's work was so important?

Optional: Beyond the Lesson

Go to the Harriet Beecher Stowe Time Line online to see how Mrs. Stowe's life intersected with the abolition events of the time. Items on the time line are clickable links to explore.

Activity 2. Optional: Harriet Beecher Stowe Time Line (Online)

Name _____   Date _____

Guided Reading: Chapter 49

1. Identify these people:

   • Harriet Beecher Stowe: _____

   • Lyman Beecher: _____

   • Abraham Lincoln: _____

2. Harriet became more concerned with the issue of slavery after she moved with her

   family to _____, where she saw the boats on the Ohio River carrying slaves to be sold at slave markets.

3. A visit to the state of _____ reinforced her displeasure with the system of slavery.

4. At the encouragement of her sister-in-law, Harriet wrote the book _____, which sold 10,000 copies in its first week of publication in 1852.

5. According to Chapter 49, what was Harriet trying to show in her book?

   • _____

   • _____

Use the map of the Underground Railroad, 1861, to answer the following question.

6. Harriet Stowe lived for a while in Cincinnati, Ohio, an important city in the history of slavery and abolition. Find Cincinnati on the map. Can you identify two facts about the city's location that help explain its influence on abolition events of the time?

   _____

   _____

Think Back

7. Chapter 49 notes that Uncle Tom's Cabin was the first American novel to show blacks as real people. It made people care about the issue of slavery. In what ways were Uncle Tom's Cabin and the Underground Railroad linked to the growing conflict over slavery?

_____

_____

_____

_____

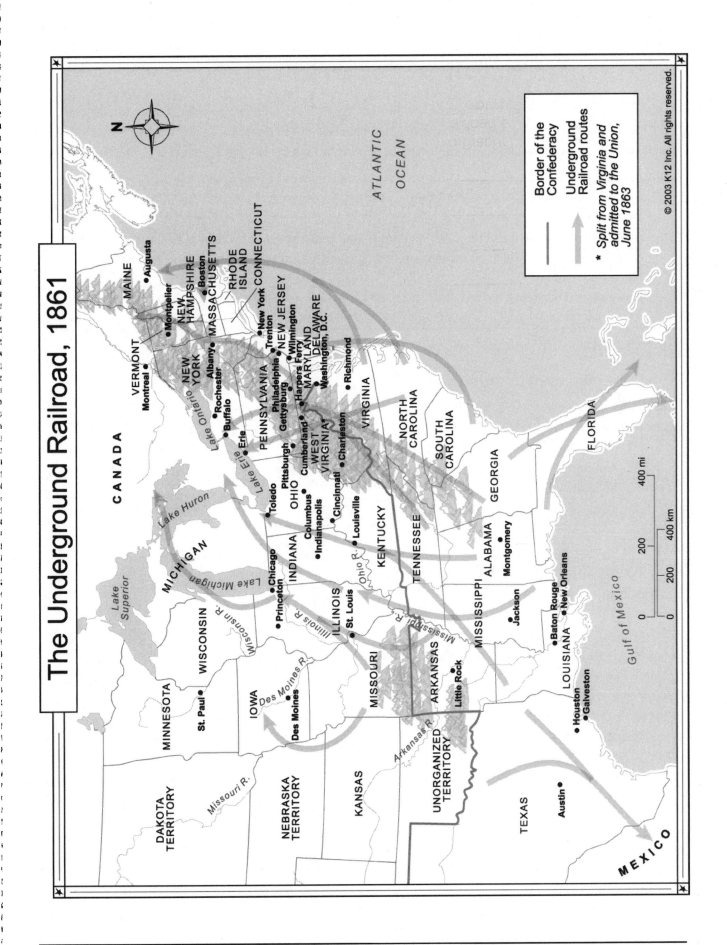

The Underground Railroad, 1861

Border of the Confederacy

Underground Railroad routes

* Split from Virginia and admitted to the Union, June 1863

© 2003 K12 Inc. All rights reserved.

Student Guide
Lesson 11: Against Slavery: John Brown

People still debate whether fiery abolitionist John Brown was a hero or a traitor. He wanted to end slavery so badly that he marched into the town of Harpers Ferry and seized the arsenal. His violent actions got him into trouble. In 1859, the debate about John Brown reflected how divided the North and South had become.

Lesson Objectives

- Summarize the way in which John Brown worked to end slavery and evaluate the effectiveness of his methods.
- Analyze the quote from Lincoln, "Old John Brown has been executed for treason against a State. We cannot object, even though he agreed with us in thinking slavery wrong. That cannot excuse violence, bloodshed, and treason."
- Compare and contrast the goals and actions of Harriet Beecher Stowe and John Brown.

PREPARE

Approximate lesson time is 60 minutes.

Materials

For the Student

Working Against Slavery

A History of US (Concise Edition), Volume B (1790-1877) by Joy Hakim

History Journal

LEARN
Activity 1: Old John Brown (Offline)
Instructions
Read

John Brown had a good goal. He wanted to end slavery. Unfortunately, he used violence to try to reach his goal. It didn't work. His plan for a slave uprising failed, but his words inspired Northerners while they angered Southerners.

Read Chapter 50, pages 254–258.

Discuss

1. How might the Dred Scott case have affected John Brown's views about the way to end slavery?
2. How did John Brown try to end slavery? In what ways was he effective? In what ways was he ineffective?
3. How did abolitionists feel about John Brown's trial? How did Southerners feel about it?
4. Do you think John Brown was a hero-martyr (someone who suffers or dies for a cause) or a rebel-traitor (someone who betrays his country)? Why?

Use What You Know

Abraham Lincoln said:

"Old John Brown has been executed for treason against a State. We cannot object, even though he agreed with us in thinking slavery wrong. That cannot excuse violence, bloodshed, and treason."

What did Lincoln mean?

Compare and contrast Harriet Beecher Stowe and John Brown's actions on the Working Against Slavery sheet. Have an adult review your answers.

Optional: Beyond the Lesson

John Brown's actions, trial, and execution were well known in America in the years leading up to the Civil War. People began to sing a song called "John Brown's Body."

Find out more about the song and listen to the words by visiting a PBS site called the "History of 'John Brown's Body.' "

ASSESS

Lesson Assessment: Against Slavery: John Brown *(Online)*

You will complete an online assessment covering the main points of this lesson. Your assessment will be scored by the computer.

LEARN

Activity 2. Optional: John Brown's Body *(Online)*

Name _____   Date _____

Working Against Slavery

Compare and contrast the goals and actions of Harriet Beecher Stowe and John Brown. Write the goals and actions of each person in the circle under his or her name. In the middle section, write the goals and actions they had in common.

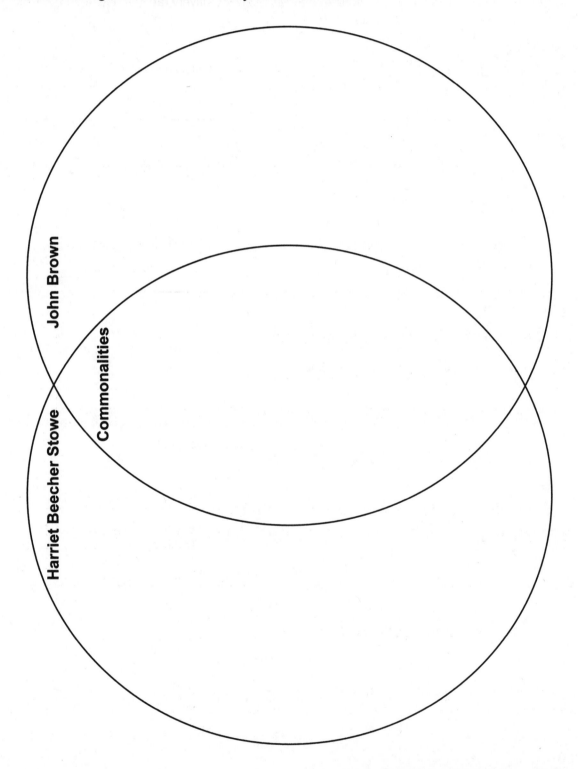

Student Guide
Lesson 12: Abraham Lincoln: Larger Than Life

Abraham Lincoln's life was characterized by the strength born of frontier living, a love of learning, and opposition to the injustices of slavery. Lincoln went from being a schoolboy in Kentucky and Indiana, to being an unsuccessful businessman, then a lawyer and politician in Illinois, and finally the sixteenth president of the United States. Along the way, he rose above human hatred by attacking slavery rather than the people who practiced it.

Lesson Objectives
- Describe the pre-presidency life and character of Abraham Lincoln, including his frontier youth, love of learning, and ability to see the moral issues in political questions.

PREPARE

Approximate lesson time is 60 minutes.

Materials
For the Student

A History of US (Concise Edition), Volume B (1790-1877) by Joy Hakim

History Journal

LEARN
Activity 1: On the Way to the Presidency *(Offline)*
Instructions
Read

You may have heard a lot about Abraham Lincoln as president, but how much do you know about his earlier life? What was he like? What did he do? How did he end up being one of the greatest presidents we've ever had?

Find out how Lincoln grew up in the woods of Kentucky and Indiana, and then moved to New Salem, Illinois, to start his career. After a brief period as an unsuccessful businessman, he became a politician. He moved to Washington, D.C., when he was elected president of a very divided nation. Through it all, he never stopped learning.

Read Chapter 51, pages 259–263, and Chapter 52, pages 264–266.

Discuss

1. How would you describe Abraham Lincoln?
2. If you could ask Abraham Lincoln a question, what would it be?

Optional: Beyond the Lesson

To find out more about Abraham Lincoln, visit Abraham Lincoln Online.

Activity 2. Optional: Abraham Lincoln *(Online)*

Optional: Beyond the Lesson

Student Guide
Lesson 13: Unit Review

You have finished the unit, Slavery, Sectionalism, and the Road to Civil War. It's time to review what you've learned. You will take the Unit Assessment in the next lesson.

(This review might refer to topics presented in optional lessons in this unit.)

Lesson Objectives

- Demonstrate mastery of important knowledge and skills taught in previous lessons.

PREPARE

Approximate lesson time is 60 minutes.

Materials

For the Student

🖳 Outline Map of the United States

A History of US (Concise Edition), Volume B (1790-1877) by Joy Hakim

History Journal

LEARN
Activity 1: A Look Back (Offline)
Instructions
History Journal Review

Review what you've learned in this unit by going through your History Journal. You should:

- Look at activity sheets you've completed for this unit.
- Review unit vocabulary words.
- Read through any writing assignments you did during the unit.
- Review the assessments you took.

Don't rush through; take your time. Your History Journal is a great resource for a unit review.

Online Review

Use the following to review this unit:

- The Big Picture
- Time Line

Fifty States

Practice identifying the 50 states by labeling the Outline Map of the United States.

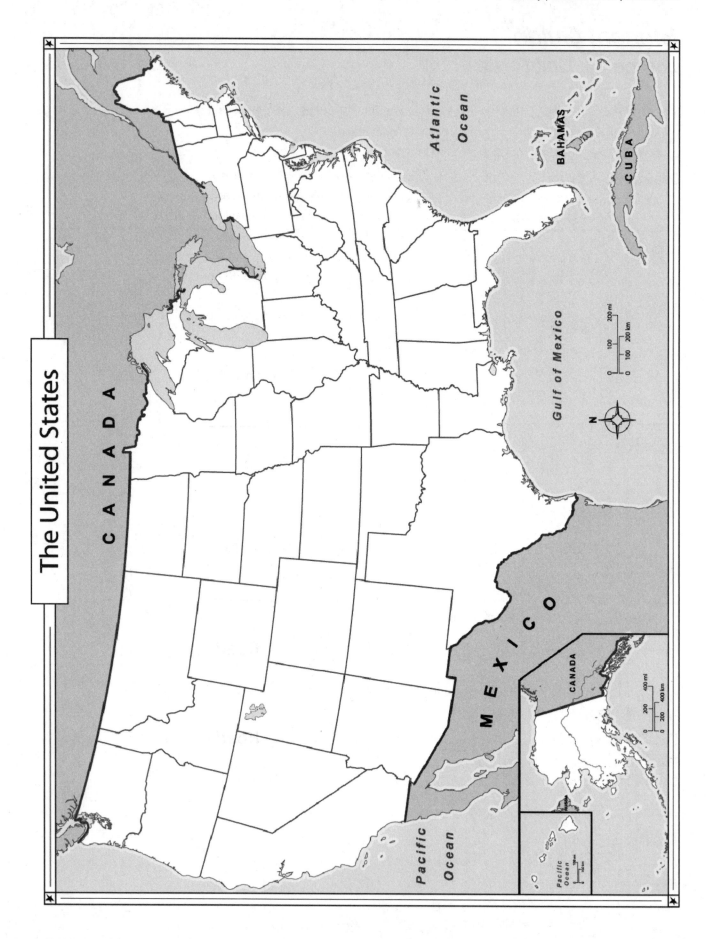

The United States

Student Guide
Lesson 14: Unit Assessment

You've finished this unit! Take the Unit Assessment, and then read on for the next lesson.

Lesson Objectives

- Describe the Underground Railroad.
- Describe the risks some people took to escape slavery or help others do so.
- Summarize the way in which Harriett Beecher Stowe worked to end slavery.
- Summarize the way in which John Brown worked to end slavery and evaluate the effectiveness of his methods.
- Recognize that there was diversity of opinion on the issue of slavery and secession in 1850.
- Summarize the goals of the Missouri Compromise (Compromise of 1820) and the Compromise of 1850.
- Explain why antislavery people such as Daniel Webster were willing to compromise on the issue of slavery.
- Explain the argument and decision in the Dred Scott case.
- Describe the pre-presidency life and character of Abraham Lincoln, including his frontier youth, love of learning, and ability to see the moral issues in political questions.

PREPARE

Approximate lesson time is 60 minutes.

Materials

For the Student

A History of US (Concise Edition), Volume B (1790-1877) by Joy Hakim

History Journal

ASSESS

Unit Assessment: Slavery, Sectionalism, and the Road to Civil War, Part 1 *(Online)*

Complete the computer-scored portion of the Unit Assessment. When you have finished, complete the teacher-scored portion of the assessment and submit it to your teacher.

Unit Assessment: Slavery, Sectionalism, and the Road to Civil War, Part 2 *(Offline)*

Complete the teacher-scored portion of the Unit Assessment and submit it to your teacher.

LEARN

Activity 1: Chapters 53 and 54 *(Offline)*

Instructions
Read On

All wars are terrible, but the worst are those fought within a nation. In the case of the United States, two great issues hung in the balance—states' rights versus central government, and slavery versus liberty.

After you take the Unit Assessment, read about the beginning of the Civil War and the attack on Fort Sumter in South Carolina. Find out how Lincoln tried to win the support of the border states and keep the issue of slavery off the battlefield.

Read Chapter 53, pages 268–271, and Chapter 54, pages 272–276. Be prepared to discuss the basic principles that separated North and South in 1861 and to summarize the challenges Lincoln faced as the nation went to war.

Vocabulary

Write a brief definition for the following terms in your History Journal:

- civil war
- states' rights
- Yankees
- border state

Student Guide
Lesson 1: An Uncivil War

The Civil War answered questions the Founders couldn't or wouldn't answer. Which has greater power, the states or the central government? Can a state nullify a federal law? Who is a citizen? Can slavery exist in a country born with the Declaration of Independence? These are some of the issues you will explore in this unit.

Abraham Lincoln's victory in the election of 1860 convinced Southerners that their way of life was doomed if they stayed in the Union. Many white Southerners believed that their culture could not survive without slavery. So, after much talk about pulling out of the Union, the South finally did it.

Lesson Objectives

- Define *civil war*, *Yankees*, and *border state*.
- List the advantages of the North (more people, industry, and food) and of the South (skilled fighters, outdoorsmen, Southerners' belief that they were fighting for their land) as the war began.
- Identify Richmond as the capital of the Confederacy and Jefferson Davis as its president.
- Summarize the challenges that Lincoln faced, including the importance of border states and the dilemma of the slavery issue.
- Identify the basic principles that separated North and South in 1861, including differing views on slavery and the right to leave the Union.

PREPARE

Approximate lesson time is 60 minutes.

Materials

For the Student

Time to Fight

Who's Going to Win?

A History of US (Concise Edition), Volume B (1790-1877) by Joy Hakim

History Journal

LEARN
Activity 1: War Between the States *(Offline)*

Instructions

Check Your Reading (Chapter 53, pages 268–271, and Chapter 54, pages 272–276)

Review Chapters 53 and 54. Complete the Time to Fight sheet. Have an adult check your answers.

Discuss

Discuss the following with an adult.

Reread the quote by Abraham Lincoln in the margin on page 274. In the quote, Lincoln is discussing the importance of the border states to the North. Explain why Lincoln considered Maryland, Kentucky, Missouri, and Delaware—the border states—vital to the Northern cause.

Use What You Know

Complete the Who's Going to Win? sheet. Share your chart and your prediction with an adult.

Read On

For many Southerners, preparations for war seemed like a game. But both sides quickly realized that war was serious and deadly.

Read Chapter 55, pages 277–282.

Vocabulary

You'll see the term *rebels* as you read. Write a brief definition for it in your History Journal.

Name _____ Date _____

Time to Fight

1. The main issue in the Civil War was _____.

2. Another issue in the Civil War was that Southerners believed in _____

   _____ and the right to leave the _____.

3. The states that pulled out of the Union called themselves the _____

   _____ of America.

4. Two other names for Northerners were _____ or

   _____.

5. The Confederate government was headquartered in _____,

   _____.

6. Four slave states that touched both North and South were undecided at first about joining the Confederacy or staying in the Union. These states were called

   _____ states.

Name _____   Date _____

Who's Going to Win?

Both the North and the South expected a short war, and each side was convinced that it would win. In order to understand the challenges each side faced, complete the chart listing the advantages that each side had over the other side as war began. Use the advantage bank and details from your reading. Share your chart with an adult. The first one is done for you.

Advantage Bank
skilled fighters   more factories (industry)   outdoorsmen
more food   determination   more men to fight (large population)
belief that they were fighting for their land

Northern Advantages	Southern Advantages
more men to fight (large population)	

Making Predictions

The _____ will win the war because _____

_____

_____

_____

450

Student Guide
Lesson 2: It Begins

After the attack on Fort Sumter, soldiers for both sides confidently marched off to battle. One of the first casualties was the idea that it would be a quick, glorious war. Chaos and bloodshed at Manassas (Bull Run) hinted at the tragedy to come.

Lesson Objectives
- Locate on a map the states that seceded and the border states.
- Summarize the attitude of most soldiers as believing the war would be quick and glorious and the reasons they were incorrect, including new weapons and lack of experience.
- Identify on a map and explain the significance of Fort Sumter as initiating the war.
- Identify on a map and explain the significance of the first battle at Bull Run (Manassas) as changing attitudes about war in both the North and the South.

PREPARE

Approximate lesson time is 60 minutes.

Materials

For the Student

Battles of the Civil War

map of Battles of the Civil War, 1861-1865

A History of US (Concise Edition), Volume B (1790-1877) by Joy Hakim

History Journal

LEARN
Activity 1: You Were There (Offline)
Instructions
Check Your Reading (Chapter 55, pages 277–282)

Review Chapter 55 by completing the following activity in your History Journal. Share your account of the battle with an adult.

You are a reporter observing the battle of Manassas (Bull Run). At the end of the battle, you rush into a telegraph office in Washington, D.C., to cable news of the battle to your home office. Your message must be 25 words or less, so you must give only the essential information. Describe the scenes and the battle. Try to use all your senses as you describe the battle.

Learn from Maps

Maps can help you understand why historical events happened where they did. Refer to the map of the Battles of the Civil War, 1861–1865, to complete the Battles of the Civil War activity sheet.

Optional: Beyond the Lesson

Take a virtual tour of Manassas or read more about the history of the battlefield at the Manassas National Battlefield Park Home Page.

Activity 2. Optional: Manassas National Battlefield Park *(Online)*

Name _____ Date _____

Battles of the Civil War

Refer to the map of Battles of the Civil War, 1861–1865, to answer the following questions.

1. Name the border states. _____

_____

_____

2. Was the battle of Manassas fought in Union or Confederate territory? _____

3. Why was Manassas a logical place to have a battle? _____

_____

_____

_____

4. Why do you think so many battles were fought in Virginia? _____

_____

_____

_____

5. Why were so many battles fought near rivers and railroads? _____

_____

_____

_____

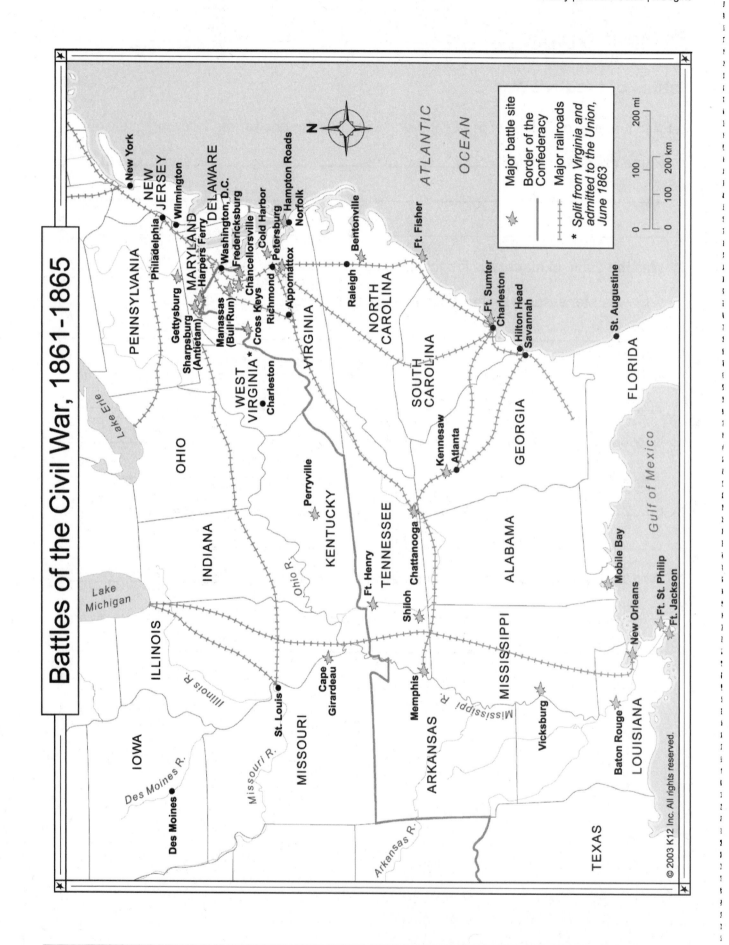

Battles of the Civil War, 1861–1865

Legend:
- ★ Major battle site
- — Border of the Confederacy
- ┼┼┼ Major railroads
- * Split from Virginia and admitted to the Union, June 1863

Scale: 0 — 100 — 200 mi / 0 — 100 — 200 km

Labels on map:

ATLANTIC OCEAN

New York, NEW JERSEY, Wilmington, DELAWARE, Philadelphia, PENNSYLVANIA, Harpers Ferry, Washington, D.C., MARYLAND, Fredericksburg, Chancellorsville, Cold Harbor, Hampton Roads, Norfolk, Gettysburg, Manassas (Bull Run), Sharpsburg (Antietam), Cross Keys, Richmond, Petersburg, Appomattox, WEST VIRGINIA *, Charleston, VIRGINIA, Bentonville, Raleigh, NORTH CAROLINA, Ft. Fisher

Lake Erie, OHIO, Lake Michigan, INDIANA, ILLINOIS, Illinois R., IOWA, Des Moines R., Des Moines

Perryville, KENTUCKY, TENNESSEE, Ft. Henry, Shiloh, Chattanooga, Ohio R., SOUTH CAROLINA, Ft. Sumter, Charleston, Hilton Head, Savannah, Kennesaw, Atlanta, GEORGIA, St. Augustine, FLORIDA

St. Louis, MISSOURI, Missouri R., Cape Girardeau, Memphis, ARKANSAS, Mississippi R., Arkansas R., MISSISSIPPI, ALABAMA, Vicksburg, Mobile Bay, New Orleans, Ft. St. Philip, Ft. Jackson, Baton Rouge, LOUISIANA, TEXAS, Gulf of Mexico

© 2003 K12 Inc. All rights reserved.

Student Guide
Lesson 3: North Versus South

The harsh realities of the Civil War shattered families and ended the romantic notion that war was glorious. New weapons changed the rules of war. Improvements in communication and transportation made it a war like no other. In fact, some say it was the first modern war.

Lesson Objectives

- Compare and contrast life in the North and the South in 1861, including Northern urbanization versus Southern pastoral life, and different social structures.
- Describe Civil War soldiers and give some reasons so many died, including the use of new weapons and old tactics.
- Explain how the Civil War differed from earlier wars.
- Demonstrate mastery of important knowledge and skills taught in previous lessons.
- Define *civil war*, *Yankees*, and *border state*.
- List the advantages of the North (more people, industry, and food) and of the South (skilled fighters, outdoorsmen, Southerners' belief that they were fighting for their land) as the war began.
- Identify the basic principles that separated North and South in 1861, including differing views on slavery and the right to leave the Union.
- Locate on a map the states that seceded and the border states.
- Summarize the attitude of most soldiers as believing the war would be quick and glorious and the reasons they were incorrect, including new weapons and lack of experience.
- Identify on a map and explain the significance of the first battle at Bull Run (Manassas) as changing attitudes about war in both the North and the South.

PREPARE

Approximate lesson time is 60 minutes.

Materials

For the Student

Guided Reading: Chapters 56 and 57

A History of US (Concise Edition), Volume B (1790-1877) by Joy Hakim

History Journal

LEARN
Activity 1: The First Modern War *(Offline)*

Instructions
Read

Father against son, brother against brother, friend against friend. The personal toll of the war was incredible.

Read Chapter 56, pages 283–286, and Chapter 57, pages 287–291. Complete the Guided Reading: Chapters 56 and 57 sheet. Have an adult check your answers.

Vocabulary

You'll see these terms as you read. Write a brief definition for each term in your History Journal. Also indicate which term describes the North and which term describes the South at the time of the Civil War.

- urban
- pastoral

Optional: Beyond the Lesson

Read excerpts from Civil War diaries kept by soldiers, women, and others at The Valley of the Shadow: Searchable Civil War Diaries website.

ASSESS
Mid-Unit Assessment: North Versus South (*Online*)
You will complete an online Mid-Unit Assessment covering Lessons 1, 2, and 3. Your assessment will be scored by the computer.

LEARN
Activity 2. Optional: Civil War Diaries (*Online*)

Name _____ Date _____

Guided Reading: Chapters 56 and 57

1. The author writes that the Civil War "was a war that split families." Give two examples from the text that support her statement. _____

_____

_____

2. In what ways was the North becoming an urban society? _____

_____

3. Who had great opportunity in the South? Who did not? _____

_____

4. Virginia Senator James M. Mason said, "I look upon it [the Civil War] then, sir, as a war of… one form of society against another form of society." What do you think he meant by this? _____

_____

_____

5. How was the United States different after the Civil War? _____

_____

_____

6. What was the median age of the Civil War soldier? _____

7. When the war started, the ranks of both armies were filled with _____.
Later, governments paid cash _____ for volunteers. Eventually, both
sides had to _____ men.

8. Before the war, most soldiers had been _____.

9. What was the most common cause of death for soldiers? _____

10. Why did new rifled guns, new types of bullets, and new cannons result in more deaths than in previous wars? _____

_____

_____

11. Besides the new weapons, how did the Civil War differ from earlier wars and become known as the first modern war? _____

_____

_____

12. List the two things that surprised you most as you read Chapters 56 and 57. _____

_____

_____

Student Guide
Lesson 4: Generals North and South

The South had plenty of well-trained, competent generals. In the North, it was a different story. One Northern general came up with a plan to win the war, but people thought it was nonsense when he said the plan would take several years. President Lincoln was forced to find another general.

Lesson Objectives
- Describe the Anaconda Plan as the strategy for Union victory.
- Identify Ulysses S. Grant as the general who led the Union to victory by outlasting the enemy and winning many battles.
- Identify Robert E. Lee as the leader of Confederate forces and recognize that he chose to leave the Union out of loyalty to his state.

PREPARE

Approximate lesson time is 60 minutes.

Materials
For the Student
- The Plan
- Who Am I?

A History of US (Concise Edition), Volume B (1790-1877) by Joy Hakim

History Journal

LEARN
Activity 1: Who's In Charge? *(Offline)*
Instructions
Read

Read Chapter 58, pages 292–294, and Chapter 59, pages 295–299. Complete the following activity sheets:

- The Plan
- Who Am I?

Discuss your answers with an adult.

Name _____   Date _____

The Plan

General Winfield Scott had a plan to win the war against the South. Look at the map of Major Battles of the Civil War in Chapter 66 to understand General Scott's plan. Locate Charleston and Savannah, two major Southern ports. Find the Mississippi River. Then, use details from your reading to chart the effects the actions of the Northern army would have on the South if the North followed General Scott's plan.

Action by the North	Result on the South
1. Blockade Southern posts	
2. Gain control of the Mississippi River	
3. Send Union armies from the East and West	

4. What was the name of General Scott's plan? _____

Name _____ Date _____

Who Am I?

Read the following statements. Decide to which general or generals the statement applies and write the name(s) on the line. (Names may be used more than once, and some statements should have more than one name.)

1. I am opposed to slavery and secession, but I can't fight against my own people or my state. Who am I?

   _____

2. I am a general in the Union Army. Who am I?

   _____

3. I was called into service to lead the Union troops because I can outkill or outlast my enemy. Who am I?

   _____

4. I came up with the Anaconda Plan. Who am I?

   _____

5. I am a Confederate general during the Civil War. Who am I?

   _____

6. I don't like to fight. I keep hesitating and making excuses for why I don't follow Lincoln's orders. Who am I?

   _____

7. Some say that I am the finest general that America has produced. Who am I?

   _____

Student Guide
Lesson 5: The War Moves Out to Sea

The Civil War was also fought at sea. During the war, the Confederates built a new kind of ship called an *ironclad*. The Union navy secretly built its own ironclad. The battle between the Confederate *Virginia*, or *Merrimack*, and the Union *Monitor* marked the beginning of a new era in warfare.

Lesson Objectives

- Identify Farragut as the Southerner who commanded Union ships to capture the Mississippi River.
- Identify ironclad ships—including the *Monitor* (Union) and the *Merrimack*, or *Virginia* (Confederate)—as one of the reasons the Civil War is considered a modern war.
- Describe the innovation of the ironclad ship and its importance in warfare.
- Describe the Anaconda Plan as the strategy for Union victory.
- Identify Ulysses S. Grant as the general who led the Union to victory by outlasting the enemy and winning many battles.

PREPARE

Approximate lesson time is 60 minutes.

Materials

For the Student

map of Battles of the Civil War, 1861-1865

War at Sea

A History of US (Concise Edition), Volume B (1790-1877) by Joy Hakim

History Journal

LEARN
Activity 1: Battling Ironclads *(Offline)*
Instructions
Read

Read Chapter 60, pages 300–305, and then complete the War at Sea sheet. Have an adult check your answers.

Learn from Maps

On the map of Battles of the Civil War, 1861–1865, locate and highlight the following Southern ports:

- New Orleans
- Savannah
- Charleston/Fort Sumter
- Hampton Roads

Also, highlight the labels for the Mississippi River, Gulf of Mexico, and Atlantic Ocean.

Optional: Beyond the Lesson

Take a virtual tour of the *Monitor* at the PBS/Nova website *Lincoln's Secret Weapon*.

ASSESS
Mid-Unit Assessment: The War Moves Out to Sea *(Online)*
You will complete an online assessment covering the main points of this unit. Your assessment will be scored by the computer.

LEARN
Activity 2. Optional: The *Monitor* *(Online)*

Name _____   Date _____

War at Sea

1. At the beginning of the Civil War, almost all ships were made of _____.

   During the war, the Confederates began to coat the sides of some of their ships with

   _____ .

2. These new warships were known as _____ .

3. The use of these ships is one of the reasons why the Civil War is considered a modern

   war. Why were they so effective in battle? _____

   _____

4. The _____ was the first Confederate ironclad.

5. The _____ was the first Union ironclad.

6. Many naval battles took place on the Atlantic Coast and the Gulf of Mexico. But some

   took place on inland rivers. Name one of these rivers. _____ Who was

   the Union commander that captured this river? _____

7. Why might he have fought for the Confederacy instead of the Union? _____

   _____

Imagine you're the captain of one of the old wooden Union warships. You narrowly escape destruction by the Confederate ironclad *Virginia*. Write a report to the head of the Union navy about what happened and what you saw. Discuss your report with an adult.

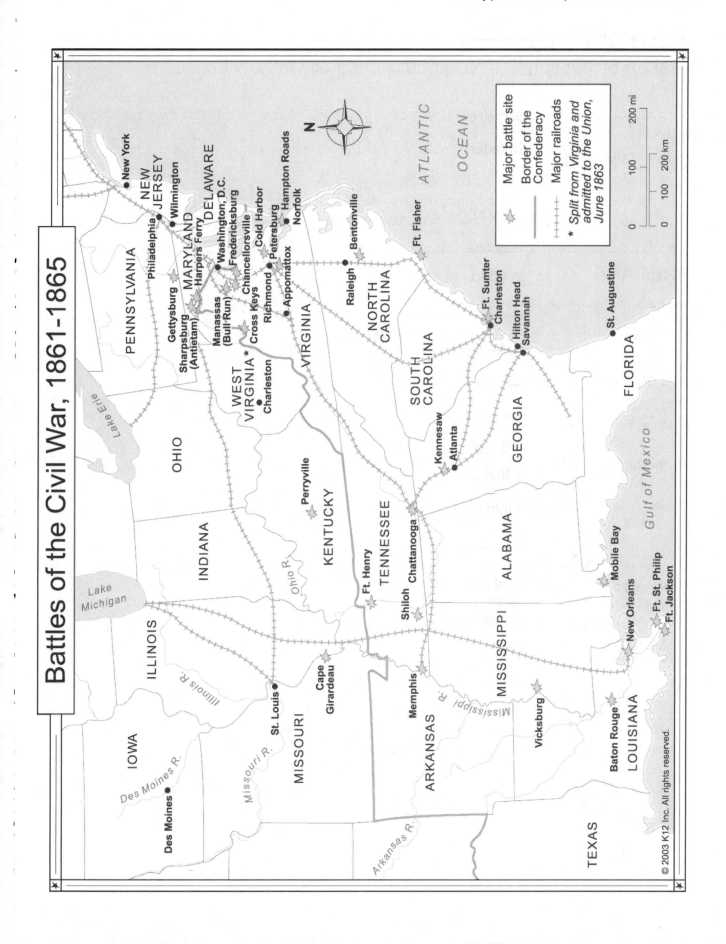

Battles of the Civil War, 1861–1865

Student Guide
Lesson 6: (Optional) Through the Eyes of Mathew Brady

The photography of Mathew Brady brought the reality of the Civil War to many Americans. His photos showed the harsh conditions soldiers faced at the front.

Lesson Objectives
- Identify Mathew Brady as the major photographer of the Civil War.
- Recognize the impact of photography on the public's perception of the war.
- Analyze Brady photos online to gain understanding of the Civil War.

PREPARE

Approximate lesson time is 60 minutes.

LEARN
Activity 1. Optional: Putting the Civil War Into Focus *(Offline)*
Instructions
Analyze Photographs

Mathew Brady was the most important Civil War photographer. Brady took photos of camps, hospitals, men getting ready for battle, and men after the battle. For the first time, the American public could see what the war was like. They could see that war was not all about fancy uniforms and marching bands. It was harsh. It was uncertain. It was dangerous. It was deadly.

Visit the National Portrait Gallery's website: Mathew Brady's World: Brady and the Civil War. Read the three paragraphs of text about Brady and his work. Then visit The Civil War as Photographed by Mathew Brady at the National Archives.

Look at two photos, which you'll find near the bottom of the page:

- # 7, Wounded Soldiers in a hospital
- # 15, Camp of the 44th New York Infantry near Alexandria, VA

Click on the Photo Analysis Worksheet, which you'll find at the bottom of the National Archives page. Print two copies of the sheet. Fill in one sheet for each of the photographs.

Student Guide
Lesson 7: Proclaiming Emancipation

President Lincoln changed the Civil War with his Emancipation Proclamation. The war had been a fight to save the Union; now it was also a battle for human freedom.

Lesson Objectives

- Evaluate the Emancipation Proclamation in terms of freeing slaves and its impact on the goals of the war.
- Explain the significance of the Battle of Antietam in terms of lives lost, the firing of McClellan, and psychological impact.
- Locate Antietam on a map.

PREPARE

Approximate lesson time is 60 minutes.

Materials

For the Student

Dying to Make Men Free

Map of Battles of the Civil War, 1861-1865

A History of US (Concise Edition), Volume B (1790-1877) by Joy Hakim

History Journal

LEARN
Activity 1: Freeing the Slaves *(Offline)*
Read

Read Chapter 61, pages 306–312, to learn about Lincoln's Emancipation Proclamation.

Vocabulary

You'll see these terms as you read. Write a brief definition for each term in your History Journal

- emancipation
- proclamation

Complete the Dying to Make Men Free sheet. Have an adult check your answers.

Discuss

In what ways did the Emancipation Proclamation carry out the promises of the Declaration of Independence? Discuss your thoughts with an adult.

Learn from Maps

Locate Antietam on the map of Battles of the Civil War, 1861–1865.

Instructions
Read

Read Chapter 61, pages 306–312, to learn about Lincoln's Emancipation Proclamation.

Vocabulary

You'll see these terms as you read. Write a brief definition for each term in your History Journal

- emancipation
- proclamation

Complete the Dying to Make Men Free sheet. Have an adult check your answers.

Discuss

In what ways did the Emancipation Proclamation carry out the promises of the Declaration of Independence? Discuss your thoughts with an adult.

Learn from Maps

Locate Antietam on the map of Battles of the Civil War, 1861–1865.

ASSESS

Lesson Assessment: Proclaiming Emancipation *(Online)*
You will complete an online assessment covering the main points of this lesson. Your assessment will be scored by the computer.

Name _____   Date _____

Dying to Make Men Free

1. President Lincoln needed a Union victory. He got it at the battle of

    _____ , fought near the town of Sharpsburg, Maryland.

2. That battle was the _____ day of the war, because both North and
    South suffered such terrible casualties.

3. Who did Lincoln send home after the Battle of Antietam for failing to go after the

    Confederate army? (Circle the correct answer.)

    (A) Lee

    (B) Farragut

    (C) Brady

    (D) McClellan

4. The battle gave Lincoln the victory he needed to make the _____
    Proclamation.

5. What does emancipation mean? _____

6. What does proclamation mean? _____

7. The Emancipation Proclamation announced that _____ .
    (Circle the correct answer.)

    (A) the South could leave the Union

    (B) slaves in the rebel states were free

    (C) the North would end the war immediately

    (D) slaves in every part of the country were free

8. After the Emancipation Proclamation, the freeing of the slaves became one of the

    North's _____ of the war.

9. Frederick _____ was a former slave who rejoiced in the Emancipation
    Declaration.

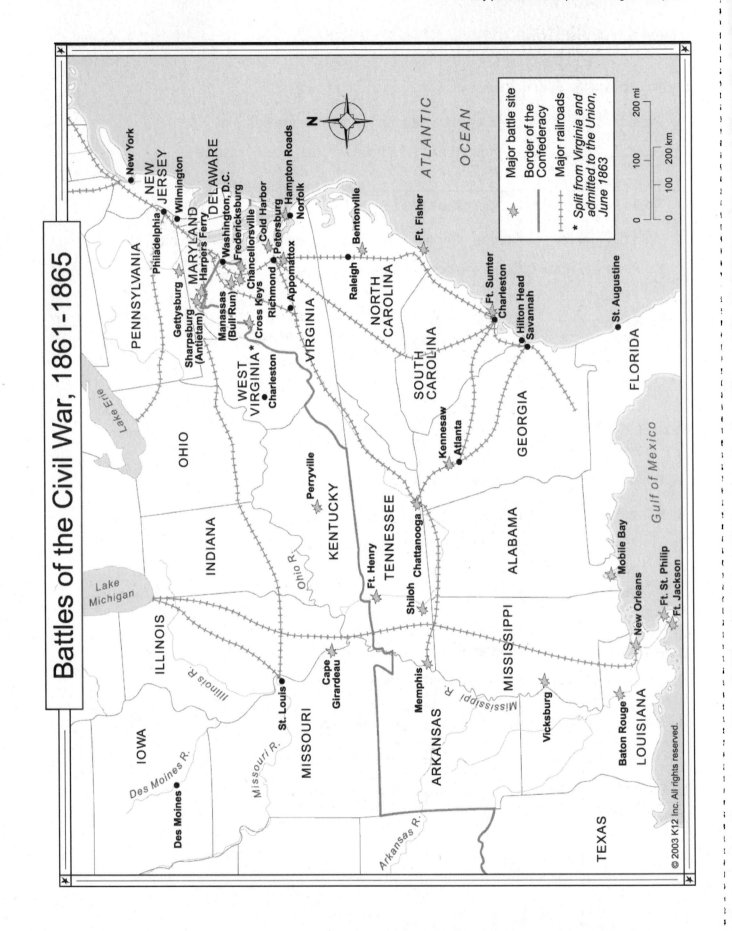

Battles of the Civil War, 1861-1865

Student Guide
Lesson 8: Fighting More Than a War

Despite opposition and prejudice, black soldiers fought with valor for the Union army. Their courage in the fight for liberty changed attitudes toward blacks in the North.

Lesson Objectives
- Summarize the story of the 54th Massachusetts Regiment and its role in changing Northern attitudes.
- Explain the reasons for the refusal to allow blacks in the Union army at the start of the war.

PREPARE

Approximate lesson time is 60 minutes.

Materials
For the Student
> Frieze Analysis
> Revolution of the Public Mind
> A History of US (Concise Edition), Volume B (1790-1877) by Joy Hakim
> History Journal

LEARN
Activity 1: Black Troops in the Union Army (Offline)
Instructions
Read

Read Chapter 62, pages 313–316. Complete the Revolution of the Public Mind sheet.

Use What You Know

Go online to the National Gallery of Art to visit the Shaw Memorial Home Page. Complete the Frieze Analysis Sheet as you analyze the frieze. A *frieze* (freez) is an artwork that is a sculptured or ornamented band, often on a building.

Read On

The Civil War was changing. Blacks were now fighting in the Union army. And civilians, too, began to feel the hardships of war as the fighting came closer to home. Read about that now in Chapter 63, pages 317–325, and Chapter 64, pages 326–328.

You'll see the term *total war* as you read. Write a brief definition for it in your History Journal.

Name _____   Date _____

Frieze Analysis

Observation

1. Study the frieze for two minutes. Begin by forming an overall impression of the frieze and examining individual items. Then divide the frieze into quadrants and study each section to see what new details you find. Use the website's magnifier to help you examine the memorial.

2. What is the main object in the frieze? What story is it trying to tell?

   _____

   _____

   _____

3. Are any there any symbolic images in the frieze?

   _____

   _____

   _____

4. Use the chart below to list people, objects, and activities in the frieze.

People	Objects	Activities

Inference

1. Based on what you have observed, what story do you think the frieze is trying to tell?

_____

_____

_____

2. What themes are present in the frieze?

_____

_____

_____

3. Is there a message in the frieze? If so, what is that message?

_____

_____

_____

Questions

1. What questions does this frieze raise in your mind?

_____

_____

_____

2. Where could you find answers to them?

_____

_____

_____

Name _____ **Date** _____

A Revolution of the Public Mind

1. At the start of the Civil War, the Northern armies _____.

    (A) sent blacks to the front lines

    (B) would not let blacks fight

    (C) gave blacks the most dangerous jobs

    (D) only accepted black soldiers from Massachusetts

2. True or false? At the beginning of the Civil War, many people believed that blacks could not fight. _____

3. How were enslaved blacks forced to contribute to the Confederate war effort?

    _____

    _____

    _____

    _____

4. Name the black regiment that charged a Confederate fort in Charleston Harbor.

    _____

5. How did this regiment turn Northern ideas about black soldiers upside down?

    _____

    _____

    _____

6. What did a reporter mean when he said there was a "revolution of the public mind"?

    _____

    _____

    _____

Student Guide
Lesson 9: Gettysburg and Vicksburg

The Civil War was fought mainly on Southern land, which caused problems for Southern civilians. Confederate General Robert E. Lee wanted the North to suffer too, so he marched his army north to Gettysburg, Pennsylvania. By the time the Confederates retreated, both sides had lost thousands of soldiers. While General Lee was meeting defeat at Gettysburg, Union General U.S. Grant was victorious and took the city of Vicksburg in Mississippi.

Lesson Objectives
- Define the term *total war* and explain its purpose.
- Describe Lee's reasons for moving into the North.
- Identify the major reason for the high casualties at Gettysburg as the use of traditional tactics in a day of more modern weapons.
- Label Gettysburg and Vicksburg on a map and explain Vicksburg's strategic importance.
- Identify the battle at Gettysburg as the turning point of the war in the east and Vicksburg as the turning point in the west.

PREPARE

Approximate lesson time is 60 minutes.

Materials
> For the Student
>> This Is War!
>> A History of US (Concise Edition), Volume B (1790-1877) by Joy Hakim
>> History Journal

LEARN
Activity 1: Three Days at Gettysburg *(Offline)*
Instructions
Check Your Reading (Chapter 63, pages 317–325, and Chapter 64, pages 326–328)

Review Chapters 63 and 64. Complete the This Is War! sheet. Have an adult check your answers.

Locate and highlight the labels for the Battle of Gettysburg and the Battle of Vicksburg on the map of Civil War Battles, 1861–1865 (from Lesson 2: It Begins).

Use What You Know

In your History Journal, explain why *total war* was an effective war strategy used by the North, and how the strategy contributed to the Battle of Gettysburg.

Optional: Beyond the Lesson

Take a virtual tour of Gettysburg, explore interactive maps, or read more about the Battle of Gettysburg and the Gettysburg National Military Park online.

Activity 2. Optional: Gettysburg *(Online)*

Name _____   Date _____

This Is War!

Complete the following chart using information from Chapter 63.

Cause	Effect
1. Northern soldiers needed wood for tent supports.	
2. Northern soldiers took over Southern houses and needed fuel to keep warm.	
3. Northern soldiers wanted fresh meat and vegetables to supplement teir army diet of coffee, bacon, and hardtack.	
4. Northern generals realized that marching through land in the South helped the war effort.	
5. General Lee wanted the North to suffer.	
6. Gettysburg townsfolk heard that soldiers were in their area.	
7. Yankee soldiers located on Cemetery Ridge.	
8. Lee's troops charged using an old-fashioned military tactic of fighting in a long, deep formation.	

9. Which battle reversed the war in the East in favor of the Union? _____

10. Which battle reversed the war in the West in favor of the Union? _____

11. Vicksburg was an important victory for the Union, because the Union now controlled the

_____ River.

Student Guide
Lesson 10: Important Words

Several months after the battle at Gettysburg, a ceremony was held to honor the soldiers who died there. President Lincoln gave his now famous two-minute speech, the Gettysburg Address.

Lesson Objectives

- Analyze the Gettysburg Address to gain understanding of its meaning.
- Summarize the story of the 54th Massachusetts Regiment and its role in changing Northern attitudes.
- Explain the reasons for the refusal to allow blacks in the Union army at the start of the war.
- Define the term *total war* and explain its purpose.
- Describe Lee's reasons for moving into the North.
- Identify the major reason for the high casualties at Gettysburg as the use of traditional tactics in a day of more modern weapons.
- Label Gettysburg and Vicksburg on a map and explain Vicksburg's strategic importance.
- Identify the battle at Gettysburg as the turning point of the war in the east and Vicksburg as the turning point in the west.

PREPARE

Approximate lesson time is 60 minutes.

Materials

For the Student

Ideas and Words

A History of US (Concise Edition), Volume B (1790-1877) by Joy Hakim

History Journal

LEARN
Activity 1: The Gettysburg Address *(Offline)*
Instructions
Read

Read Chapter 65, pages 329–332.
Use What You Know

Read the Gettysburg Address in Chapter 65 aloud. After you have read it, complete the Ideas and Words sheet to help you understand Lincoln's purpose in giving the speech. Have an adult check your answers.
Look Back

Review your work from Lessons 8, 9, and 10.

Optional: Beyond the Lesson

Lincoln wrote several drafts of the Gettysburg Address. Copies of the speech, written in Lincoln's own hand, exist today. To learn about the changes he made to his speech and what techniques are used to preserve the actual papers, go online to The Gettysburg Address at the Library of Congress Exhibition.

ASSESS
Mid-Unit Assessment: Turning Points and Words (*Online*)

You will complete an online Mid-Unit Assessment covering the main points of this unit. Your assessment will be scored by the computer.

LEARN
Activity 2. Optional: Drafts of the Gettysburg Address (*Online*)

Name _____   Date _____

Words and Ideas

Listed in the chart are some ideas and concepts that Lincoln wanted to share with the public after the Battle of Gettysburg. Match the actual words in the Gettysburg Address with Lincoln's ideas. Draw a line to connect the words with the ideas.

Lincoln's Ideas	Lincoln's Words
Referred to the American Revolution (1776)	"Now we are engaged in a great civil war, testing whether that nation, or any nation so conceived and so dedicated, can long endure."
Upheld the idea (expressed in the Declaration of Independence) of liberty and equality for ALL	"…that from these honored dead we take increased devotion to that cause for which they gave the last full measure of devotion…"
The Civil War was a test of democracy.	"Four score and seven years ago our fathers brought forth on this continent, a new nation…"
The reason for the ceremony	"…and that government of the people, by the people, for the people…"
The dead inspire the living.	"…conceived in Liberty, and dedicated to the proposition that all men are created equal."
Reaffirmed the idea of government by consent of the people	"We have come to dedicate a portion of that field, as a final resting place for those who here gave their lives that that nation might live."

In your own words, and in one sentence, tell what you think Lincoln's purpose was in giving the Gettysburg Address.

_____

_____

Student Guide
Lesson 11: Almost Over

It would take a bold move to end the war. Northerners were tired of fighting; Southerners' land and homes were in peril. President Lincoln was up for reelection, and even he didn't think he could win. When two Union generals finally turned the tide for the North, the end was in sight.

Lesson Objectives

- Describe the Union strategy late in the war as an attempt to end the war as quickly as possible by trapping Lee's army.
- Identify Sherman as the general who captured Atlanta and used total warfare in Georgia and the Carolinas.
- Explain why Lincoln was able to win a second term in office.

PREPARE

Approximate lesson time is 60 minutes.

Materials

> For the Student
>> Match It Up
>
> A History of US (Concise Edition), Volume B (1790-1877) by Joy Hakim
>
> History Journal

LEARN
Activity 1: When Will It End? *(Offline)*

Instructions
Read

Read Chapter 66, pages 333–339. Complete the Match It Up sheet by matching statements on the left with the correct answer on the right. Have an adult check your answers.

Use What You Know

Imagine you are General Grant. In your History Journal, write a letter home to your wife, Julia, explaining why you decided to besiege Petersburg.

Name _____   Date _____

Match It Up

Draw a line between the statements or words that go together.

Reason for Northern strategy to end the war quickly	Petersburg
What Grant would have to do in order to be victorious	Sherman
Supply center for Lee's army	Pontoon bridges
How Grant crossed the James River	The longer fighting continued, the more likely Northerners would give up
General who captured Atlanta and used total warfare in Georgia and the Carolinas	The capture of Atlanta by the Union army
Change that made a difference and allowed Lincoln to be re-elected	Trap the Confederate army and lay siege

Student Guide
Lesson 12: Hope and Sorrow

As the war came to a close, Lincoln saw hope amid the destruction. While Grant and Lee hammered out the terms of surrender, Lincoln and Congress moved ahead to amend the Constitution to end slavery.

Lesson Objectives

- Summarize the surrender at Appomattox Courthouse and explain why it is considered "generous."
- Describe the change in Lincoln's views on slavery between his first and second elections.
- Summarize Lincoln's view of Reconstruction as one of generosity and kindness to North and South.

PREPARE

Approximate lesson time is 60 minutes.

Materials

For the Student

Guided Reading: Chapters 67 and 68

A History of US (Concise Edition), Volume B (1790-1877) by Joy Hakim

History Journal

LEARN
Activity 1: It's Over! (Offline)
Instructions
Read

Complete the Guided Reading: Chapters 67 and 68 sheet as you read Chapter 67, pages 340–343, and Chapter 68, pages 344–347. Have an adult check your answers.

Discuss

Unlike the terms of surrender in some wars, the terms of surrender for the South following the Civil War were very generous. In fact, President Lincoln worked hard to ensure that the South and Southerners were not punished (any more than the war had already punished them). Think about what might have happened if Lincoln and the North had punished the South by making them pay all the costs of the war or by charging all Confederate soldiers with treason. Discuss your ideas with an adult.

Name _____ Date _____

Guided Reading: Chapters 67 and 68

Use the word bank to fill in the blanks.

```
                        Word Bank

   Reconstruction        slavery      amendments        home

   Appomattox Court House      guns       purpose        horses

          punish        sidearms        treason
```

When Lincoln was first elected president, he hoped to prevent war by allowing

(1) _____ in the United States. As time went on, he saw the

(2) _____ of the war as putting an end to slavery. Once the Civil War

was over, President Lincoln did not intend to (3) _____ the South. He felt
everyone had suffered enough. He wanted to help the South, and the whole country, rebuild.

The process of rebuilding the country following the Civil War was called

(4) _____. The official surrender by General Lee to General Grant

occurred at (5) _____, and the terms were generous to the South.

The terms of surrender said that the Southern soldiers could go (6) _____

and would not be prosecuted for (7) _____. It also said

that they must surrender their (8) _____, but could keep their

(9) _____. Officers were allowed to keep their

(10) _____.

In order to make the achievements of the war permanent, three (11) _____
were added to the U.S. Constitution.

Student Guide
Lesson 13: Unit Review

You have finished the unit, The Civil War. It's time to review what you've learned. You will take the Unit Assessment in the next lesson.

Lesson Objectives

- Demonstrate mastery of important knowledge and skills taught in previous lessons.

PREPARE

Approximate lesson time is 60 minutes.

Materials

For the Student

    🖳 Outline Map of the United States

    A History of US (Concise Edition), Volume B (1790-1877) by Joy Hakim

    History Journal

LEARN
Activity 1: A Look Back *(Offline)*
Instructions
History Journal Review

Review what you've learned in this unit by going through your History Journal. You should:

- Look at activity sheets you've completed for this unit.
- Review unit vocabulary words.
- Read through any writing assignments you completed during the unit.
- Review the assessments you took.

Don't rush through; take your time. Your History Journal is a great resource for a unit review.

Online Review

Use the following to review this unit online:

- The Big Picture
- Time Line

Fifty States

How many states can you identify? Print the Outline Map of the United States and see.

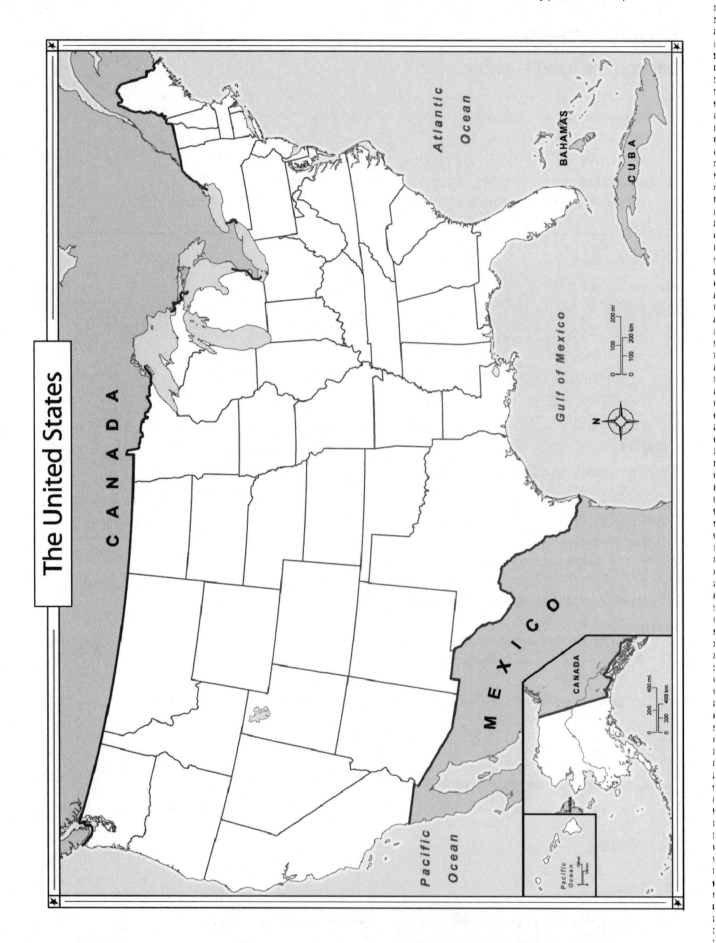

The United States

CANADA

MEXICO

Atlantic Ocean

BAHAMAS

CUBA

Gulf of Mexico

Pacific Ocean

CANADA

Pacific Ocean

Student Guide
Lesson 14: Unit Assessment

You've finished this unit! Take the Unit Assessment.

Lesson Objectives

- Demonstrate mastery of important knowledge and skills in this unit.
- Define *civil war*, *Yankees*, and *border state*.
- List the advantages of the North (more people, industry, and food) and of the South (skilled fighters, outdoorsmen, Southerners' belief that they were fighting for their land) as the war began.
- Identify Richmond as the capital of the Confederacy and Jefferson Davis as its president.
- Identify the basic principles that separated North and South in 1861, including differing views on slavery and the right to leave the Union.
- Summarize the attitude of most soldiers as believing the war would be quick and glorious and the reasons they were incorrect, including new weapons and lack of experience.
- Identify on a map and explain the significance of the first battle at Bull Run (Manassas) as changing attitudes about war in both the North and the South.
- Describe the Anaconda Plan as the strategy for Union victory.
- Identify Ulysses S. Grant as the general who led the Union to victory by outlasting the enemy and winning many battles.
- Identify Robert E. Lee as the leader of Confederate forces and recognize that he chose to leave the Union out of loyalty to his state.
- Identify ironclad ships—including the *Monitor* (Union) and the *Merrimack*, or *Virginia* (Confederate)—as
- one of the reasons the Civil War is considered a modern war.
- Evaluate the Emancipation Proclamation in terms of freeing slaves and its impact on the goals of the war.
- Explain the significance of the Battle of Antietam in terms of lives lost, the firing of McClellan, and psychological impact.
- Explain the reasons for the refusal to allow blacks in the Union army at the start of the war.
- Define the term *total war* and explain its purpose.
- Identify the battle at Gettysburg as the turning point of the war in the east and Vicksburg as the turning
- point in the west.
- Identify Sherman as the general who captured Atlanta and used total warfare in Georgia and the Carolinas.
- Summarize the surrender at Appomattox Courthouse and explain why it is considered "generous."
- Describe the change in Lincoln's views on slavery between his first and second elections.
- Summarize Lincoln's view of Reconstruction as one of generosity and kindness to North and South.

PREPARE

Approximate lesson time is 60 minutes.

ASSESS

Unit Assessment: The Civil War, Part 1 *(Online)*

Complete the computer-scored portion of the Unit Assessment. When you have finished, complete the teacher-scored portion of the assessment and submit it to your teacher.

Unit Assessment: The Civil War, Part 2 *(Offline)*

Complete the teacher-scored portion of the Unit Assessment and submit it to your teacher.

Student Guide
Lesson 1: Tragedy

When the Civil War ended in 1865, slavery was over and the federal government controlled the reunited country. The war had taken a terrible toll. Reconstruction plans tried to deal with the tough problems, but tragic events and huge obstacles made it incredibly difficult.

Lincoln had a plan for reuniting the country and helping the newly freed slaves make the transition to full citizenship. But before he could implement his plan, he was assassinated.

Lesson Objectives

- Define *Reconstruction* and *assassin*.
- Describe Lincoln's assassination and identify John Wilkes Booth as the assassin.

PREPARE

Approximate lesson time is 60 minutes.

Materials

> For the Student
>
> > Who or What Am I?
> >
> > A History of US (Concise Edition), Volume B (1790-1877) by Joy Hakim
> >
> > History Journal

LEARN
Activity 1: Goodbye, Mr. Lincoln *(Offline)*
Instructions
Read

Read Chapter 69, pages 348–352. Complete the Who or What Am I? sheet. Have an adult check your answers.

Use What You Know

Read the feature titled "The Whole World Bowed in Grief" in Chapter 69. Respond to the following in your History Journal. Use specific quotes or words from the writing. Share your answers with an adult.

1. Who is the author?
2. What type of document is this? (For example, a letter, a diary entry?)
3. Choose two ideas or quotes that illustrate what the author thought of President Lincoln.
4. Choose one quote from the document that tells you how others felt about President Lincoln's death.

Read On

Read Chapter 70, pages 353–356. As you read, try to identify some of the social and economic issues the United States faced at the end of the Civil War.

Name _____ Date _____

Who or What Am I?

Use the word bank to complete the sheet.

Word Bank		
Reconstruction	John Wilkes Booth	Civil War
Ford's Theatre	newly freed slaves	assassin

1. I am the war that tested a free, democratic government where people rule themselves. What am I?

   _____

2. I am Lincoln's vision for bringing North and South together into a united nation. What am I?

   _____

3. I am the people who needed schooling, land, and jobs when the war ended. Who am I?

   _____

4. I am the actor who shot President Lincoln. Who am I? _____

5. I killed the president for fanatical political reasons. What am I? an _____

6. I am the place where President Lincoln was shot. What am I? _____

Student Guide
Lesson 2: New Era, New President

Lincoln wanted to rebuild the country gently, but his assassination deprived the nation of his patience and wisdom. The new president, Andrew Johnson, was a Southerner loyal to the Union. Unfortunately, he was stubborn and uncompromising when the country needed flexible and understanding leadership.

Lesson Objectives

- Identify the social and economic issues the United States faced at the end of the Civil War.
- Summarize Lincoln's approach to Reconstruction.
- Describe the strengths and weaknesses Andrew Johnson brought to the presidency.

PREPARE

Approximate lesson time is 60 minutes.

Materials

For the Student

Reconstruction: For or Against

A History of US (Concise Edition), Volume B (1790-1877) by Joy Hakim

History Journal

LEARN
Activity 1: Rebuilding (Offline)
Instructions
Check Your Reading (Chapter 70, pages 353–356)

Did you identify some of the social and economic issues the United States faced at the end of the Civil War? Discuss these with an adult.

Use What You Know

Reconstruction was a tough time. People had strong opinions about what needed to be done. Unfortunately, those opinions often conflicted. During the next few lessons, you will keep track of the actions taken by various people and groups to either promote (For) or obstruct (Against) the goals of Reconstruction.

As you come across them in your reading, list the actions in the appropriate columns on the Reconstruction: For or Against sheet. You will be asked to explain to an adult why the actions you included either promoted or obstructed Reconstruction. The list you create will serve as a useful review tool. If you fill the page, draw a line down the middle of a blank page and continue your list.

There are some sample entries on the list to get you started. Compare your answers to those in the Learning Coach Guide.

Look Back

Review your work in this lesson and read the Flash Cards before you take the assessment.

Read On

Read Chapter 71, pages 357–361. As you read, continue adding to the Reconstruction: For or Against sheet.

ASSESS

Lesson Assessment: New Era, New President (*Online*)

You will complete an online assessment covering the main points of this lesson. Your assessment will be scored by the computer.

Name _____   Date _____

Reconstruction: For or Against

Reconstruction was a tough time. People had strong opinions about what needed to be done. Unfortunately those opinions often conflicted. List actions taken by individuals or groups to either promote (For) or obstruct (Against) the goals of Reconstruction in the appropriate columns.

For	Against
Both Republicans and Democrats supported Andrew Johnson at first.	Some Northerners thought the Rebel leaders should be hanged

Student Guide
Lesson 3: Executive Efforts

The government faced a huge challenge trying to bring the Confederate states back into the Union. The Freedmen's Bureau helped African Americans adjust to their new lives, but it was not easy. Although many people had fought and died for justice during the Civil War, there were many attempts to undermine justice during Reconstruction. In the South, black codes forced African Americans back into conditions similar to slavery. White supremacy groups such as the Ku Klux Klan terrorized opponents.

Lesson Objectives

- Identify the Freedmen's Bureau and describe the kind of work it did.
- Summarize the ways in which some white Southerners denied justice to blacks.
- List political questions that had to be addressed during Reconstruction.

PREPARE

Approximate lesson time is 60 minutes.

Materials

For the Student

Black Codes

A History of US (Concise Edition), Volume B (1790-1877) by Joy Hakim

History Journal

LEARN
Activity 1: Presidential Reconstruction (Offline)
Instructions
Check Your Reading (Chapter 71, pages 357–361)

Add to the Reconstruction: For or Against sheet if you did not do this while you read Chapter 71. What ideas and events did you read about in this chapter that contributed to the problems of Reconstruction? How did people try to solve the problems? Compare your answers to those in the Learning Coach Guide. Discuss the items you listed with an adult. Explain why you think each action promoted or obstructed the goals of Reconstruction.
Use What You Know

Black codes were laws passed by Southern states. They violated the constitutional rights of African Americans and forced them to live in conditions that were a lot like slavery.

On the Black Codes sheet, match the code with the constitutional right that it violated. Discuss your answers with an adult.

Discuss

Discuss the following with an adult:

The Ku Klux Klan still exists today. In the past, members of the Klan have committed hate crimes. Many people still consider the Klan a hate group. Are they a legal organization? What kinds of hate crimes are committed today? By whom? Against whom? Have any laws been passed that address hate crimes?

Look Back

Review your work in this lesson and review the Flash Cards before you take the assessment.

Read On

The Civil War had been fought over the issues of slavery and states' rights—issues that would determine what the nation stood for. As Reconstruction developed, it was clear that those issues had not been settled.

Read Chapter 72, pages 362–365, and Chapter 73, pages 366–369. Continue adding to the list on the Reconstruction: For or Against sheet.
Here are a few examples of new items to include: The Civil Rights Act of 1866 nullified the black codes [For]; Northerners went South to help [For]; President Johnson vetoed the Civil Rights law [Against].

Vocabulary

As you read, write a brief definition for each of the following terms in your History Journal.

- carpetbagger
- scalawag

ASSESS

Lesson Assessment: Executive Efforts (*Online*)
You will complete an online assessment covering the main points of this lesson. Your assessment will be scored by the computer.

Name _____ Date _____

Black Codes

Match each code with the right that is being violated. Write the appropriate constitutional amendment in the blank after each code. You may want to first review the excerpt from each amendment.

Constitutional Amendments:

1st Amendment: Congress shall make no law… abridging the right of the people peaceably to assemble.

2nd Amendment: … the right of the people to keep and bear Arms, shall not be infringed.

6th Amendment: In all criminal prosecutions, the accused shall enjoy the right… to be confronted with the witnesses against him; to have compulsory process for obtaining witnesses in his favor.

13th Amendment: Neither slavery nor involuntary servitude… shall exist within the United States, or any place subject to their jurisdiction.

14th Amendment: All persons born or naturalized in the United States… are citizens of the United States and of the State wherein they reside. No State shall make or enforce any law which shall abridge the privileges or immunities of citizens of the United States; nor shall any State deprive any person of life, liberty, or property, without due process of law; nor deny to any person within its jurisdiction the equal protection of the laws.

Black Codes:

1. Every Negro is required to be in the regular service of some white person or former owner, who shall be held responsible for the conduct of that Negro. _____

2. No public meetings or congregations of Negroes shall be allowed after sunset. Such public meetings may be held during the day with the permission of the local captain in charge of the area. _____

3. No Negro shall be permitted to preach or otherwise speak out to congregations of colored people without special permission in writing from the government.

_____

4. A Negro may not testify against a white person in a Court of Law. _____

5. It shall be illegal for a Negro or a person of Negro descent to marry a white person.

   _____

6. No Negro shall be permitted outside in public after sundown without permission in writing from the government. A Negro conducting business for a white person may do so but

   only under the direct supervision of his employer. _____

7. No Negro shall sell, trade, or exchange merchandise within this area without the special

   written permission of his employer. _____

8. No Negro who is not in the military service shall be allowed to carry firearms of any kind or weapons of any type without the special written permission of his employers.

   _____

Student Guide
Lesson 4: Legislative Labors

Two amendments addressed the causes of the Civil War. The 13th Amendment abolished slavery. The 14th Amendment weakened states' rights and made the federal government the guardian of individual liberty. Radical Republicans in Congress took control of Reconstruction from the president. They had federal troops occupy the South. The doors of government were opened to blacks, who now had the right to vote.

Lesson Objectives
- Identify the ways in which the government attempted to give blacks full citizenship.
- Explain the impact of the 14th Amendment on the federal balance of power.
- Describe the effects of congressional Reconstruction (as opposed to presidential Reconstruction).

PREPARE

Approximate lesson time is 60 minutes.

Materials
For the Student
> The 14th Amendment Digest
>
> A History of US (Concise Edition), Volume B (1790-1877) by Joy Hakim
>
> History Journal

LEARN
Activity 1: Congressional Reconstruction (Offline)
Instructions
Check Your Reading (Chapter 72, pages 362–365, and Chapter 73, pages 366–369)

If you did not add to the Reconstruction: For or Against sheet while you read Chapters 72 and 73, do this now. What ideas and events did you read about in these chapters that affected the problems of Reconstruction? How did people try to solve the problems?

Discuss the ideas you listed with an adult. Explain why you think each item promoted or obstructed the goals of Reconstruction.

Use What You Know

The 13th Amendment is pretty simple. It ended slavery. But the 14th Amendment is not so simple. It settled the issue of states' rights, but it also did a lot more than that.

Reading laws and other legal text can be hard because they usually aren't written in plain English. To understand them, sometimes it helps to cross out words that distract from the basic meaning. It also helps to circle crucial words that are difficult or uncommon. Once you've looked up definitions of the circled words, you can reread the parts that haven't been crossed out.

Read passages from the 14th Amendment on the 14th Amendment Digest sheet, and explain in your own words what you think they mean. We've already crossed out parts and circled the difficult, but important, words for you. Try it yourself the next time you read legal text. Compare your answers to those in the Learning Coach Guide.

Look Back

Review your work and look at the Flash Cards before you take the assessment.

_____

ASSESS

Lesson Assessment: Legislative Labors (*Online*)

You will complete an online assessment covering the main points of this lesson. Your assessment will be scored by the computer.

Name _____   Date _____

The 14th Amendment Digest

Read the passages from the 14th Amendment below, and explain in your own words what you think the passages mean. Some words have been crossed out to make the major part of the sentence clearer to you. These words are important, but you will be able to understand the sentence without them. Other words that may be uncommon or difficult have been circled. If necessary, find the meaning of these words in a dictionary.

"All persons born or naturalized in the United States, ~~and subject to the jurisdiction thereof~~, are citizens of the United States ~~and of the State wherein they reside~~."

1. This means: _____

_____

"No State shall make ~~or enforce~~ any law which shall (abridge) the (privileges) ~~or immunities~~ of citizens of the United States; nor shall any State deprive any person of life, liberty, or property, without due process of law; nor deny to any person ~~within its jurisdiction~~ the equal protection of the laws."

2. This means: _____

_____

"Representatives shall be (apportioned) ~~among the several States according to their respective numbers~~, counting the whole number of persons in each State, excluding Indians not taxed."

3. This means: _____

_____

The following statement summarizes the impact that the 14th Amendment had on the federal balance of power. Complete the statement by filling in the blanks with either the term *federal* or *state*.

According to the 14th Amendment, if an individual believed that the state violated his civil

rights, that person could sue the _____ in _____ court. This meant

that the _____ government, not the _____, would decide on the

constitutionality of the individual's claim. This gave a lot of power to the Supreme Court, a

part of the _____ government, and took power from the _____ .

Student Guide
Lesson 5: Single-Minded Stevens

Thaddeus Stevens was fiercely determined to win justice for blacks. The clash between Congressman Stevens and the equally strong-willed president, Andrew Johnson, set the stage for one of the great trials in American history—the first impeachment of a U.S. president.

Lesson Objectives

- Define *radical*.
- Identify the leader of the Radical Republicans.
- Define *impeachment* and explain its purpose.

PREPARE

Approximate lesson time is 60 minutes.

Materials

For the Student

How Does Impeachment Work?

A History of US (Concise Edition), Volume B (1790-1877) by Joy Hakim

History Journal

LEARN
Activity 1: One Radical Republican *(Offline)*
Instructions
Read

Read Chapter 74, pages 370–373, to learn about Thaddeus Stevens. His fierce honesty and strong convictions set in motion a tremendous constitutional power struggle.

On the Reconstruction: For or Against sheet, add new information to your continuing list of problems and solutions following the Civil War. What ideas and events did you read about in this chapter that added to the problems of Reconstruction? What were the ways people tried to solve these problems?

Vocabulary

As you read, write the definitions for the following terms in your History Journal.

- radical
- impeach

Use What You Know

The U.S. Constitution, Article 2, Section 4, states: *The President, Vice President and all civil officers of the United States, shall be removed from office on impeachment for, and conviction of, treason, bribery, or other high crimes and misdemeanors.*

The impeachment process is complicated. The Founders did not want it to be easy to remove an official, especially a president, from office. But knowing the basics will help you understand the events of the past and the difficult decisions our nation's leaders sometimes face.

Complete the How Does Impeachment Work? sheet. You will use this activity sheet in the next lesson.

Name _____   Date _____

How Does Impeachment Work?

The Constitution includes a process called impeachment that allows Congress to bring to trial U.S. government officials accused of serious misconduct. To impeach someone means to charge him or her with a crime or some other misdeed.

The Founders included the impeachment process in the Constitution so the American people would have a way to remove officials who break the law or abuse their power in a serious way. Congress has the power to impeach presidents, vice presidents, cabinet officers, federal judges, or any other civilian U.S. official—except members of Congress. It's not easy to impeach someone, though. It's a long, complicated process. Let's see how the basics work.

- Step 1: Only the U.S. House of Representatives has the power to begin the impeachment process against a U.S. official. So first, House members must debate whether or not the official deserves to be charged with crimes or serious misconduct.

- Step 2: After debate, the House votes on whether or not to bring charges. If a majority of the House members vote yes, then the official is said to be "impeached." That is, the official has been accused of crimes or serious misconduct, and now must stand trial.

- Step 3: Next, the process moves to the U.S. Senate, where the trial takes place. The Senate sits as a jury and hears the charges against the impeached official. During the trial, senators listen to evidence and arguments about whether the official should be found guilty of the charges.

- Step 4: At the end of the trial, the senators vote on whether the evidence proves that the official is guilty of the charges. If two-thirds of the senators vote guilty, then the official is convicted.

- Step 5: Someone who is impeached and convicted doesn't go to jail or pay a fine. The punishment is that the individual is removed from office. The Senate may also prohibit that person from ever again holding office in the U.S. government. He or she may also be tried in a regular court of law. If convicted there, the punishment could involve a fine or jail time.

The nation held its breath in 1868 as Andrew Johnson faced the first presidential impeachment. Only twice since then has Congress started the process against presidents. In 1974, the House of Representatives was on the verge of bringing charges against President Richard Nixon, but Nixon resigned his office rather than face impeachment. In 1998, the House charged President Bill Clinton with lying under oath. The Senate held a trial but found him not guilty. So, like Andrew Johnson, Clinton was impeached by the House but not convicted in the Senate—and therefore he stayed in office.

The House of Representatives has voted to impeach officials only 16 times since the nation's founding. Only seven of those people were then convicted in the Senate. They were all judges who were removed from the bench.

Use what you have just learned about the impeachment process to fill in the blanks below. The letters in the boxes will spell out an important process of our political system's checks and balances.

1. The process of removing an official from office is defined in

   Article 1, Section 2 of the ___ ___ ___ ___ ___ [ ] ___ ___ ___ ___ ___ ___.

2. Offenses that may bring charges are ___ ___ ___ [ ] ___ ___ or serious misconduct.

3. Andrew Johnson and Bill Clinton were both [ ] ___ ___ ___ ___ ___ ___ ___ ___ who were impeached.

4. Who brings charges? the ___ ___ ___ ___ [ ]

5. Who acts as the jury? the ___ ___ ___ ___ ___ [ ]

6. The House may not charge members of [ ] ___ ___ ___ ___ ___ ___ ___.

7. Conviction occurs if ___ ___ ___ ___ ___ [ ] ___ ___ ___ ___ of the senators vote guilty.

Student Guide
Lesson 6: A President on Trial

The fate of President Johnson rested on a single vote. In an act of courage, Senator Edmund Ross of Kansas voted "not guilty"—and in favor of preserving the balance of power between Congress and the presidency.

Lesson Objectives

- Explain how Andrew Johnson's impeachment affected the balance of power in the U.S. government.
- Identify Edmund Ross and his view of Johnson's impeachment.
- Describe the process of impeachment under the U.S. Constitution.

PREPARE

Approximate lesson time is 60 minutes.

Materials

For the Student

Senator Ross Votes Not Guilty

A History of US (Concise Edition), Volume B (1790-1877) by Joy Hakim

History Journal

LEARN
Activity 1: Just Cause? *(Offline)*
Instructions
Read

Use the How Does Impeachment Work? sheet from the Single-Minded Stevens lesson to trace the impeachment of President Johnson as you read Chapter 75, pages 374–377.

Use What You Know

Review our federal government's systems of checks and balances in the online activity, Checks and Balances. Drag each small box to one of the three choices, which are the legislative branch (U.S. Capitol), executive branch (White House), and judicial branch (U.S. Supreme Court).

Complete the Senator Ross Votes Not Guilty sheet.

Name _____   Date _____

Senator Ross Votes Not Guilty

The impeachment of President Andrew Johnson in 1868 was more than a struggle between the president who supported Abraham Lincoln's policy of lenient Reconstruction and the Radical Republicans of Congress who wished to treat the South as "conquered lands." It was also a struggle between two branches of the U.S. government.

Each branch of government has its own powers under the Constitution. (To review the three branches of government, complete the Checks and Balances activity online.) Each branch can also check the power of the other two so that no one branch or person becomes too powerful.

During Reconstruction, some members of Congress tried to make the legislative branch more powerful than the executive. They wrote a law that took away the president's power to fire his own cabinet members (Tenure of Office Act). When Andrew Johnson challenged that law, he was impeached. It was at Johnson's impeachment trial in the U.S. Senate that Senator Edmund Ross became a key player.

As the trial progressed, it became clear that the Radical Republicans did not intend to give Johnson a fair trial. Evidence in his favor was excluded. Bribery was rampant.

Thirty-six votes were needed for the two-thirds majority required for conviction. Thirty-five senators said they planned to vote against Johnson. Edmund Ross was the only senator who refused to judge the president before hearing all the evidence.

Ross's party and his constituents in Kansas bombarded him with letters and telegraph messages demanding conviction. He was spied upon, offered bribes, and harangued daily. The Radical Republicans threatened him with political ruin if he did not vote for conviction.

Ross listened to the evidence. He voted not guilty, but the cost was enormous.

Ross's career in politics was over. Neither he nor any of the Republicans who voted against conviction were ever elected to the Senate again. When he returned to Kansas, Ross and his family suffered social isolation, physical attacks, and near poverty. If he had voted differently, he might have had an excellent career in the Senate and in future politics. Edmund Ross was intelligent, articulate, and popular. He threw it all away for one act of conscience. But he told his wife, "Millions of men cursing me today will bless me tomorrow for having saved the country "

Ross understood that his vote wasn't only about an individual president. Years later, he explained why he had sacrificed his career.

> *"In a large sense, the independence of the executive… branch of the government was on trial. If the President must step down… from partisan considerations [political reasons], the office of the President would… be… ever after subordinated to [controlled by] the legislative… This government had never faced so insidious [menacing] a danger…"*

Two decades after the trial, Congress repealed the law that Johnson had challenged and eventually the Supreme Court declared it unconstitutional.

1. What law did President Johnson challenge, resulting in his impeachment?

   _____

2. Why was Senator Ross under so much pressure?

   _____

   _____

3. Why did Ross vote as he did?

   _____

   _____

   _____

4. At what stage was the impeachment process halted?

   _____

5. Suppose Johnson had been convicted. What would have happened next?

   _____

Student Guide
Lesson 7: Turning Back

Corruption, lack of leadership, and lack of popular support for Reconstruction allowed the old guard to slip back into power in the South. In 1877, a political deal led President Rutherford Hayes to call an end to Reconstruction. By the close of the decade, black Southerners found themselves under the leash of a new master—a fool named Jim Crow.

Lesson Objectives
- Define and describe *sharecropping* and explain why it kept people in poverty.
- Describe the ways many Southern whites denied blacks rights after Reconstruction ended.
- Summarize the problems many Southern whites believed were caused by Reconstruction.

PREPARE

Approximate lesson time is 60 minutes.

Materials
For the Student

Sharecropping: A Cycle of Debt

A History of US (Concise Edition), Volume B (1790-1877) by Joy Hakim

History Journal

LEARN
Activity 1: Cycle of Debt *(Offline)*
Instructions
Read

Learn about the failure of Reconstruction as you read Chapter 76, pages 378–382. Continue adding to your list on the Reconstruction: For or Against sheet. Identify the ideas and events that either promoted (For) or obstructed (Against) the goals of Reconstruction.

Vocabulary

As you read, write the definitions for the following terms in your History Journal.

- Jim Crow
- segregation
- sharecropper

Use What You Know

Read and complete the Sharecropping: A Cycle of Debt sheet.

Name _____   Date _____

Sharecropping: A Cycle of Debt

What is sharecropping?

After the Civil War, many blacks fled the violence and poverty of the South and moved to the North and to the West. Most blacks, however, had no choice but to remain on the farms and plantations. They were uneducated, poor, and did not know how to live outside of slavery.

Many planters had a lot of land but very little money to pay wages. A sharecropping system developed. Former slaves and poor whites agreed to work a plot of land owned by someone else, often a former master, in exchange for a share of the crop. They signed contracts. The landowner provided land, a house, work animals, tools, and seed.

The problem with the system was that a sharecropper needed food, clothing, and other supplies, but he would not receive any money until the crop was harvested and sold. The sharecropper was forced to rely on credit from stores owned by the landowner to take care of his family. The sharecropper would pay back the landowner after the harvest.

At harvest time the crop was divided between the sharecropper and the landowner and sold. There was not usually enough profit to let the sharecropper pay off the debt, and take care of his family until the next harvest. The sharecropper had to continue to borrow from the landowner. The sharecropper could not leave the land until he was out of debt, but that rarely happened. Some dishonest landowners made sure that never happened. They knew the former slaves could not read or understand the accounting books, so they tricked them.

When sharecroppers realized they could not get out of debt, some of them tried to flee to the North. Those who were caught and arrested were forced to work as prison laborers.

Although sharecropping replaced slavery after the Civil War, usually that only meant the family was bound to a landowner rather than a slave owner.

A sharecropper is a person who lives and raises crops on land that belongs to someone else in exchange for a share of the crop or its profits.

A tenant farmer is a person who farms on rented land.

Both tenant farmers and sharecroppers were trapped by unfair practices that forced them to remain in debt.

Cycle of Debt

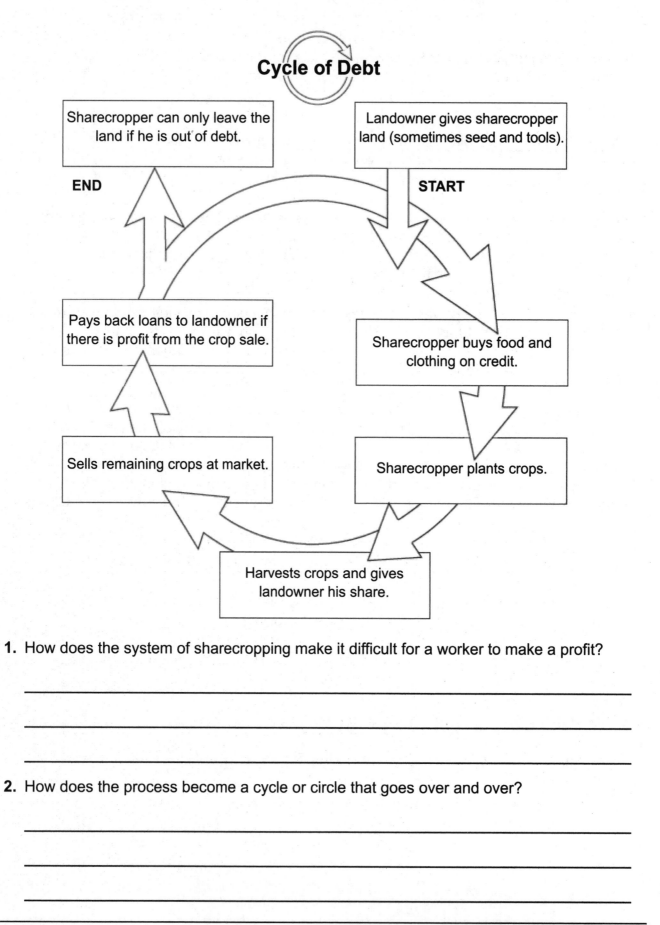

Sharecropper can only leave the land if he is out of debt.

END

Landowner gives sharecropper land (sometimes seed and tools).

START

Pays back loans to landowner if there is profit from the crop sale.

Sharecropper buys food and clothing on credit.

Sells remaining crops at market.

Sharecropper plants crops.

Harvests crops and gives landowner his share.

1. How does the system of sharecropping make it difficult for a worker to make a profit?

_____

_____

_____

2. How does the process become a cycle or circle that goes over and over?

_____

_____

_____

3. The vast majority of sharecroppers couldn't read or keep their own books (accounts). How did this hurt people who sharecropped with dishonest landowners?

_____

_____

_____

_____

_____

4. Did sharecropping solve the problems of the former slaves?

_____

_____

_____

_____

_____

5. The text indicated the slaves had nowhere to go and no home once they were set free. What problems would this create?

_____

_____

_____

_____

_____

Student Guide
Lesson 8: Unit Review

You have finished the unit, Rebuilding a Nation. It's time to review what you've learned. You will take the Unit Assessment in the next lesson.

Lesson Objectives
- Demonstrate mastery of important knowledge and skills in this unit.

PREPARE

Approximate lesson time is 60 minutes.

Materials

For the Student

A History of US (Concise Edition), Volume B (1790-1877) by Joy Hakim

History Journal

Keywords and Pronunciation

impeach : to charge a public official with crimes or misconduct

Jim Crow : a system of laws that began in the late 1800s that forced blacks to use separate and inferior facilities

Ku Klux Klan : an organization formed in the South in 1866 that used lynching and violence to intimidate and control blacks and others

radical : someone who promotes extreme or revolutionary changes in existing laws, practices, or conditions

Reconstruction : the time period after the Civil War (1865 to 1877) in which the nation tried to reorganize and remake the South without slavery

segregation : the practice of separating racial, ethnic, or religious groups from one another, especially in public places

sharecropper : a person who lives and raises crops on land that belongs to someone else in exchange for a share of the crop or its profits

LEARN
Activity 1: A Look Back (Offline)
Instructions
History Journal Review

Review what you've learned in this unit by going through your History Journal. You should:

- Look at activity sheets you've completed for this unit.
- Review unit vocabulary words.
- Read through any writing assignments you completed during the unit.
- Review the assessments you took.

Don't rush through; take your time. Your History Journal is a great resource for a unit review.

Student Guide
Lesson 9: Unit Assessment

You've finished this unit! Take the Unit Assessment.

Lesson Objectives

- Summarize Lincoln's approach to Reconstruction.
- Describe the strengths and weaknesses Andrew Johnson brought to the presidency.
- Identify the Freedmen's Bureau and describe the kind of work it did.
- Summarize the ways in which some white Southerners denied justice to blacks.
- Identify the ways in which the government attempted to give blacks full citizenship.
- Explain the impact of the 14th Amendment on the federal balance of power.
- Describe the effects of congressional Reconstruction (as opposed to presidential Reconstruction).
- Define *radical*.
- Define *impeachment* and explain its purpose.
- Explain how Andrew Johnson's impeachment affected the balance of power in the U.S. government.
- Define and describe *sharecropping* and explain why it kept people in poverty.
- Describe the ways many Southern whites denied blacks rights after Reconstruction ended.
- Summarize the problems many Southern whites believed were caused by Reconstruction.

PREPARE

Approximate lesson time is 60 minutes.

ASSESS

Unit Assessment: Rebuilding a Nation, Part 1 *(Online)*

Complete the computer-scored portion of the Unit Assessment. When you have finished, complete the teacher-scored portion of the assessment and submit it to your teacher.

Unit Assessment: Rebuilding a Nation, Part 2 *(Offline)*

Complete the teacher-scored portion of the Unit Assessment and submit it to your teacher.

Student Guide
Lesson 10: (Optional) End-of-Year Review: Units 1–4

You've finished! Now it's time to pull together what you have learned this year. You've learned a lot, so we'll review it unit by unit. Let's start by taking a quick look at the first four units. Ready?

Lesson Objectives

- Demonstrate mastery of important knowledge and skills taught in the first semester.

PREPARE

Approximate lesson time is 60 minutes.

Materials

For the Student

Unit Snapshot

A History of US (Concise Edition), Volume A (Prehistory to 1800) by Joy Hakim

History Journal

LEARN
Activity 1. Optional: End-of-Year Review: Units 1–4 *(Offline)*
Instructions
History Journal Review

Review your History Journal. For each unit, look over:

- Completed work
- Maps
- Vocabulary
- Assessments

Online Review

Go online and review Units 1–4 by looking at the Big Picture for each unit. These are located in the Unit Review lesson for each unit.

Complete the Unit Snapshot sheet for each unit as you review the Big Pictures.

Name _____   Date _____

Unit Snapshot: Unit _____

Categorize important information from this unit.

Significant People	Significant Events

Significant Places	Symbols of the Period
	(What do you associate with this time period? Example: 1840s—covered wagons)

What was your favorite lesson? Why?

Name _____   Date _____

Unit Snapshot: Unit _____

Categorize important information from this unit.

Significant People	Significant Events

Significant Places	Symbols of the Period
	(What do you associate with this time period? Example: 1840s—covered wagons)

What was your favorite lesson? Why?

Name _____ Date _____

Unit Snapshot: Unit _____

Categorize important information from this unit.

Significant People	Significant Events

Significant Places	Symbols of the Period
	(What do you associate with this time period? Example: 1840s—covered wagons)

What was your favorite lesson? Why?

Name _____   Date _____

Unit Snapshot: Unit _____

Categorize important information from this unit.

Significant People	Significant Events

Significant Places	Symbols of the Period
	(What do you associate with this time period? Example: 1840s—covered wagons)

What was your favorite lesson? Why?

Student Guide
Lesson 11: (Optional) End-of-Year Review: Units 5–7

Let's review the next three units. Get ready to revisit the American Revolution and the creation of the Constitution.

Lesson Objectives

- Demonstrate mastery of important knowledge and skills taught in the first semester.

PREPARE

Approximate lesson time is 60 minutes.

Materials

For the Student

Unit Snapshot

A History of US (Concise Edition), Volume A (Prehistory to 1800) by Joy Hakim

History Journal

LEARN
Activity 1. Optional: End-of-Year Review: Units 5–7 *(Offline)*
Instructions
History Journal Review

Review your History Journal. For each unit, look over:

- Completed work
- Maps
- Vocabulary
- Assessments

Online Review

Go online and review Units 5–7 by looking at the Big Picture for each unit. These are located in the Unit Review lesson for each unit.

Complete the Unit Snapshot sheet for each unit as you review the Big Pictures.

Name _____   Date _____

Unit Snapshot: Unit _____

Categorize important information from this unit.

Significant People	Significant Events

Significant Places	Symbols of the Period
	(What do you associate with this time period? Example: 1840s—covered wagons)

What was your favorite lesson? Why?

Name _____   Date _____

Unit Snapshot: Unit _____

Categorize important information from this unit.

Significant People	Significant Events

Significant Places	Symbols of the Period
	(What do you associate with this time period? Example: 1840s—covered wagons)

What was your favorite lesson? Why?

Name _____   Date _____

Unit Snapshot: Unit _____

Categorize important information from this unit.

Significant People	Significant Events

Significant Places	Symbols of the Period
	(What do you associate with this time period? Example: 1840s—covered wagons)

What was your favorite lesson? Why?

Student Guide
Lesson 12: (Optional) End-of-Year Review: Units 8–11

Are you ready to review some more? Let's revisit the exciting changes taking place in America in the first half of the nineteenth century. How much do you remember about the changes in transportation and technology, the settling of new land in the West, and the reform movements?

Lesson Objectives
- Demonstrate mastery of important knowledge and skills taught in the second semester.

PREPARE

Approximate lesson time is 60 minutes.

Materials
For the Student

Unit Snapshot

A History of US (Concise Edition), Volume B (1790-1877) by Joy Hakim

History Journal

LEARN
Activity 1. Optional: End-of-Year Review: Units 8–11 (Offline)
Instructions
History Journal Review

Review your History Journal. For each unit, look over:

- Completed work
- Maps
- Vocabulary
- Assessments

Online Review

Go online and review Units 8–11 by looking at the Big Picture for each unit. These are located in the Unit Review lesson for each unit.

Complete the Unit Snapshot sheet for each unit as you review the Big Pictures.

Name _____   Date _____

Unit Snapshot: Unit _____

Categorize important information from this unit.

Significant People	Significant Events

Significant Places	Symbols of the Period
	(What do you associate with this time period? Example: 1840s—covered wagons)

What was your favorite lesson? Why?

Name _____   Date _____

Unit Snapshot: Unit _____

Categorize important information from this unit.

Significant People	Significant Events

Significant Places	Symbols of the Period
	(What do you associate with this time period? Example: 1840s—covered wagons)

What was your favorite lesson? Why?

Name _____ Date _____

Unit Snapshot: Unit _____

Categorize important information from this unit.

Significant People	Significant Events

Significant Places	Symbols of the Period
	(What do you associate with this time period? Example: 1840s—covered wagons)

What was your favorite lesson? Why?

Student Guide
Lesson 13: (Optional) End-of-Year Review: Units 12–14

You've almost finished! There are just three more units to review. Let's take another look at what happened in America before, during, and after the Civil War.

Lesson Objectives
- Demonstrate mastery of important knowledge and skills taught in the second semester.

PREPARE

Approximate lesson time is 60 minutes.

Materials

For the Student

Unit Snapshot

A History of US (Concise Edition), Volume B (1790-1877) by Joy Hakim

History Journal

LEARN
Activity 1. Optional: End-of-Year Review: Units 12–14 *(Offline)*
Instructions
History Journal Review

Review your History Journal. For each unit, look over:

- Completed work
- Maps
- Vocabulary
- Assessments

Online Review

Go online and review Units 12–13 by looking at the Big Picture for each unit. These are located in the Unit Review lesson for each unit. **Note:** There is no Big Picture for Unit 14.

Complete the Unit Snapshot sheet for each unit as you review the Big Pictures.

Name _____   Date _____

Unit Snapshot: Unit _____

Categorize important information from this unit.

Significant People	Significant Events

Significant Places	Symbols of the Period
	(What do you associate with this time period? Example: 1840s—covered wagons)

What was your favorite lesson? Why?

Name _____   Date _____

Unit Snapshot: Unit _____

Categorize important information from this unit.

Significant People	Significant Events

Significant Places	Symbols of the Period
	(What do you associate with this time period? Example: 1840s—covered wagons)

What was your favorite lesson? Why?

Name _____   Date _____

Unit Snapshot: Unit _____

Categorize important information from this unit.

Significant People	Significant Events

Significant Places	Symbols of the Period
	(What do you associate with this time period? Example: 1840s—covered wagons)

What was your favorite lesson? Why?

Student Guide
Lesson 14: End-of-Year Assessment

You've reviewed all the units. You're ready for the end-of-year assessment. Take the assessment, and then take a well-deserved break—you've learned a lot this year.

Lesson Objectives

- Identify the social and economic issues the United States faced at the end of the Civil War.
- Identify the Freedmen's Bureau and describe the kind of work it did.
- Summarize the ways in which some white Southerners denied justice to blacks.
- Identify the ways in which the government attempted to give blacks full citizenship.
- Explain the impact of the 14th Amendment on the federal balance of power.
- Define *radical*.
- Define *impeachment* and explain its purpose.
- Locate the Bering Sea and land bridge on a map or globe.
- Trace the migration route of the earliest Americans.
- Locate the regions where Inuit live on a map.
- Locate on a map the area where the cliff dwellers lived.
- Identify geographic reasons for diversity among Native American groups.
- Identify Columbus as the first explorer to attempt to reach East Asia by sailing west from Europe.
- Recognize that plants, animals and diseases were exchanged among continents as a result of European exploration.
- List at least four plants, three animals, and one disease that were part of the Columbian Exchange.
- Describe the economic and religious motives for French exploration and colonization in North America.
- Identify the area of North America claimed by the French and the routes of major explorers.
- Identify the area of North America claimed by England.
- Describe England's motives for exploration and colonization as the desire to gain wealth and form model societies.
- Identify the role of tobacco in the economic success of Jamestown.
- Explain the beginnings of slavery in Virginia as a way to fill the need for field workers, and the difference between an indentured servant and a slave.
- Describe the Mayflower Compact as an early form of self-government in Plymouth and William Bradford as the governor.
- Describe plantation life for owners, women, slaves, and small farmers.
- Explain the causes of the French and Indian War as competition between France and England for land and power.
- Identify and describe the Stamp Act.
- Identify Sam Adams and Patrick Henry as opposition leaders.
- Explain the reasons for choosing George Washington to command the Continental Army, including his experience and character.
- Recognize the Enlightenment ideas Jefferson used in the Declaration of Independence.
- Read and analyze the Declaration of Independence to gain understanding of its meaning.
- Explain the significance of the Declaration of Independence in unifying people for the war effort.

- Identify individuals who came from Europe to aid the American cause, including the Marquis de Lafayette, Baron Friedrich von Steuben, and Haym Salomon.
- Describe the difficulties George Washington faced as commander of the Continental Army, including a small, unstable army, lack of supplies, and need to use retreat as a way to save the army.
- Identify Cornwallis as the leader of the British forces and Alexander Hamilton as aide to George Washington.
- Identify the Articles of Confederation as the first government of the United States and describe its weaknesses, including the lack of an executive and of taxing power.
- Summarize the reasons for and major provisions of the Northwest Ordinance.

PREPARE

Approximate lesson time is 60 minutes.

ASSESS

Course Assessment: MS American History Before 1865 End-of-Year Assessment *(Online)*

You will complete an online assessment covering the main points of this course. Your assessment will be scored by the computer.